ISBN 978-0-282-94987-7
PIBN 10874334

1 MONTH OF
FREE
READING

at

www.ForgottenBooks.com

By purchasing this book you are eligible for one month membership to ForgottenBooks.com, giving you unlimited access to our entire collection of over 1,000,000 titles via our web site and mobile apps.

To claim your free month visit:
www.forgottenbooks.com/free874334

English
Français
Deutsche
Italiano
Español
Português

www.forgottenbooks.com

Mythology Photography **Fiction**
Fishing Christianity **Art** Cooking
Essays Buddhism Freemasonry
Medicine **Biology** Music **Ancient**
Egypt Evolution Carpentry Physics
Dance Geology **Mathematics** Fitness
Shakespeare **Folklore** Yoga Marketing
Confidence Immortality Biographies
Poetry **Psychology** Witchcraft
Electronics Chemistry History **Law**
Accounting **Philosophy** Anthropology
Alchemy Drama Quantum Mechanics
Atheism Sexual Health **Ancient History**
Entrepreneurship Languages Sport
Paleontology Needlework Islam
Metaphysics Investment Archaeology
Parenting Statistics Criminology
Motivational

COLLECTIONS

OF THE

MINNESOTA

HISTORICAL SOCIETY

VOLUME IX.

ST. PAUL, MINN.
PUBLISHED BY THE SOCIETY.
APRIL, 1901.

kettles on for cooking. A cellar was dug near the front of the camp; and a table was made at the rear end, opposite the door. This describes the average lumber camp of the Minnesota pineries during the early years, from 1847 to 1860.

The modern logging outfit is different. Two bob-sleds are placed one behind the other, and are fastened by two chains crossed in the center. With a tackle and fall, logs are rolled up and loaded on these sleds, sometimes to the height of ten feet. Horses or oxen are used on the tackle, and a load takes from four to ten thousand feet of logs.

It is made possible to draw these very heavy loads by icing the ruts of the logging roads. At the beginning of the logging season, and occasionally afterward, whenever snow-storms or continued wearing make it needful, water tanks on runners are drawn along the roads, supplying a small stream at each side. The resulting narrow courses of ice bear up the sleds under the great weight.

The manner of felling the trees also shows an important change from the old methods. Instead of chopping them down with axes, as was formerly done, they are sawed off at the stump.

Temporary lumbering camps of the present time, for use during one or two winters, are warmly built log-houses with perpendicular sides, well supplied with windows, and are in many other respects better than when I began logging on the Mississippi and Rum rivers. The more permanent camps have partitions dividing them into a kitchen, dining-room, and sitting-room, on the main floor, with bedrooms upstairs. The sitting-room is heated by a large stove, and the kitchen has the best and largest modern cooking range. In a single camp fifty choppers and teamsters may be comfortably lodged. They eat breakfast and supper at the camp, going to their work, often two miles away, before light in the short days of winter, and returning after dark. They are provided with abundant and well prepared food, for which their hard manual labor gives a keen appetite.

LUMBERMEN OF ST. ANTHONY AND MINNEAPOLIS PRIOR TO 1860.

The pioneer lumbermen of the upper Mississippi region, who were engaged in our great logging and lumber manu-

.facturing industries before the Civil war, are named in the following list, with dates of their coming to St. Anthony or Minneapolis. It will be remembered that these two towns or cities, on opposite sides of the Mississippi, were not united under the latter name until the year 1872. The dates given for firms and companies indicate the year of beginning of their work in lumbering. A few residents of St. Paul, as Borup and Oakes, and John S. Prince, having business interests in St. Anthony and Minneapolis, are also included, with the earliest years of accounts of their logs in the surveyor's records.

With nearly all whose names appear in this list, I was personally acquainted. Only very few of them are left with me to the present time. They well performed their work as founders of Minnesota and of its largest city.

The list is compiled from the records of the surveyor general's office. It comprises more than a hundred names of individuals and firms. They are arranged in the chronologic order of their coming to live at Minneapolis, or, in connection with firms and companies, of their first engaging in business here. In some instances a residence of a few years in Minneapolis preceded the appearance of the name in the surveyor's records. Franklin Steele and Roswell P. Russell had lived a long time previously within the limits of. the present state of Minnesota, having come respectively in 1837 and 1839 to Fort Snelling.

Each proprietor or firm used a special mark to designate their logs for separate accounts and payments, when the logs of many different owners were mixed together in the booms and drawn out for sawing, or when they were rafted together for sale to southern manufacturers.

1847.

Caleb D. Dorr.
Ard Godfrey.
Roswell P. Russell.
Daniel Stanchfield.

Franklin Steele, Caleb Cushing, and Co.
Charles W. Stimpson.
Calvin A. Tuttle.

1848.

Joseph R. Brown.
Silas M. Farnham.
Summer W. Farnham.

John Rollins.
Samuel Stanchfield.

1849.

Reuben Bean.
Rufus Farnham.
Isaac Gilpatrick.
John Jackins.
Isaac E. Lane.
Silas Lane.

James A. Lennon.
John G. Lennon.
James McMullen.
John W. North.
Anson Northup.
Joseph P. Wilson.

1850.

Joel B. Bassett.
Henry Chambers.
Thomas Chambers.
Charles Chute.

Richard Chute.
Gordon Jackins.
William Jackins.

1851.

John Berry.
Mark T. Berry.
John T. Blaisdell.
Robert Blaisdell.
George A., Camp.
Dan S. Day.

J. W. Day.
Joseph Day.
Leonard Day.
Joseph Libbey.
Marshall and Co.
Benjamin Soule.

1852.

William Hanson.
F. G. Mayo and Brothers.
Frank Rollins.

Russell, Gray and Co.
Ensign Stanchfield.

1853.

Henry T. Welles.

1854.

A. M. Fridley.
McKenzie and Estes.
D. W. Marr.

Stanchfield and Co.
Ambrose Tourtelotte.

1855.

F. C. Barrows.
Borup and Oakes.
Camp and Reynolds.
Chapman and Co.
John Dudley.
Farnham and Stimpson.
Gray and Libbey.
Jackson and Blaisdell.
Jewett and Chase.
James A. Lovejoy.
Stephen Lovejoy.
McIntosh and Estes.

McKnight and King.
John Martin.
Clinton Morrison.
Dorilus Morrison.
David Nichols.
John S. Pillsbury.
Stanchfield and Brown.
Daniel Stimpson.
Tourtelotte and Co.
George Warren and Co.
Welles and Co.

1856.

Ames, Howell and Co.
Ames and Hoyt.
John Banfil.
Daniel Bassett.
Cathcart and Co.
Josiah H. Chase.
L. P. Chase.
Robert Christie.
Farnham and Co.
Gray and Leighton.
John G. Howe.
James McCann.

Richard J. Mendenhall.
Morrison and Tourtelotte.
Elias Moses.
W. M. Nesmith.
Olmstead and Ames.
John S. Prince.
Rotary Mill Co.
I. Sanford.
Stanchfield and McCormack.
William A. Todd.
Woodbury and Co.
Ivory F. Woodman.

1857.

W. H. Chamberlain.
William W. McNair.

William D. Washburn.
Wensinger and Co.

1858 (none added).

1859.

Jonathan Chase.
W. E. Jones.

Orlando C. Merriman.

EARLY LUMBER MANUFACTURING ABOVE MINNEAPOLIS.

In 1860, business reverses and the death of my wife and children caused me to remove from Minneapolis, and after a year of travel I settled in Davenport, Iowa. There I again married and engaged in the lumber trade until 1889, when I returned to Minneapolis, to spend my declining years in the city whose first growth and earliest industries sprang from my exploration of the Upper Mississippi pineries. It is not proposed, therefore, to extend this history beyond the year 1860, excepting as it is partly given in biographic sketches and in the tables of statistics.

Joseph Libbey, who came to St. Anthony with his family early in 1851, was the first to cut and haul logs above the junction of the Crow Wing and Mississippi rivers. Several years passed before any other lumberman went so far north, the next being Asa Libbey. When the best pineries adjoining the Rum river began to be exhausted, the loggers went up the Mississippi to Pine and Gull rivers and many other streams forming its headwaters, which I had partly explored in February, 1848, predicting that the timber supply in that region would far outlast a generation.

Within the subsequent period of more than fifty years, logging and lumber manufacturing have been developed beyond any extent which could then be expected. Railroads for lumbering have been built, during the last ten years, in the large district reaching north from Brainerd to Leech, Cass, and Bemidji lakes, and also northward from the mouths of Swan and Deer rivers, to bring the timber of areas many miles distant from any stream capable of floating and driving logs; and, in some instances, after the country has been stripped of its merchantable pine, the rails of long lines and branches have been taken up to be laid again for the same use in other belts of pine forest on and near the principal watersheds. Large districts have yielded all or nearly all their available pine timber; but some extensive tracts of this most valuable timber yet remain. In the progress of railroad logging, probably the pine supply of the Upper Mississippi region will continue many years; and its resources of excellent hardwood timber, well adapted for building, furniture, and a very wide range of wood manufacturing, almost wholly neglected to the present time, seem practically inexhaustible.

During the period preceding the Civil War, lumber manufacturing was begun, on a small scale, in Anoka, Elk River, St. Cloud, and Little Falls, besides numerous smaller towns and settlements, some of which, as Watab and Granite City, existed only a few years.

In the winter of 1853-'54 the first dam and sawmill at Anoka were built by Caleb and W. H. Woodbury. In 1860 this water-power and sawmill were bought by James McCann, the mill having then only one sash-saw, with a capacity of 6,000 feet of lumber daily.

Other early sawmills in Anoka county included one built in 1854 by Charles Peltier on the Clearwater creek near Centerville, which was operated during five years; a large steam sawmill built by Starkey and Petteys in 1857 at their village of Columbus, in the present township of this name, but this mill was burned after a few years and the village disappeared; and a mill at St. Francis, built in 1855 by Dwight Woodbury.

In Sherburne county, Ard Godfrey and John G. Jameson built the first dam and sawmill, in 1851, at the rapids of the Elk river, where four years later the village of Orono was sur-

veyed and platted, now forming the western part of the town
of Elk River. This mill had only a single sash-saw, and was
capable of sawing about 3,000 feet daily.

In Princeton a steam sawmill was built in 1856 by William
F. Dunham and others; and a sawmill run by water-power
was built by Samuel Ross in 1858. Their daily capacity, respectively, was about 6,000 feet and 3,000 feet.

At Monticello two large steam sawmills were built in 1855
and 1856, each having a daily capacity of about 25,000 feet.
The first was operated many years, but the second was burned
in 1858, and was never rebuilt.

At Clearwater a dam and sawmill were built in 1856, but
were washed away by a flood when nearly ready to begin sawing. The next year a second sawmill on the Clearwater river,
a mile above the former, was built by Herman Woodworth;
and in 1858 a steam sawmill was erected by Frank Morrison
on or near the site of the first mill. Each of these later mills
continued in operation about twenty years.

At St. Cloud, one of the earliest enterprises was the erection of a steam sawmill in 1855 by a company consisting of J.
P. Wilson, George F. Brott, H. T. Welles and C. T. Stearns. It
was burned and was rebuilt the next year. Its site was that
of the Bridgman upper mill. In 1857, Raymond and Owen
erected their first factory for making doors, sash, and blinds,
which was carried away by ice in 1862, but was rebuilt the
same year.

The old village of Watab, which was platted in 1854 and
flourished during several years but was afterward abandoned,
situated on the Mississippi in Benton county, about four miles
north of Sauk Rapids, had a steam sawmill, which was built
in 1856 by Place, Hanson, and Clark.

In Morrison county, the first sawmill was built at Little
Falls by James Green, in 1849, and was operated by different
owners until 1858, when it was washed away. Extensive out-
lay was made by the Little Falls Manufacturing Company,
during the years 1856 to 1858, in building a dam and mills;
but they were destroyed by a flood in the summer of 1860.
Near the mouth of Swan river, on the west side of Pike rapids,
Anson Northup built a steam sawmill in 1856, and operated
it two years. On the Skunk river, in the east part of this

county, at a distance of nearly twenty miles from Little Falls, a steam sawmill and a considerable village, called Granite City, were built in 1858 and ensuing years; but the site was abandoned at the time of the Indian outbreak in 1862, and was never reoccupied.

Northward from Morrison county, the present large development of lumber manufacturing at Brainerd, Aitkin, and other places on the Northern Pacific railroad, which was built through this region in 1870 and 1871, belongs to a period considerably later than that which is the theme of this paper. More recent lines of railway, in several instances constructed chiefly or solely for their use in lumbering, with numerous large sawmills and a vast yearly production of manufactured lumber, are situated yet farther north within the Mississippi drainage area.

The continuation of this subject, however, must be left for other and younger writers. Let those who have shared in the great expansion of the lumber industry during the later period narrate its steps of advance, as I have attempted to give the records of the early time which included my exploration and work.

Biographic Sketches.

Among those who were my associates in the years 1847 to 1860, Severre Bottineau and Charles Manock are well remembered as companions of travel by canoe and afoot during the earliest years when I was cruising through the pineries of Rum river and the upper waters of the Mississippi. The determination of the areas occupied by pine timber available for logging, and the estimation of the amounts that would be yielded from different tracts on the many streams of that great region, led many others also to prospect or cruise in search of the most desirable areas for lumbering. This was my principal work during a large part of each year up to the time of my appointment as surveyor general of logs and lumber. It was the custom of the cruiser to supply himself with some provisions, a blanket, a rifle or shotgun with plenty of ammunition, and a good stock of matches to start the nightly campfire, and then to go alone, or with one or two comrades, into the pathless forests, there to collect the information and

23

estimates needed, remaining weeks or sometimes even months in the woods, and subsisting mostly on game, fish, and berries.

Manock was hired to accompany my first expedition for his aid as a hunter, and we seldom lacked an abundance of wild meat. He was a good cook, and always performed the usual work of preparing the camp and meals.

Severre Bottineau, as previously noted, was a younger brother of Pierre, the well known guide. He was a stout and athletic fellow, accustomed to the hardships of exploring. His acquaintance with four languages, French, English, Ojibway, and Dakota, made him very serviceable in my dealings with the Indians. It should be added, too, that both Manock and Bottineau were mixed-bloods, thoroughly understanding the temperament, inclinations, and usages, of the two great tribes or nations of red men who then occupied and owned nearly all of what is now Minnesota. Young Bottineau, intelligent, friendly, fond of conversation, and always good-natured, was my companion during all the first year, until September, 1848.

It would be a pleasure to me to write further of these men, but I am unable to do so, or even to state whether either of them may be still living.

There are many among the hundred or more who were engaged in lumbering here during those early years of whom I would wish to write my high appreciation and friendship; but the proper limits of the present paper forbid this, even if the biographic information for so many of the old pioneers were sufficiently known to me. Six of them, however, I may be permitted to select, namely, Franklin Steele, Caleb D. Dorr, Sumner W. Farnham, John Martin, Dorilus Morrison, and John S. Pillsbury, in the chronologic order of their coming to Minnesota, of whom short biographic sketches, with portraits, are placed here to give, by these examples, a view of the sterling integrity, business sagacity, and indomitable energy and perseverance, which characterized the pioneer lumbermen of our North Star State.

FRANKLIN STEELE

was born in Chester county, Pennsylvania, May 12th, 1813. At the age of twenty-four years, in 1837, he came to Fort Snelling, and thence went to the St. Croix falls and took a land

claim, building a log cabin to secure ownership of the water-power there. In 1838 he received a federal appointment as sutler of Fort Snelling. In April, 1843, he was married, in Baltimore, to Miss Anna Barney, a granddaughter of Commodore Barney of the United States Navy, and also, by her mother, of Samuel Chase, one of the Maryland signers of the Declaration of Independence. The part taken by Mr. Steele in the improvement of the water-power at the falls of St. Anthony, and in the early development of logging and manufacturing lumber here, has been noted in the foregoing pages. In 1851 he was elected by the legislature as one of the first Board of Regents of the University of Minnesota; and by his gifts and personal interest he aided largely in establishing and sustaining this institution. In 1854 he built a suspension bridge connecting St. Anthony and Minneapolis, which was the first bridge to span the Mississippi in any part of its course from lake Itasca to its mouth. In 1862 he was active to aid the settlers who had been driven from their homes by the Sioux outbreak and massacre. To the close of his life, September 10th, 1880, he was one of the most eminent and public-spirited citizens of his adopted state. Mr. Steele began the utilization of the falls of St. Anthony, and lived to see the city which he so largely aided to found there grow to have 48,000 people. Another has justly written, "His life was peculiarly unselfish, and largely devoted to the prosecution of public measures, of which others have chiefly reaped the benefits."

CALEB D. DORR

was born at East Great Works (now Bradley), in Penobscot county, Maine, July 9th, 1824. He had worked several years in the pineries of the Penobscot river, cutting and driving logs, before he came to St. Anthony in the autumn of 1847, arriving here October 1st. He was employed mainly during 1848 in the construction of the first dam and sawmill of Steele, Cushing, and Company, at the falls of St. Anthony; and in the spring and summer of that year he built the first boom above the falls. Late in the autumn of 1847 he had cut pine in the vicinity of Little Falls and Swan river, intended for the St. Anthony dam and boom; and in 1848 he ran the first rafts and drives of logs from the upper Mississippi river to St. An-

thony, which my logging crew had cut during the preceding winter, as narrated in an earlier part of this paper. On the 4th of March, 1849, in a visit east after his first year in Minnesota, he married Celestia A. Ricker of Maine.

Mr. Dorr brought the first machine used at St. Anthony for making shingles, in 1850. During many years he was one of the principal lumbermen of the upper Mississippi, cutting logs chiefly on the Rum river. In 1866 he accepted the office of boom master, and held it many years. He is still living in Minneapolis, where he has held numerous positions of honor and trust, one of the earliest being as an alderman in the first city council of St. Anthony, in 1858.

SUMNER W. FARNHAM

was born in Calais, Maine, April 2nd, 1820. His father was a surveyor of logs and lumber on the St. Croix river, which forms the boundary between Maine and New Brunswick, and the son inherited a strong inclination for the lumber business. At the age of fourteen years he began work with his father about the sawmills, and four years later went into the pine woods to cut logs on his own account. In 1840 he bought a sawmill, and ran it four years. In September, 1847, he left Calais and came west. After examining the lumbering prospects of eastern Michigan and wintering in the lead-mining region of southwestern Wisconsin, he arrived at Stillwater in the spring of 1848. He was at first employed in logging by his friend, John McKusick, who had previously come from the same part of Maine. On the way up the Mississippi, the steamer which brought Mr. Farnham had been pushed ashore by a gale, with drifting ice, near the site of Lake City, and there I first met him, aiding the captain in his endeavors to get the boat again into the water. This was while I was on my way to Galena, partly for the business of Mr. Steele in relation to capital supplied from the east for the improvements at St. Anthony Falls. The next winter Mr. Farnham went into the woods of Rum river as foreman of one of my logging camps. In the next two summers, he did the greater part of the work of clearing this river of its driftwood, opening it for log-driving from its upper tributaries.

During 1850 and several ensuing years, Mr. Farnham was very profitably engaged in logging and lumber manufacturing.

June 1st, 1851, he was married to Miss Eunice Estes, a daughter of Jonathan Estes, an immigrant from Maine. In 1854, with Samuel Tracy, he opened the first bank in St. Anthony, which continued in business until 1858. It was then closed, on account of the prevailing financial depression, and all the depositors were fully paid, though at a considerable loss of the capital invested by Mr. Farnham and his partners. In 1860 he associated with himself James A. Lovejoy, forming the lumber firm of Farnham and Lovejoy, which continued in this business twenty-eight years, until Mr. Lovejoy's death. Their total production of manufactured lumber is estimated to have exceeded 300,000,000 feet.

As early as 1849, Mr. Farnham was one of the founders of the Library Association of St. Anthony. In 1852, and again in 1856, he was a member of the Territorial Legislature. He also served as assessor and afterward as treasurer of St. Anthony, and during the Civil War was appointed with others to raise money for the relief of soldiers' families. Throughout his long life, he has honorably fulfilled his part in the promotion of the best interests of his city and state, and still lives in Minneapolis, but his health was broken by paralysis several years ago.

JOHN MARTIN

was born in Peacham, Vermont, August 18th, 1820, and was early inured to hard work on his father's farm. In 1839 he took employment as a fireman on a steamboat plying on the Connecticut river, and in time became its captain. After five years he went with this steamboat to North Carolina, and there was engaged in freighting on the Neuse river during several years. In 1849, returning to Peacham, he was married to Miss Jane B. Gilfillan. Soon afterward, he went to California, by the way of the Isthmus of Panama, and spent a year in placer gold mining. Next he returned and lived as a farmer two or three years in Vermont. But an adventurous temperament led him to the Northwest in 1854. Having found in St. Anthony opportunities for good investments in lumbering, and believing that the little village of that time would become a great commercial metropolis, he went back to Vermont, sold his farms, and early in 1855 came to reside permanently here.

During that year he became interested in Mississippi steamboating, and aided to form a company for navigating the river to St. Anthony. Subsequently he was captain of the steamer Falls City, named for St. Anthony, where it had been built, and made regular trips far down the Mississippi. Through the ensuing forty years, he has engaged very successfully in lumbering, operating many sawmills, with lumber yards in Minneapolis and St. Paul; in flour manufacturing, becoming president of the Northwestern Consolidated Milling Company at Minneapolis, which owns several large mills; and in banking, and railway building. He still lives amid the scenes of his life work, in review of which a friend says: "Thus Captain Martin's life, in a private and unostentatious way, has been full of labor, inspired by sagacity, reaching success, and contributing to the common weal. . . . . He enjoys in fullest measure the respect and confidence of his neighbors and acquaintances, and has occupied a large place in the growth of Minneapolis."

DORILUS MORRISON

was born in Livermore, Maine, December 27th, 1814, his father, a farmer of Scotch lineage, having been one of the early settlers of that state. Dorilus became a merchant in Bangor, a part of his business being to furnish supplies to lumbermen for their winter logging camps. In 1854, he first came to Minnesota for the purpose of purchasing pine lands for himself and others. Being very favorably impressed with the advantages here for lumbering, he returned to Maine, disposed of his large business interests there, and came, with his family, in the spring of 1855, to reside in St. Anthony. During several years following, he lumbered on the Rum river and its branches, supplying logs to Lovejoy and Brockway, who had leased the St. Anthony sawmills. He was a director, and at times was president, of the Minneapolis Mill Company, which constructed a dam and canal for utilization of water-power on the west side of the river, at first largely employed in sawing lumber, and now in manufacturing flour. He built a sawmill, opened a lumber yard, and conducted all branches of the business from cutting the logs in the woods to the sale of the manufactured lumber. His sons, George H. and Clinton Morrison, in 1868, succeeded him in lumber manufacturing.

DORILUS MORRISON.

J. T. Pilloberry

Besides his very extensive work in Minnesota, Mr. Morrison had lumber yards in Davenport, Iowa, and in Hannibal, Mo. His yard and stock in Davenport I bought in 1863, and continued in business there as his successor during twenty-five years.

In 1856, he was the first president of the Union Board of Trade of St. Anthony and Minneapolis. In 1864 and 1865 he was a member of the state senate. In 1867, when Minneapolis was incorporated as a city, Mr. Morrison was elected its first mayor, and in 1869 he again held this office.

He was one of the principal members of the construction companies which in the years 1870 to 1873 built the Northern Pacific railroad through Minnesota and onward to the Missouri river; and during many years afterward he was a director of this great railroad corporation. He was one of the founders of the Minneapolis Harvester Works. During the later part of his life, he was for several terms a member of the city Board of Education, and was long a member of the Board of Park Commissioners of Minneapolis. From its beginning, he was one of the chief supporters of the Athenæum Library, which is now a part of the city public library. After a most active and eminently useful life, spent in Minnesota for its last forty-two years, he died June 26th, 1897.

JOHN S. PILLSBURY

was born in Sutton, New Hampshire, July 29th, 1827. His education was limited to the common schools of his native town; and from the age of sixteen to twenty-one years he was a clerk in the general country store of his brother, George A. Pillsbury, then of Warner, N. H. He was afterward in mercantile partnership during two years with Walter Harriman, of Warner, who was his senior by ten years, and who was twice elected governor of New Hampshire, in 1867 and 1868. Mr. Pillsbury was next engaged two years as a merchant tailor and cloth dealer in Concord, N. H. In 1853 he began a tour of observation throughout the western states, and in June, 1855, came to Minnesota, and settled at St. Anthony, now the east part of Minneapolis, which has ever since been his home. Returning east for a visit, he married Miss Mahala Fisk, in Warner, N. H., November 3rd, 1856.

In St. Anthony he engaged in the hardware business with George F. Cross and Woodbury Fisk, his brother-in-law. The firm prospered, until, at the same time with the financial panic of 1857, their store was burned at a loss of about $38,000, without insurance. Beginning anew, Mr. Pillsbury reorganized the business, and by hard work and honesty of dealing made his establishment the leading hardware house of the Northwest. His trade consisted largely of supplies for lumbermen and millwrights, and it was continued until 1875, being then relinquished to give attention more fully to lumbering and flour milling.

During the past twenty-five years, Mr. Pillsbury has been actively interested in logging and the manufacture of lumber. Through the greater part of this time, the Gull River Lumber Company, under his general supervision as president, has carried on a very extensive business, cutting logs in the pineries of Gull river and a large adjoining district, and sawing the lumber at Gull River station and Brainerd.

In 1869, with his nephew, Charles A. Pillsbury, he established the flour-milling firm of C. A. Pillsbury and Company, which later included his brother, George A. Pillsbury, and another nephew, Fred C. Pillsbury. This firm built and operated several large flouring mills, one being the largest in the world, capable of producing 7,000 barrels of flour daily. In 1890 this immense business, with that of other prominent flour manufacturers in Minneapolis, was sold to an English syndicate, for which Mr. John S. Pillsbury continues to share in the management of these mills as an American director.

By his distinguished public services for Minnesota, Mr. Pillsbury has won the enduring gratitude of all her citizens. In 1860 and ensuing years, he was an alderman of St. Anthony; in 1864 and onward, a member of the state senate; and in 1876 to 1882 he was for three successive terms the governor of this commonwealth. In 1861 he rendered very efficient aid in organizing regiments of Minnesota volunteers for the Civil War, and in 1862 raised and equipped a mounted company for service against the Sioux outbreak in Minnesota.

In 1863, Mr. Pillsbury was appointed a regent of the State University, in which position he has continued to the present time, constantly giving most devoted care to the upbuilding

o.' this great institution of learning. Financial difficulties which beset the University in its early years were met and overcome by Mr. Pillsbury's wise direction; and its steady growth to its rank as one of the largest and best universities of the United States has been in great part due to his watchfulness, persistent efforts, and personal influence. One of its chief buildings was donated by him, and is named in his honor.

The private benefactions of Governor Pillsbury and his wife have been many and generous, but unostentatious. Their noble devotion to the welfare of the community, the city, and the state, leads all who know them to wish very heartily for each of them long continuance of life, with all the blessings that kind Providence can give.

STATISTICS.

For the early years, to 1855, the following statistics of lumber production are derived, approximately, from the scalers' record books; and for the ensuing years from reports of the surveyors general of logs and lumber, beginning in 1856. The summary of these reports was published during many years in the governors' messages, and afterward in the reports of the commissioners of statistics.

As the printing of this paper has been delayed, I am able to include the figures for the year 1899. The table thus comprises a period of fifty-two years.

Year.	Feet.	Year.	Feet.
1848	2,000,000	1874	222,466,520
1849	3,500,000	1875	172,775,000
1850	6,500,000	1876	200,371,277
1851	8,830,000	1877	137,081,140
1852	11,600,000	1878	141,380,530
1853	23,610,000	1879	189,422,490
1854	32,944,000	1880	255,306,080
1855	36,228,314	1881	298,583,190
1856	41,230,000	1882	390,507,510
1857	44,434,147	1883	361,295,800
1858	42,117,000	1884	384,151,420
1859	29,382,000	1885	378,160,690
1860	45,000,000	1886	322,260,820
1861	41,196,484	1887	254,056,690
1862	40,000,000	1888	407,009,440
1863	21,634,700	1889	287,977,130
1864	35,897,618	1890	344,493,790
1865	108,328,278	1891	425,765,260
1866	72,805,100	1892	505,407,898
1867	113,867,502	1893	428,172,260
1868	115,889,558	1894	459,862,756
1869	146,782,530	1895	539,012,678
1870	121,438,640	1896	385,312,226
1871	117,206,590	1897	527,367,710
1872	179,722,250	1898	533,179,510
1873	197,743,150	1899	678,364,430

The great expansion and ratios of growth of this industry
during the half century are more concisely indicated in a second table, formed by addition of successive parts of the preceding table, these parts being then added to give their aggregate amount.

	Feet.
1848 to 1850, three years	12,000,000
1851 to 1860, ten years	315,375,461
1861 to 1870, ten years	817,840,410
1871 to 1880, ten years	1,813,475,027
1881 to 1890, ten years	3,428,496,480
1891 to 1899, nine years	4,482,444,728
Total, fifty-two years	10,869,632,106

A considerable amount of other pine lumber, however, is
cut in this district, doubtless as much as a tenth and perhaps
even more than a fifth of that here tabulated, which fails to
appear in the official returns. The whole lumber product to
the present time has therefore equalled or exceeded twelve
billion feet. Fully two-thirds of this amount, or about eight
billion feet, have been sawn in Minneapolis.

Allowing six dollars per thousand feet as the average
value of this lumber at the sawmills, it will be seen that its
total value in this district has amounted, in round numbers,
to $75,000,000, the sawn lumber of Minneapolis having been
worth $50,000,000.

In the census of 1890, the city of Minneapolis was reported
to have thirty-nine establishments engaged in lumber manufactures, including, besides the sawing of logs, the many plan-
ing mills and the various mills and factories for making sash,
doors, blinds, laths, shingles, etc. Their aggregate capital
invested was somewhat more than $10,000,000; their combined
number of employees was 3,894, receiving $1,800,000 in yearly
wages; and the value of their products, for a year, was $9,626,-
975.

Since that date, within the last nine years, the lumber business has undoubtedly increased more than fifty per cent. in
Minneapolis; and for the entire district, taking into consideration the many towns and hamlets whose chief industry is lumber manufacturing, it has quite certainly doubled.

A. L. Larpenteur

RECOLLECTIONS OF THE CITY AND PEOPLE OF ST. PAUL, 1843-1898.

BY AUGUST L. LARPENTEUR.

"There's a Divinity that shapes our ends,
Rough-hew them how we will."

I am requested by our worthy Secretary to make some remarks upon the early settlement of our beloved state and the city of St. Paul in particular, for your edification. I shall endeavor to do so in as simple and interesting a manner as I am capable of, under the circumstances. In my early days the benefits of a classical education were not easily acquired, and not within the reach of everyone, as to-day; hence, you will pardon me if l my tale unfold incoherently. As a plea for my undertaking to perform this, my duty, I, as well as every other old settler, owe it to posterity.

The development of the great Northwest was not due alone to the graduates of the Harvards, Yales, Princetons, or William and Marys, but largely to the noble and sturdy class of pioneers, the *coureurs des bois*, the Indian traders. 'Twas they who first penetrated these vast forests and plains, and by their traffic with the natives soon paved the way for large cities like Chicago, Cincinnati, St. Louis, and St. Paul, to be built upon their once "happy hunting grounds." These traders were brave men, many of them men of refinement, choosing this vocation because it brought them close to nature and nature's God. Few but us old settlers can realize the worldly paradise we had here, and no one better than we can understand the reluctance with which the Indians left it.

Before civilization desecrated it, I may say, it was a land flowing with milk and honey. We had game of all kinds

---

*Read at the monthly meeting of the Executive Council, September 12, 1898.

right at our door, and were not circumscribed by game laws; fish of every variety abounded in our many lakes; and a day's ride from where we stand would bring us into buffalo herds. Some great inland seas, and other lakes of less magnitude, but all containing pure, limpid water, shone forth with the re-flection of the sun, like so many diadems in the crown of some fairy queen. When Father Hennepin made his report to Louis XIV ("le Grand Roi," as he was called), the king dubbed him "le Grand Menteur" (the big liar). He could not believe such a country could exist, and the good friar had not half told all there was, or that could be said about it. And little did I think, when a boy in Maryland, studying my geography in a Baltimore county schoolhouse, that I would ever see the Falls of St. Anthony. Nor was it my intention, when I left home, to come in this direction; hence, I have adopted the above text. The part which I took in the formation of our state and city was purely accidental. Some of our most worthy and honored citizens came here for a purpose, as governors, judges, etc.; but I came here for "romance alone," to take of nature all she had to give and give nothing in return. This idea came to me from circumstances which I shall treat upon later on.

KINDRED, AND MIGRATION TO ST. PAUL.

My grandfather was a great admirer of Napoleon, and one of his strong adherents, a member of the National Guard, and, after Waterloo, he could not be contented with a Bourbon dynasty. Therefore, in 1816, he packed his grip and came to America, and settled near Baltimore. His family consisted of three boys and one girl. My father was the eldest. His name was Louis. The second was Eugene, who became a worthy citizen of this state and died in 1877, loved and respected by all who knew him. The youngest was named Charles, and of him I shall speak later.

My father married a Miss Simmons, of Mount Washington, Baltimore county. Her father was a drummer in the war of 1812, and was what was called "an Old Defender," a society that has now become extinct. They were among those who defended the city of Baltimore from the invasion of the British, and killed their General Ross at the battle of North Point.

When I was about six years old, my mother died, leaving myself and an only brother. We were taken to our grandfather's, and with him I made my future home. Grandmother, before dying, enjoined my grandfather to care for and have me in his keeping, and truly the good man did, and for years we were inseparable.

My uncle Charles, the youngest of the family, being rather of a romantic disposition and not well disposed to manual labor, embraced the first opportunity to gratify his ambition. A friend of our family, Colonel Johnson, had for some time been an Indian agent at St. Louis for the Sacs and Foxes, and for various tribes along the Missouri. He came to Baltimore for the purpose of receiving his portion of an estate that had been left him. A part of that portion consisted of twenty-five negroes. In course of conversation with grandfather, Col. Johnson said he would like Charles, my uncle, to accompany him out west as far as St. Louis. Here was Charles' opportunity, and he embraced it at once, his father being willing. This was in 1828. His autobiography is now in the hands of the publisher, Francis P. Harper, of New York, as edited by Dr. Elliott Coues, of Washington City, from his diary, which, when published, I shall be pleased to present to this Historical Society.

Charles Larpenteur had been in the West about eight years, five of which had been spent in the Indian country, when he made us his first visit. I was then a lad going to school. He brought with him a variety of Indian curiosities, among which were complete suits of an Indian chief and his squaw, all trimmed with beads and the quills of the fretful porcupine. The squaw's dress just fitted me, and he dressed me up for exhibition to our friends; and he, as the great chief, would give the war whoop, and go through their various antics, much to our edification. From that moment, I made up my mind that I would see and realize some of this, and traverse the vast plains, of which he gave us such glowing accounts.

We were still suffering from the effects of the panic of 1837, and in 1841 my uncle Eugene, who was occupying the old homestead, the "Pimlico farm," made up his mind that he would go west, upon the solicitation of his brother Charles.

Thereupon I got the consent of my grandfather to accompany him as far as St. Louis. We came from Baltimore to Harrisburg, Penn., by rail and canal, and also by canal to Hollidaysburg; crossed the Allegheny mountains, descending an inclined plain to Johnstown; travelled from Johnstown to Pittsburg by canal; and thence down the Ohio river by boat to Cairo, and up the Mississippi river to St. Louis, Mo., reaching the latter point about October first. My intention was to remain in St. Louis during the winter, and go up into the Indian country on the upper Missouri with my uncle Charles in the following spring, as we then expected him down in charge of a fleet of Mackinaw boats loaded with their winter's catch of furs. But, as fate would have it, the company sent him the other way among the Blackfeet Indians, toward the headwaters of the Yellowstone river and the great Park, which then was unknown, but today is recognized as one of our most precious national treasures.

This vast country was owned by various tribes of Indians, and California had not yet been ceded to the United States government by Mexico. All traders had to receive a license permitting them to trade, or even to travel or hunt, within these territories. The country was full of game of all kinds, and the Indians lived "like gods." The buffalo roamed in their midst without fear, as if placed there by a bountiful Providence for their special benefit. The fur trade was of vast importance; and, as the Hudson Bay Company, of British America, often encroached upon this territory, American traders kept close to the line in opposition to them. My uncle Charles' services being very valuable to the company, he was induced to remain in the country. Therefore, the fleet of the American Fur Company arrived in St. Louis in the spring of 1843 without him, as it did the spring previous, and I abandoned for that season again the hope of reaching the plains of the upper Missouri. In the meantime, I remained in the family of my uncle Eugene, and assisted him in his vocation. The spring following his arrival he leased about five acres of ground upon which there was a comfortable little house, situated on Chouteau avenue, near Chouteau's pond, for the purpose of market gardening; and the two years I remained with him our crops were simply immense. But

we could get nothing for them. There was no money. The few dollars he had brought with him from the East he had placed in the hands of a friend, who afterwards failed, producing a crisis; and two years later, with the remnant of the wreck, he returned to Baltimore, and to the old homestead, Pimlico, where he remained until he came to St. Paul in 1849.

By the treaty proclaimed June 15th, 1838, the Sioux Indians, comprising the bands of Wabasha, Red Wing, Kaposia, Black Dog, Lake Calhoun, Shakopee, and Good Road, ceded to the United States government all their lands east of the Mississippi river, thus opening up this country to settlement. No longer was any license required to trade with the Indians. The country was free to all. Quite a number of persons became engaged along the St. Croix river in lumbering, and others in trading with Indians for furs.

In the spring of 1843 a friend of ours, Mr. William Hartshorn, whose business was buying furs, made a trip up the Mississippi river as far as Fort Snelling. Previous to this, a mission had been established by the Reverend Father Galtier, in 1841, some six miles below Fort Snelling, and dedicated to St. Paul. Around this mission a few families of refugees from Fort Garry and employees of the Fur Company had settled, among whom were Benjamin and Pierre Gervais, Joseph Rondo, Pierre Bottineau, Abraham Perry, Vital Guerin,* Scott Campbell, Francois Morin, Menock Dyerly, James R. Clewett, Sergeant Richard W. Mortimer, and Edward Phalen. The only accessible landing for boats was near this mission chapel of St. Paul, in consequence of the high bluffs between that point and the fort, and hence the vicinity of the mission became the site of our beautiful city, and its name was given for the patron saint of the chapel.

When my friend reached this point, a gentleman boarded the boat and joined the party for the fort. This was Mr. Henry Jackson, who with his wife had located here the fall previous. He had traded with the Indians, and had accumulated quite a quantity of furs. These Mr. Hartshorn bought, and at the same time formed a copartnership with Mr. Jackson. Returning to St. Louis, and buying an outfit for the firm, he

---

*Mr. Guerin's first name has been often misspelled Vetal, in accordance with its pronunciation.

called upon me, giving me a history of his venture and intentions for his future trade in this new and but little known Indian country. He said there were half-breeds from the British
American districts who visited St. Paul for the purpose of
trade and all spoke French, and as I spoke that language he
would like my services. Here was my opportunity. I had a
chance at last presented me to see a live Indian; and, being
tired of waiting for a place in the Missouri country, I engaged
myself to this firm for an indefinite period at eight dollars per
month and expenses. I was glad to get anything. A man's
services had scarcely any value at all, and what he produced
about the same. Oats sold for six cents per bushel; dressed
hogs at one and a half cents per pound; and porter-house steak
at five cents per pound, with all the liver you desired thrown in.
St. Louis county and city orders were selling at forty cents on
the dollar. Such was the state of things at that time.

Having made the needed purchases, and consummated
our engagement, I left St. Louis on the steamer Iowa with an
oufit, September 1st, 1843. At Galena, one of the most important points between St. Louis and Fort Snelling, in consequence of its great lead mines, which were at that period
attracting as many prospectors as California at a later day,
we reshipped all our outfit on board the Steamer Otter. Capt.
Scribe Harris was in command, and Capt. Thomas Owens was
clerk and supercargo. We reached our destination here September 15th, 1843, just fourteen days after our departure from
St. Louis. This was considered quite a quick trip. Just think
of the difference in time now. The Otter was a small side-
wheel steamer, propelled by a single engine. She had a very
loud voice, and you could hear her escape for miles.

POPULATION AND TRADE IN 1843.

Upon my arrival, I found my employer's partner, Mr.
Henry Jackson, and his estimable wife, with whom I was
soon made to feel at home, and for many years I was pleased
to look upon her as a mother and friend. Society was crude,
but pure and devoid of affectation. The white population,
taken all together at that date, in the vast territory that
now includes the great state of Minnesota, the two Dakotas,
parts of Wisconsin and Iowa, and all the country across the

Missouri river to the Pacific coast, did not exceed three hundred. To-day we count them by the millions. The Indian and the buffalo have disappeared and given place to habits of civilization, with its railroads, electric cars, rules of etiquette, and conventional customs. We found this country new. We were beyond the bounds of civilization, beyond the frontier. The former we enjoy to-day with all its advantages; but the latter, the frontier, where is it? Can any man tell? It has disappeared forever.

Our trade was with the natives, and with them I became exceedingly interested. I acquired in a very short time sufficient knowledge of their language to get along nicely with them in their trade, and in a couple of years became quite proficient. In fact, I was obliged immediately to study up the language, because I needed to use it as soon as the fur season commenced, which was in November. All furs are considered in their prime at that season; mink, otter and coon, in particular. I was usually sent out to their hunting grounds with various articles for trading, and I would pick up a good many muskrat skins that others knew little about. The country abounded in game, and I soon became an expert in the chase.

Competition was great in those days. One had to keep on the alert, for the American Fur Company regarded the fur trade as exclusively their own, and when Louis Robert, James W. Simpson, and Hartshorn & Jackson, came upon the scene, they were looked upon as intruders. I remember on one occasion, it was a Christmas eve, we were all enjoying ourselves at citizen Robert's; I believe it was on the occasion of the celebration of the marriage of his niece to Mr. Simpson. About ten o'clock I withdrew, having my train already loaded, and started out with Scott Campbell as my interpreter, and Acka-wasta as my guide. We reached Little Canada about midnight, and camped by the side of that beautiful lake, with nothing but a Mackinaw blanket for my covering. Old Scott Campbell was very fond of his nips, and he and the old Indian were having a jolly good time, while I was attending to the domestic affairs necessary for our comfort. Having felled a good-sized oak tree, preparatory to making our camp fire, old man Campbell rose up in order to help me, when he stumbled

24

over the log and fell head foremost into three feet of snow, and before I could dig him out I thought he would smother.

I had not been long in the country before it became neces-sary that I should have an Indian name. One day, "Techa," Old Bets' brother, came into the store, and being quite a wag, from some act of mine, he baptized me "Wamduska," the ser-pent, and by that name I have been known from St. Paul to the British line and wherever there was a Dakota Indian. I soon learned to speak their language fluently, and have always re-tained their confidence and good will.

The Indians then received their annuities with commend-able regularity, and for many days after the yearly payment the old traders and their visitors would enjoy to their hearts' content a lively game of poker, and a stranger who would happen to come around was sure to be amused. Such old fellows as Donald McDonald, William A. Aitkin, and some others, the names of whom I have now forgotten, could enter-tain the most adept, and give them a percentage besides. On one occasion, I remember one of my employers about the Christmas holidays thought he would make a trip up among these traders, because, having sold more goods for cash than was desirable, and having no use for the money until spring, he wished to invest it in buying some of their furs for cash. Taking a friend along, he remained away about ten days, re-turning without money or furs. He said that upon their ar-rival, they found it impossible to invest their cash in furs. The traders would not sell. Their returning home without furs and without money was accounted for by the statement that on their way down, just a little above Anoka, while they were on the river, the ice gave way and they were precipitated into the water and lost the saddle-bags containing their money and came near losing their lives besides. They resolved to go back at once, after procuring rakes and other tools, in hopes that they might be able to recover the saddle-bags and the money. Next morning bright and early they started back, taking me along. We reached "Anoka Sippi" (Rum river) about camping time, but, a thaw having come on, in the morn-ing we could not cross the river. The snow had nearly all gone, hence we were obliged to return without further search for that money bag. 'Twas just as well, for although I was

not a very bright boy, and had many things yet to learn, 'twas just as I had surmised. The company's money got into a hole before it reached that in the Mississippi river. Oh, these old traders were a jolly set, and whenever you came in contact with them they always left you something to remember them by.

[1]The old firm dissolved shortly after that, and divided their stock, Mr. Hartshorn removing his post to a place situated where the Central Police station is to-day, on Third street at the head of Hill street. This house was built of hewn logs by Sergeant Mortimer, and contained three rooms, a bedroom at one end, a store room at the other, and a living room, which served both as kitchen and parlor, in the center, with a huge fireplace in one corner, built of stone and topped off with a flour barrel.

MARRIAGE, AND OUR PIONEER STORE AND HOME.

Before this dissolution took place, in the year 1845 I married my wife, the sister of the late Bartlett Presley. She came up from St. Louis for that purpose, as this was to be our future home, and I had not the means to make the trip to St. Louis to bring her up. You see it was economy to have her come and have the hymeneal knot tied here, and also showed a good example to our friends hereabout. Mr. Hartshorn's family being still in St. Louis, it became very convenient for him to have us take charge of his domestic as well as his commercial affairs, and hence the situation accommodated us all along the line. We would have been put to considerable inconvenience had Mr. Hartshorn not been able to avail himself of this location.

Sergeant Mortimer having died, Mrs. Mortimer was left a widow with four or five children. About this time William Evans, an old soldier and acquaintance of the Mortimers, whose time had expired, having received an honorable discharge, took a claim on what is now called Dayton's Bluff. They became engaged. Henry Jackson being at the time a justice of peace, they presented themselves before him to have the nuptial service performed. From some cause or other, he declined to do it, saying he did not feel that he had authority to perform the ceremony, but he would draw up a contract

binding them to have the rite performed as soon as it could be legally done. The contract was drawn and duly signed, and as Mr. and Mrs. Evans could not occupy both places, they elected to take for their home Dayton's Bluff. Thus Mr. Hartshorn got the original Mortimer claim. Mr. and Mrs. Evans lived happily a number of years on the bluff, when they sold their claim to Mr. Lyman Dayton, after which they moved to Cottage Grove, and in that vicinity have both gone to their reward.

Moving into our new quarters, we soon began to make our little home as comfortable as circumstances would permit. Many times it became very monotonous and lonesome for this young wife. The nearest neighbors we had were Mrs. John R. Irvine on the south, Scott Campbell on the east, and, in order after these, the families of Vital Guerin, Benjamin Gervais, James W. Simpson, then a bachelor, and, finally, on the extreme edge of the bluff, on the corner of Jackson and Bench streets, were Henry Jackson and his estimable wife. Mr. and Mrs. Irvine were our nearest and most congenial neighbors. My wife was accustomed to spend much of her leisure time with them, their house being in sight and within a stone's throw of ours.

At times it used to be very lively about the shop, that is, during the fur season, when sometimes we would have so many Indians lying about the floor you could scarcely move around without stepping on one. We always had to keep them over night and feed them besides. Trading was mostly done at night anyway, as they did not like to pass the fur company's place of business at Mendota when they could be seen, for some of them were owing the company. Oh! the Indian is human, and don't you forget it!

Let me say right here, we owe a debt of gratitude to the wives and mothers of the old settlers and pioneers of Minnesota. It is to them that many of us owe the blessings we now enjoy in this North Star State. Many of them left the comforts of home, and friends, loving mothers and doting fathers, to follow us adventurers into an unknown land, and how well they have done their part! Many of us would have fallen by the wayside, but by their prayers and helping hands they have bidden us rise again, and thus we were enabled to face

the stern realities of life. Such were the wives of the old set-
lers, and to them is due all praise for the benefits we are all
enjoying here to-day.

To one of these I may say I am indebted for being able to
be with you this evening. It was a dark and dismal night.
My wife had retired. I was about closing up. There were yet
a few embers aglow in the fireplace, when a knock was heard
at the door. We were alone. I opened the door, when an
Indian came in, seating himself by the fire. I was in hopes
that after he had warmed himself he would get up and go
away. I entertained him as well as I could, but he became
very abusive, and before I could think he drew his knife and
was in the act of making a plunge at me, when my wife in her
white sleeping gown appeared in the door, thus diverting his
attention, which gave me the opportunity of grabbing his hand
in which he held the knife, and disarming him. I was his
equal then. I left him a fit subject for the cemetery, and
threw him over the bluff. Next morning he crawled up and
came into the house, and I assisted him to perform his ablu-
tions and gave him a good breakfast. We parted friends, and
were friends ever thereafter. Such scenes as these were not
infrequent to wives and mothers of the pioneers of Minnesota.

On another occasion, by appointment, my mother and my
sister and her husband met me in St. Louis on their
way to Minnesota to make it their future home. I had been
there purchasing my spring stock, and had shipped all aboard
the steamer Excelsior, commanded by Capt. James Ward. We
reached home, all well, and with nothing out of the usual
course of things happening. The next morning after our arrival, my brother-in-law was helping to open a crate of crockery ware which stood in the stock in front of my store, and
my mother and sister were standing upon the porch, when a
band of Ojibway Indians, coming down Jackson street, made
an attack upon some Sioux Indians, shooting into Forbes'
store, and killing one squaw, the sister of Old Bets. You all
know Isaac P. Wright. He is a particular friend of mine, but
I must say that, in his zeal and enthusiasm, he sometimes
deviates from veracity. In an article which he wrote giving
a description of this affair, he says: "At the time of the attack, A. L. Larpenteur was opening a crate of crockery ware

and had his hands full of plates and dishes; he was so frightened that he let them fall out of his hands, and they broke all to pieces." Now, you all know it was Wright that was frightened, and not Larpenteur.

Going into the house, my sister "roasted" me to a turn for bringing them here to be scalped, and for some time they were hard to be conciliated. Finally, like Claude Melnotte with Pauline Deschapelles, I located them on the bank of Lake Como, where they still reside.

HOSTILITIES BETWEEN THE OJIBWAYS AND SIOUX.

In the spring of 1842, the year before I came here, a war party of Ojibway Indians made an attack upon Little Crow's band of Sioux at Kaposia, close south of St. Paul, killing some eighteen or twenty of their best soldiers. They came from the St. Croix, and early in the morning of the attack they secreted their men in ambush along the coulie just below the present fish hatchery, where the old poor farm used to be. From there at early dawn, they started two scouts to make a demonstration on the village. Before they reached the site of the village, however, they came upon Francis Gammel's house. Two Sioux squaws were hoeing potatoes, a little patch of which they had in the yard. They shot and scalped the poor women, and from this an alarm was given. The Sioux on the village side, west of the Mississippi, immediately started as many as they could in pursuit. The scouts kept in sight, but at sufficient distance to be out of danger, and thus led the Sioux completely into the ambush, when the fight began, and eighteen of the Sioux fell at the first fire. Quite a number of the Ojibways were killed outright, and some of the wounded were dispatched afterwards by the women who followed in the rear. Old Bets told me that she dismembered one. He was a tough fellow, and, her hatchet being dull, she had a deal of hard work before she could accomplish her object satisfactorily.

Three years previous to this attack, two Ojibways, hiding in ambush, near Lake Harriet, had killed a Sioux, immediately after many hundred Ojibways, having smoked the pipe of peace with the assembled Sioux at Fort Snelling, had departed northward by two routes for their homes. The Ojib-

ways were, therefore, pursued and overtaken by the Sioux, their hereditary enemies, and two battles were fought, one in the valley of the Rum river and the other at Stillwater, on the ground where now stands our state penitentiary. Mrs. Carli, still living, the sister of the late Joseph R. Brown, told me the last time I saw her, not long ago, that she saw the Stillwater battle. The Sioux were victorious in both those battles, and, having taken many scalps, returned in triumph.

In the attack against Kaposia, old Bets' brother "Techa," called Jim, lost his leg. It was broken below the knee and hung by a fragment. He took his knife and cut it off himself, and thus became his own surgeon. It healed, and the year following, when I became acquainted with him, he had made himself a wooden leg of the most improved style. He was known to the later settlers as "Peg-Leg Jim." Old Bets' oldest son, Taopi, who long afterward, in 1862, aided to save white settlers from massacre, and became one of General Sibley's most trusty scouts, was also wounded in this fight, whence he received this name (Taopi, the Wounded). For a long time, even after I came here, the excitement in regard to this raid by the Ojibways was the topic of almost every day's conversation, and an Ojibway Indian was supposed to be hidden behind every bush.

THE JACKSON HOTEL, WITH AN ANECDOTE.

The Northwestern territory began about this time to attract more or less attention from tourists, and Henry Jackson was obliged to furnish to them shelter and accommodation such as he could afford from the scanty means he had at hand. His hospitality soon became known, and there were at all times some guests stopping at his caravansary. About this time there were several permanent boarders stopping with him: W. G. Carter, a cousin; Thomas Sloan, a stockman; and W. Renfro, a Virginian, a good fellow, who had wandered out west to get rid of society. There was also a Mr. Joseph Hall, a native of Wilmington, Delaware, a carpenter by trade. These boarders, with the balance of us, constituted the regular household of the Jackson Hotel.

This man Hall, poor fellow, was about half-witted, and very fond of the society of ladies. He spent all his earnings,

on the arrival of every boat, and on other occasions, for sweet-
meats and delicacies with which to treat them, all of which
was very nice and commendable in him, of course; but, as
there must be always some bitter with the sweet, our friend
Renfro, being considerable of a wag, thought we must have
a little fun at poor Hall's expense. Consequently, calling
him aside one day, he said: "Yesterday, while taking my
usual walk out on the road leading into the interior, I met a
couple of nice girls. They inquired of me if I knew Mr.
Joseph Hall. I told them I did. They told me they were
about getting up a suprise party for Michel LeClaire, and that
they would require your assistance, that they would be pleased
to meet you here about dusk to-morrow evening, in order to
make the necessary preliminary arrangement, and that you
should be sure to bring a friend along."

This road coincided nearly with the course of Jackson
street. It extended out beyond the Dawson residence, and
thence on toward the Rice lakes, being an old road of the Indians, used by them in going out to their hunting ground every
fall. From the description of the girls, Hall knew them at once.
Everything being arranged, the following evening four fellows started out arrayed in war paint, blanket, and gun
loaded to the muzzle with blank cartridges. No. 1, Henry
Jackson, was stationed, in ambush, on the extreme outpost;
No. 2, William G. Carter, was stationed about 200 yards this
way; No. 3, Thomas Sloan, was stationed about 200 yards
farther in; No. 4, Mr. Blank, was stationed nearer in, farthest
from the enemy. At the proper time, Mr. Renfro, with Mr.
Hall, came along, earnestly engaged in conversation, passing
the concealed pickets all right, to the extreme outpost, pre-
cisely where the girls were to be. All at once, Jackson rose
up out of the brush, articulating some Ojibway word,
blanket over his shoulder, and fired his piece. Renfro fell to
the ground, at the same time saying "Hall, save yourself; I
am killed." The poor fellow issued a yell of distress and
started on a canter, reaching outpost No. 2, when a salute was
given him, and another quickly from No. 3, and, as he rushed
past, before you could think, No. 4 gave him the coup de
grace. Such yelling and running was never seen nor heard of

since. He made his way to what was known later as the Baptist hill. An Ojibway half-breed, Mr. Pierre Bottineau, lived there, and at that very time a ball was going on at his house. Mr. Hall made his way there and gave them a history of his woes, saying that he was taking a walk with his friend Renfro, when at a certain point of the road they were fired upon by Ojibway Indians, that his friend was killed, and that he escaped by a miracle.

The ball was broken up for awhile, and some of the male portion started out to investigate, taking Hall along. They could find nothing, and thought they would go over to Jackson's and see what they could learn there. They entered his store, which was also the bar room, sitting room and everything else, when lo and behold, the dead man was sitting on the counter smoking his pipe, with the other fellows alongside of him, apparently unconscious of what had happened with our neighbors. It soon became apparent that a good joke had been played on someone, and for a time the half-breeds were a little disposed to take a more serious view of the situation. But someone suggested that we throw oil upon the troubled waters, and the demijohn was passed around. All then adjourned to the domicile of neighbor Bottineau, and the ball went on again, with renewed energy, until the next morning.

Poor Hall became a victim of the Sioux outbreak, as I have since learned; and in regard to Renfro we must record that the poor fellow's career ended not less unhappily. He was a gentleman of refinement, but, unfortunately, became too fond of his cups, and I believe that for that reason he came out here to try to overcome this habit. But it was the worst place he could have come to. Edward Phelan, or Phalen, from whom lake Phalen derived its name, had his shack not far from where the palatial residence of William Hamm now stands; and when Renfro would have one of his spells come upon him, he would hie himself off to Phelan's, and there remain until he recovered. On one of these occasions he rose in the night and slipped away from Phelan's with nothing on but his drawers. It was in winter, with snow on the ground, and Phelan gave us the alarm the next morning. It having snowed a little during the night, he could not track him. Hence,

when he came in and told us of the circumstance, we all started out for a systematic search. I found him lying at full length, frozen stiff, not far from where is situated to-day the Van Slyke Court. We buried him at the head of Jackson street. May his soul rest in peace. He was a good fellow, of a kind disposition, but a victim to a morbid appetite. A lesson— but, alas, learned too late by many.

FIRST SURVEYS AND LAND CLAIMS.

In 1847 we laid out the original town plat of St. Paul, having to send to Prairie du Chien for a surveyor, Mr. Ira B. Brunson, for that purpose. The plat contained about a half mile square, bounded by Wacouta, Eighth and St. Peter streets, and the river to the point of beginning. The present Jackson street was the only accessible way to the river, and it was very steep. We drew our goods up on a sled, a forked tree with a piece bolted across the end, the stem used for the tongue, such as the farmers in Maryland and Pennsylvania used to draw rock out of their fields. With this implement Mr. Vital Guerin hauled up all our goods from the landing with his yoke of oxen. A barrel of whisky or flour made a good load. Such was Jackson street when I first saw it. From this date our city began to be known by the outside world, and immigrants began to come in.

The United States government soon subdivided the lands, and a land office was established at St. Croix Falls. We were all in Wisconsin yet, and General H. H. Sibley, Capt. Louis Robert and myself were selected by the inhabitants of the town to enter all these lands upon which the original plat was laid out, as well as lands adjoining, and then to re-convey to the various parties interested their respective pieces. We were all called squatters. Many lots had been sold, and after title had been obtained from the government, it was necessary to re-convey and perfect these titles, all of which was subsequently satisfactorily done. We anticipated some trouble at the land sale from speculators, who usually attend these sales for the purpose of outbidding the settlers. To provide against a contingency of this kind and to protect the rights of the boys, we provided ourselves with a brigade of old fellows,

some dozen or more, and they carefully guarded our tents while we went to attend the sales. General Samuel Leech was the receiver, Col. C. S. Whitney the register, and B. W. Lott the crier. All being ready, the business began. There were quite a number of bidders. When our pieces were called, we bid them in, and everything passed off in good shape; but I assure you, gentlemen, had any poor fellow attempted to put his finger in our pie, he would have heard something drop.

ORGANIZATION AND GROWTH OF MINNESOTA TERRITORY.

On our return from the land sale, we held a convention at Stillwater. The State of Wisconsin had previously been organized, and left us with a portion of her territory. At that convention we petitioned Congress to grant us a territorial organization. Our prayers were heard, and Gen. H. H. Sibley, after a hard fight, was admitted as our delegate, and the Territory of Minnesota was organized. From that date immigration poured in upon us from all quarters.

I have seen sixteen large steamers lying at our levee at one time. One day I counted sixty carpenters' tool chests being unloaded from the boats then in port. The rush then for this new Eldorado was nearly like the great tide of gold-seekers who went to California during the same years, from 1849 onward. Some learned wisdom, and stayed with us; others left for other parts. Many valuable and influential citizens came into the territory at this time. Our agricultural resources began to develop, and we were soon becoming self-sustaining, and it was not necessary any longer to import all our food. Trade with the settlers began to be of as much importance nearly as with the Indians, and we were obliged to diversify our stocks. An occasional silk dress was required, or a fashionable bonnet.

EXPERIENCES OF THE EARLY TRADERS.

In the spring of 1848, William Hartshorn had sold out his interest to his clerks, D. B. Freeman, Augustus J. Freeman, A. L. Larpenteur, and William H. Randall, Jr., who formed the firm of Freeman, Larpenteur & Co. We removed our stock into our new building, begun by Mr. Hartshorn, and

finished by the new firm. This was situated on the corner of Jackson and Second streets. The building was used later by William Constans, and finally came into the hands of the Milwaukee railroad company, and was used by them for a baggage room until torn down. When it was built this was the first building on this side of Prairie du Chien. We kept our dry goods in the second story, the groceries in the basement. A nice convenient platform for the second story was reached by huge steps, and steps ascended also to the top of the bluff at Bench street, leading up town past the Central House and uniting with Third street at Wabasha.

Before I proceed any farther, a little circumstance presents itself to my mind, which perhaps right here is as good a place to mention as I may find. One of my partners, Mr. A. J. Freeman, had rather an aggressive disposition; if there was anything going on, he was sure to be in it. One morning I was in our office, quietly attending to my business. Freeman was behind the counter waiting upon some customers, when lo and behold, the Hon. William D. Phillips, a notorious attorney at law, came into the store, and, before you could think, he had a pistol out of his pocket and pointing at Freeman's breast, saying at the same time, "Retract, or I will put a hole through you." In an instant, I picked up a fire poker and flew between them, saying, "Up with that pistol, or I'll brain you." The pistol went up, and peace was proclaimed. The pistol was one of those single-barreled shooting irons of the Derringer style, and was loaded to the muzzle. I remember now seeing the paper wad sticking out. Our attorney left here shortly after that, and I think removed to Washington, D. C.

In the spring of 1849 St. Paul began to assume cosmopolitan importance. James M. Goodhue came among us with his oracle, The Pioneer. I have in my scrap-book the veritable first number stricken off. The office was just above us, and in C. P. V. Lull's shop. Its date was Saturday, April 28th, 1849. I find, upon looking over the directory therein contained of the business and professional houses and firms, that but few are left.

I would like to record here the names and firms and different advertisements of that day. They were up and doing,

but it would require too much space and time. One, for instance: "Horse Mantua-Maker, A. R. French, on Third street, in St. Paul, is prepared to make and furnish Saddles, Harness, &c." Freeman, Larpenteur & Co. were wholesaling, and carried stock to suit the trade, quality and quantity, viz., 50 barrels of old rectified whisky, 20 barrels of sugar-house molasses, 15 boxes of cheese, etc., etc. Readers don't see that they dealt in flour. Perhaps that was taken for granted. However, be that as it may, we did our share, and our future seemed sublime.

The Winnebago Indians had been moved to Long Prairie the year before, and that event brought a deal of new business into the country. I had been accustomed to making trips every winter, and as soon as the sleighing became good I suggested to our firm that we load a couple of teams and make the rounds. I expected nothing different but that I should be selected to go; but Mr. A. J. Freeman thought it best that he should go, because he knew Gen. J. E. Fletcher, the agent, Sylvanus B. Lowry, the interpreter, and Charles Rice and N. Myrick, Jim Beatty, Marsh, and White, etc., all right. We selected a nice assortment of just such goods as we supposed would be wanted, and started my boy off in good shape with two teams. He reached Long Prairie in due time, sold all his stock, amounting to about $1,500, had a good time with these friendly traders, was well entertained (as no one knows better how to entertain than one of these old Indian traders), and started on his way home without a cent! He had fallen into the hands of the Philistines, and they had fleeced him. Arriving at Swan River, he stopped over night, and a streak of luck struck him, and he left for home in the morning with $1,200 of money. So, upon his return, in footing up the cash, he could not account for $300, all of which we charged up to "suspense" account.

A few weeks later, I told the firm, it being a little dull, that I thought I would take a trip and see what I could do. I picked out a nice assortment of goods, such as I deemed would be wanted about that time, and started with two teams, driving one myself. I reached Long Prairie in due time, put up my teams, was treated royally by the agent, Gen. Fletcher,

and others, sold a portion of my goods, and made arrangements
for leaving early the next morning. During the evening I made
several visits, and found all very much interested in making
the time pass off agreeably for me. Finding that I did not
take, one of my friends said to me, "Why, you are not like
your partner; he left $1,500 with the boys when he was up
here." I then began to get upon the track of the shortage,
and on my way back, at Swan River, I learned of his "luck,"
and concluded that, had there been more money in the pot,
he might have made his shortage good. So, when I returned,
I called Mr. Freeman to one side and told him to charge his
private account with the shortage of $300, as I had found out
all about it; and in the following fall and early winter the
firm of Freeman, Larpenteur & Co. ceased to exist. I sold it
out to John Randall & Co., of New York; and, one of the Free-
mans having died, A. J. took his portion and opened a place
of business at Rice Creek, and in about one year he closed
that out, removed east, and died. I agreed to remain with the
new firm until spring, and did so.

In the meantime I had made arrangements to build me
a store on the lot adjoining my little dwelling, on the corner of
Jackson and Third streets. This was the second frame house
built in St. Paul. The first, which had burned down, was
built by Captain Louis Robert, a little earlier. The lot above
referred to was what subsequently became lot 14, block 26,
St. Paul Proper, which I bought of David Faribault, as a claim,
for $62.50 in a horse trade. The building now occupying it is
known as the Hale Block. I had a horse which Mr. Faribault
wanted. He had a 140-foot claim at this point. My price for
the horse was $80; the price of his claim was $125. He urged
me to take the whole claim and pay him the balance when
convenient, but I dared not then assume such an obligation.
Consequently, I only took half of the lot and trusted him for
the balance, $17.50, and I believe I was two years in collecting
it, if at all.

I built my palatial dwelling upon this lot, which afterwards became the "Hotel Wild Hunter" ("Zum Wilden Jäger").
The work was done by Aaron Foster (who married one of the
widow Mortimer's girls), J. Warren Woodbury, and Jesse H.

Pomroy. The latter is still alive and with us; the other two are dead. The painting was done by James McBoal, one of the best and laziest mortals that ever lived.

RELATIVES COME TO ST. PAUL.

Times had not improved much in St. Louis and the West, and my uncle Eugene, whom I left in that city, being discouraged by losing what little money he possessed, returned to Baltimore in 1845, and took charge again of the old Pimlico farm. My grandfather who was then beginning to feel the weight of years upon him, welcomed him back. My uncle was a thorough agriculturist, and as I had had eighteen years' experience myself in that vocation,. when the agricultural advantages here began to develop, I wrote to him, giving my opinion and advising him to come out here and locate upon some of these lands while they were cheap, and that I had selected a tract which he could have if he wished.

He showed my letter to my grandfather, who said: "You have been west once, and came back disappointed. Drop the idea, and I will deed you one-half of this farm." He said, "Father, if you deed me half of this farm to-day, I will sell it to-morrow; I am going West where that boy is just as soon as I can raise the money to go with." "Well, if that is your intention, advertise the place, we will sell it, and I will go with you." The place was sold. This was the spring of 1849. The cholera was very bad that year all over the West, and especially in St. Louis. While transferring from one boat to another in St. Louis, my grandfather met some old acquaintance upon the levee, and this good friend was careful in admonishing my poor old grandfather, telling him not by any means to go up into the city, as they were dying at the rate of five hundred a day. The good old man, having been suffering for years from chronic diarrhea, fell down on the pavement and had to be carried on board the boat. He never arose again. He managed to live, however, until he reached St. Paul, when he died on the third day, fully conscious to the last. We buried him, not having a cemetery at that time, at the head of Jackson street, near Tenth street. In course

of time, Jackson street was to be graded. We removed his remains to a cemetery back of St. Joseph's Academy. Afterward, when Iglehart street was opened and graded, his remains had to be removed again, and now they lie in peace, we hope, in Calvary cemetery. Thus we had the gratification, at least, of paying a portion of the debt we owed to that good old soul for the care of me when left without a mother.

Shortly after the obsequies I took my uncle to view the country for the purpose of selecting a location. I showed him the tract which I had selected as one which suited me. That was the present Kittsondale or Midway, as it is called today. It suited him. He developed it and made a garden of the spot. Upon it he reared his family, all respectable citizens, and both he and his good wife have long since gone to their reward. "Requiescant in pace."

TREATIES WITH THE SIOUX.

The lands east of the Mississippi, obtained of the Sioux Indians by the treaty of 1837 and opened for settlement, were being taken up so fast that it became necessary for the government, through the urgency of the settlers and speculators, to acquire the lands on the west side. Hence the treaty of Mendota, August 5th, 1851. Although the previous treaty had been made and duly signed, it was not satisfactory. The Indians claimed that when ceding their lands in 1837, east of the Mississippi river, they had retained the privilege of hunting upon these lands for fifty years, or during good behavior, all of which I fully believe to be true, neither party thinking then that it would be unsafe to make such an agreement. No one would have thought that before the expiration of that time the territory would contain more than a million inhabitants and have a valuation of several hundred million dollars of taxable property.

The Mendota treaty became an absolute necessity. By that treaty, and by the slightly earlier treaty of Traverse des Sioux, made July 23d, 1851, the several Sioux bands of southern Minnesota ceded to the government nearly all their lands in this state west of the Mississippi river, and were removed to reservations on the upper part of the Minnesota river. Two

agencies were established, one about eight miles below the mouth of the Redwood river, and the other on the Yellow Medicine river. There being more or less dissatisfaction among these Indians, when the Civil War broke out, it took but little to kindle the fire of rebellion among them. The massacre of 1862 took place, and history is replete with its consequences.

TRADE WITH THE FAR NORTHWEST.

After the removal of the Indians from Mendota in the year 1852, their direct trade with St. Paul ceased; but it always remained the headquarters for outfitting traders for the various adjacent tribes. This trade extended even into Manitoba, and in that direction was of great importance. It was no uncommon sight to see from a thousand to fifteen hundred carts encamped around "Larpenteur's lake," in the western part of our present city area, loaded with buffalo robes, furs of all descriptions, dressed skins, moccasins, buffalo tongues and pemican. The latter commodity was dried buffalo meat pounded and put up in 100-pound sacks, for their winter use. It was their chief supply of food, and was husbanded with the same care by these old hunters as a farmer gives to his corn. A failure in the gathering of this crop of buffalo meat by the hunters, sometimes caused by the buffalo being scarce or driven in other directions, was as serious a matter to the inhabitants as the destruction of a farmer's wheat crop by hail storm. A voyageur, when sent out by the traders, was seldom given anything else to subsist upon but a hunk of this pemican for his daily ration. And in conversation with these old voyageurs, many of them old employees of the Hudson Bay Company, I have been told that their daily rations often were no more nor less than one load of powder and ball per day, and that, being in a country where game was in abundance, they seldom went without a meal. These traders would reach here about the first of June, having left Fort Garry, now Winnipeg, as soon as the grass had grown sufficiently for their cattle to feed upon; and, in returning, they would get back about the middle of September.

25

GAME, AND ITS DECREASE.

Game was plentiful in those days. A poor man even with an old flint-lock gun and black powder could decorate his table once in a while with a duck, goose, or a piece of venison; but to-day, alas, where are we drifting? All are preserves. The Island pass, the Rondo pass, the Baldwin pass, all are fenced in and belong to the powers. The poor man is not in it any more. We, who have been piling abuses upon our cousins across the big pond, are we not getting there, too? The consequences are rapidly being felt. To me, it matters but little. My race is nearly run. But I cannot help looking back, and comparing the difference in the times; we had the cream, you are fighting for the skimmings. Oh, could you but realize the days your ancestors enjoyed upon these grounds you are now preserving, when Sibley, Faribault, Robert and Larpenteur were taking an evening shoot at the Island pass, when Louis Robert would cry out at every falling duck, "Hie, hie, don't shoot! That's mine!" Then there was fun all along the line. It didn't matter much anyway. There was enough for all, and for the Indians besides. There was sport then; 'tis labor now.

STEAMBOAT TRAVEL, FREIGHTING, AND ADVENTURES.

Not having any railroad communication in those days, when all traffic depended upon the river, we sometimes ran down to Galena or Dubuque in the autumn to "stock up," because once the navigation closed we were in for all winter. Getting goods up by sleighs was rather expensive. In the fall of 1856 I found I needed a few more goods to carry me through the winter. Consequently, I ran down to Galena, bought what I needed, and found Capt. Louis Robert in port on his way up from St. Louis with his boat, "The Greek Slave." I had shipped my goods upon his boat, and was all ready for home, when, behold, the crew struck. His engineer, Bill Davis, who was his nephew, was all right; his pilot, George Nicholas, one of the oldest and best on the river, was all right. Monti, the mate, an old veteran of the Mexican war, was all right also, but the others of the crew wanted guaranties that, in case of a freeze-up, they would be returned to their homes free of expense.

Here was a dilemma. The captain wished to reach St. Paul with his boat so as to lay her up there all winter. It was then about the first of November. Something had to be done. Outside of the parties above named, only one cabin boy and the chambermaid remained. She called the boy to her, saying "Tom, go up town, tell Mike to come down at once and be steward of this boat, and if he refuses, tell him the first time I meet him I will cut his throat from ear to ear." Mike came down. With what we could pick up we started out for St. Paul, reached Dubuque all right, had a barge in tow when we started, and took on another at Guttenberg, also some cattle. The crew getting pretty well used up, the second morning out found us on a bar about five miles below Winona. There we lay until about four o'clock in the afternoon. Working all day, the pilot, engineer, mate and captain all exhausted, I began to believe and think we were planted on that bar for the winter.

Picking up courage, I stepped to the captain and addressed him thus: "Captain, you are sick, and need help. Give me your overshoes and overcoat and command of this boat, and I will see her through to St. Paul." The captain made a complete resignation. He said, "Larpenteur, take her." The man, as well as his crew, was exhausted, and had lost self-control. I put the captain to bed, took charge of the boat, set my spars, kept what I got, and with capstan and a few revolutions on the starboard wheel she yielded, and, from the time I took the boat, in a half hour I was at Winona. I told the boys to be patient. Seven miles above was Fountain City. It was yet light, and we would make that point, when I would put them to bed. We reached that point while yet twilight. I made all I could spare turn in, telling them that I would have them waked up at midnight, thus giving them about six hours' sleep.

A barge was to be left at this point, upon which there were some cattle. They were to be put upon the boat. All things being ready, I began the transfer of my cattle. The poor things had been abused, and were afraid for their lives, but all went well enough in transferring except an old bull.

He had been pounded over the head till he scarcely dared to move one way or the other. However, he was finally induced to step upon the staging, and there he stood neither willing to go one way nor the other. Finally I told one of the men to bring me some ear corn. I gave him one ear and patted him at the same time on the head and shoulder and offered him another ear, at the same time commanding the men to keep perfectly quiet. He approached that ear and took it, and with about four ears of corn I landed my refractory bull aboard of my boat, amid the cheers of my deck hands, thus showing that kind acts are appreciated and have their reward by a dumb animal as well as a human being.

I had all on board then turn in except the watchman. At midnight, all refreshed, I had steam ready, some hot coffee and lunch, called every man to his post, and stood on the hurricane deck the balance of that night. We landed in Stillwater about three o'clock the following afternoon. I had a horse on board of the boat and a saddle, and an idea struck me that I could reach St. Paul quicker on horseback than by boat, so I called the captain up. That was about twenty-four hours from the time I had put him to bed, and he was sleeping yet. I awoke him, delivered my charge back to him again, took my horse, and near the setting of the sun was at home with my family. The boat got in next morning and laid off for all winter.

In taking a retrospective view of those times, it makes one feel sad. What has become of those palatial steamers, the masters of which trod their decks with pride, in the knowledge of their ability to meet all responsibilities? Then the pilot—why, he was looked upon as endowed with supernatural powers! Indeed, it would seem so; for in those days there were no beacon lights around the bends, as to-day; all he had to guide him was instinct, and it was a pleasure to see such men as Wash Highs, Billy Cupps, Pleasant Cormack, Pete Lindall, John King, George Nicholas, and others, handle the wheel of a dark night. What has become of all this? Our poor Mississippi river, are you going to dry up? It makes

one who has seen her drain the product of this great valley from the Falls of St. Anthony to the balizes that guide the pilot coming in from the sea, feel that he has lost a friend.

In those days, you boarded a steamer in St. Paul for St. Louis, for instance. The cost of passage, including meals, was $10. You were four days making the trip, giving you plenty of time to get acquainted with your fellow passengers, and a wholesome rest from your arduous labors, if you had any, besides the recreation. To-day, how is it? You have scarcely time to recognize any one on board but the conductor, and we are driven at such lightning speed that many of us are landed in an insane asylum, and the word is "get out of the way or you will be run over."

The masters of our steamers in those days, were every one of them a Dewey or a Schley. There were few strikes in those days. The malcontents, if any there were, were afraid. They would say "If we kick, why, the old man will take the wheel or the engine himself, for he can run it as well as I can." Hence, they would put up with the ills they had rather than to fly to those they knew not of. These captains when treading their decks were the envy of us all, and with pleasant recollections we refer back to our friend and fellow old settler, Capt. Russell Blakeley, of the "Dr. Franklin," whom we still have with us; Capt. D. S. Harris, of the "War Eagle;" Capt. Orren Smith, of the "Nominee;" Capt. James Ward, of the "Excelsior;" Tom Rhodes, of the "Metropolitan;" Capt. Dick Gray, of the "Denmark," with calliope attachments; and John Atchison, the captain of the "Highland Mary."

I was on board when Capt. John Atchison died. I happened to be in St. Louis in the spring of 1849. I had completed my purchases and shipped all my goods on board of his boat, which was to leave in the morning. I was stopping at the Virginia Hotel. About eight o'clock in the evening, I was sitting in the rotunda of the hotel, when Capt. John came in. I asked him about the time of leaving; he said, "Early in the morning." I told him I was ready, having shipped all my goods, and would be with him. He said to me, "Larpenteur, I feel a little lonesome; come on board now." I set-

tled my bill, and, after we had walked down to the boat together, I drank a mint julep and smoked a cigar with him. Both of us retired in apparent good health as ever, about eleven o'clock. At four o'clock the following morning he was dead. Cholera was very fatal that season. His brother, Pierce Atchison, brought the boat up. I could enumerate many of these old Mississippi river steamboat captains whose memory it is a pleasure to recall. All of them were noble, generous men, and they all did their part in developing the resources of the great Northwest.

One I had almost forgotten, Captain Monfort, renowned for the Indian flute. Did anyone board his boat and possess the least bit of curiosity, he was sure to remember his Indian flute. It was an instrument about one foot long, decorated with Indian hieroglyphics and filled with flour, and when played upon it would fill the operator's eyes and face full, to his utter amazement and to the gratification of the initiated. Some would take the joke philosophically, and settle the question at the bar. Others, a little more sensitive, would not fare so well. But there was scarcely a trip in which the Indian flute of Capt. Monfort failed to get in its work.

VINDICATION AND EULOGY OF THE PIONEERS.

Now, rather than to prolong this paper unduly, I shall attempt to conclude, and will say that I am now drawing near my fourscore years of age, fifty-five of which have been passed near this spot. Fifty-five years in the life of a man is a very long time, but in the life of a country or state is but like a grain of sand upon the sea shore. What history has been written in this short space of time! Nothing equals it in the annals of the world. And, did each of us, as we pass along the rugged ways of life, make a note of current events, what an aid that would be to the future historian. Alas, we think of these things when too late. Of all the actors who were on the stage here, fifty-five years ago, there are none remaining. They have all gone. They were not bad men. They took their toddy as I do to-day from off my sideboard, while others deem it best to to be taken in their cellars.

Some historians write up Pierre Parrant, my old friend, as a very wicked man. I knew him well, and have to take issue with them. The only offense I could charge him with, if it could be called an offense, was that he sold whisky. Well, tell me who didn't. His word in a deal was as good as any other man's, whose word was good at all.

Edward Phelan (or Phalen) was one of those simple, plain, uneducated Irishmen; he stood six feet two in his stocking feet; he had been discharged honorably from the United States service, about the same time with Sergeant Mortimer. Phelan and another similarly discharged soldier, Sergeant John Hays, made claims together and built their shanty about where the electric power house is located on Hill street. One morning in September, 1839, Hays was missing. The body was recovered in the river near Carver's Cave. Phelan was arrested, taken to Prairie du Chien, there remained in prison for over six months, was tried and acquitted. He never killed Hays; the Indians have told me since that Hays was not killed by Phelan. They always spoke to me as though they knew who did kill him. After Phelan returned, he attempted to take possession of his claim, but other parties had jumped it, and he drifted lower down and took a claim and built his shanty not far from where the palatial residence of Mr. William Hamm now stands. Old Phelan was human. He took his toddy, too, but he would not injure a hair of your head, while I knew him.

They are at rest now. It matters not what the present generation has to say about these fellows. They had their faults, but are we perfect to-day, that we can go back and criticise with impunity the lives of these old pioneers, who have been the forerunners and helped us on the way to the blessings we enjoy here? I say, No. Bury their imperfections with them in their graves; keep their virtues in memory green like the sward above them.

Of a later period. I am happy to see yet with us a few of those blessed spirits whom the world would be lonesome without. Here are Nathan Myrick, Capt. Russell Blakeley, John D. Ludden, W. P. Murray, S. P. Folsom, Alexander Ramsey, and some few others; but, as they are still in the flesh,

I dare not express my sentiments regarding them and what I think of them, for fear there might be some exceptions taken. After they have retired from the sphere of action, it will be time enough then.

Before concluding, however, I will except one, you, Alexander Ramsey, our Aleck. Minnesota owes you much. You took her while in her swaddling clothes. By your wisdom and sagacity you nursed her to maturity, and then again you were called to care for her, in the nation's greatest need. By your wise and prudent judgment of men and measures, you failed not to call into your counsels the best men for your lieutenants, as demonstrated in the selection of that Christian gentleman, the poor man's friend, Gen. H. H. Sibley, capable, and honorable; and hence your administration has ever been successful. Minnesota has honored you, sir, 'tis true, but no more than you have honored her. You have always been willing to advise and confer with your constituents, and hence always will be one of us.

Your successor was somewhat different, although we all liked Willis A. Gorman. He had some peculiarities. Well, who has not? He insulted me on my first introduction to him, on the day of his arrival, when the boat landed at the foot of Jackson street, with the new governor and retinue on board. I was, like all the others, interested in seeing him come ashore, and was standing on the corner of the Merchants' Hotel, opposite to my store, when the governor came along, escorted by Col. J. J. Noah and Morton Wilkinson. Approaching me, Wilkinson said, "Governor, allow me to introduce to you Mr. A. L. Larpenteur, an old Indian trader; he is perfectly familiar with the Indians, and speaks their language; his acquaintance may be of some benefit to you." "How do you do, sir? I came here purposely to look after these Indian traders; shall see to them, sir." I thought the new governor was a scorcher, and thus the matter rested. In the course of a very short time a delegation of Indians, with Little Crow at their head, called upon the governor. Their interpreter was out of town. The governor addressed a very polite note to me, requesting me to come up to the capitol, as the Indians wished to have a talk with him. I respectfully returned his note, at the same time

reminding him of his remark on the corner by the Merchants' Hotel. Little Crow came after me, and at his request I went, and the new governor saw that man needs his fellow man, and that we are each other's keepers. We were always friends thereafter, as this little episode brought us nearer together.

Gen. H. H. Sibley was an Indian trader. Notwithstanding, when the Indian outbreak took place, you did not hesitate to call him to your aid. In so doing, the high character and integrity in which he was held by the Indians showed subsequently that you made no mistake. Had he precipitated the attack at Camp Release, as poor Custer did at Big Horn, the ninety-one hostages held by the hostile Indians would have been butchered. But, by diplomacy, the lives of all of them were saved and the hostiles were captured, without losing a man. Which of the two was the better general? 'Tis not for me in this article to say.

Minnesota, the gem of the constellation of states! I have followed your progress from infancy to maturity. I have seen you when you had to be fed as a suckling child, and ere my earthly career has closed you have contributed largely to the support of others; your hidden resources have all been developed since I saw you first. Little did I think, when stepping off the steamer Otter, September 15th, 1843, that to-day your new executive mansion would be built upon land bought by me from the government at $1.25 per acre. And again, while in pursuit of my vocation, camping with Hole-in-the-Day, the elder, at Watab, I remember casting my eyes upon those great outcrops of rock lying there, of no earthly value apparently. Yet there was a gold mine in them, and I have to-day been permitted to see specimens of this rock, artistically hewn and polished, form a part of the material out of which our capitol building is being built. It is a pleasure to me to note that our little family bickerings were finally laid at rest last July 27th, 1898, with the laying of the corner-stone of that building; but let me add, in conclusion thereto, that those who opposed the meager appropriation granted will regret their act. Within the lifetime of some of them, the state of Minnesota will contain three millions of inhabitants, and this building, large and capacious as it appears for the present needs, will

require an annex, as with our new United States postoffice building to-day.

Old settlers and fellow contemporaries, I cannot close this already too long paper, without expressing my gratification and pride, though one of the humblest among you, in being placed in your midst as one of the old settlers and pioneers of Minnesota. The brightest legacy I can leave my children is that their father was one of those who founded and helped to develop the resources of this great state. No state in our Union had a better class of men to begin its existence with. They were men of energy and intelligence,—God-fearing men, hence successful. In 1843 I found the territory of the present states of Minnesota and the two Dakotas having, if we include the soldiers at Fort Snelling, only about two hundred white inhabitants. To-day, I see these states with over two millions of people. Is it beyond the bounds of probability to say that seven years hence, "Our Minnesota" will have two millions herself? I think not.

Our climate is unsurpassed anywhere, and our winters are becoming milder every year. Those of us who passed our early days in the Middle States remember only too well the mud of early spring and late autumns, and icicles three feet long hanging from the roofs of our houses. We have none of that here. Our roads are simply perfect all the time. I look back with regret at the loss of the good sleigh rides we had here in the days of "Auld Lang Syne," which recollection at times makes us old men almost wish we were boys again.

My dear friends of this present generation, whenever you meet one of these old settlers and pioneers of the frontier, tottering toward the grave, throw the mantle of charity over him; overlook his imperfections, and remember that it was he who blazed the trees, marking out the path which made it possible for you to enjoy the blessings you possess here in the great and glorious State of Minnesota to-day.

MR. AND MRS. N. D. WHITE.

CAPTIVITY AMONG THE SIOUX, AUGUST 18 TO SEPTEMBER 26, 1862.*

BY MRS. N. D. WHITE.

. The story I bring to you includes what I saw and what occurred to myself and family during the most terrible Indian massacre that was ever known in our fair country. Fifteen thousand square miles of territory were overrun by the savages, and their trails in Minnesota were marked by blood and fire, while men, women, and innocent children were indiscriminately butchered or made prisoners.

I was born in the town of Alexander, Genesee county, New York, February 10th, 1825, my maiden name being Urania S. Frazer; and I was married to Nathan Dexter White, October 1st, 1845. The photograph reproduced in Plate XIV was taken at the completion of fifty-three years of our married life. We remained in New York state about two years, and then emigrated to Columbia county, Wisconsin, where we lived fifteen years. In the spring of 1862 we again turned our faces westward, and June 28th found us in Renville county, Minnesota.

Little did we think how soon we should pass through the terrible ordeal that awaited us. We commenced the erection of our log cabin at the base of the bluff in the valley of Beaver creek, near its opening into the wide Minnesota river valley, with stout hands and willing minds, looking hopefully forward to better times, for we thought we had selected the very heart of this western paradise for our home. Truly it was beautiful, even in its wild, uncultivated condition, with its gigantic trees in the creek valley, its towering bluffs, and the sweet-scented wild flowers. A babbling brook formed a part of the eastern boundary of our land, and its broad acres of prairie made it

*Read at the monthly meeting of the Executive Council, November 14, 1898.

desirable enough to have satisfied the wishes of the most fastidious lover of a fine farm. We had just got settled in our
new log house when the Sioux Indians who lived near us began
to be uneasy.

Little Crow's village was situated about six miles from
our house, across the Minnesota river. His warriors numbered
about eight hundred. These Indians, with their families, by
reason of the scarcity of buffaloes and other wild game, were
largely dependent upon their annuities. They were supplied
with provisions from the commissary stores at the Lower Sioux
Indian Agency, near Little Crow's village; and they also received
their annuities from the agent at this point. The summer of
that eventful year was to all appearances very favorable to
them, so far as crops were concerned. Their many cornfields,
of nearly a thousand acres, bore promise of rich yield. But
Little Crow was all the time, as was afterward proven, working upon his warriors in such a manner as to keep them excited and bloodthirsty. Indian treachery came to the surface.
We frequently saw them on the tops of the bluffs overlooking
our dwelling. They seemed to be watching for something.
When questioned, they said they were looking for Ojibways.
I think they must have held war meetings or councils, for we
often heard drums in the evening on their side of the Minnesota river several weeks before the outbreak.

Reports came to us that some of the Indians had made a
raid upon the commissary stores at the Upper Agency; but we
paid little attention to it, thinking it only a rumor.

The annuity was to have been paid in June; but, owing to
the civil war that was then raging between the United and
Confederate States, the money was delayed. The Indians were
compelled to ward off starvation by digging roots for food.
Three or four weeks previous to the outbreak, we could see
squaws almost every day wandering over the prairie in search
of the nutritious roots of the plant known to the French voyageurs as the "pomme de terre." With a small pole about
six feet long, having one end sharpened, they dug its tap-root,
which they called tipsinah, somewhat resembling a white English turnip in color, taste, and shape.

Many of the Indians had pawned their guns for provisions.
My husband had taken several in exchange for beef cattle.

Among them was Little Crow's gun. This manner of dealing with the white man was not satisfactory to them; and especially to be compelled thus to part with their guns was very hard. Knowing the treachery of the Indians, none of us should have been surprised when this desperate outbreak overwhelmed us; and yet, when the eighteenth day of August, 1862, came, with its cloudless sky, not one of the scattered settlers was prepared for the carnage and death which these cunning plotters designed for them. So secretly had each Indian performed his allotted part in the working up of this terrible tragedy in which they were to be the heartless actors and we the helpless victims.

At this time nearly every farmer was busy making hay; but my husband fortunately was on a trip to Blue Earth county, about sixty miles southeast of us. I say fortunately, because every man stood in great danger of being killed; and in all probability that would have been his fate, if he had been with us, as no men among the settlers were taken prisoners.

FLIGHT. AMBUSH, AND MASSACRE.

The first outbreak, the attack on our fleeing party, and the beginning of my captivity, were on Monday, August 18th; and I was released thirty-nine days afterward, on September 26th.

While I was busily engaged gathering up the clothing for the purpose of doing my washing on the morning of the outbreak, my daughter Julia, fourteen years old, who had been assisting at the house of Mr. Henderson, about a half mile from us, whose wife was very sick, came running in, accompanied by a daughter of Mr. J. W. Earle, and breathlessly told me that the Indians were coming to kill us, and that I must go back with them quick. This frightened me, in fact, it seemed to strike me dumb; but, suddenly recovering my thoughts, I immediately began planning what we should take with us. Soon I came to the conclusion that it would be folly to attempt to take anything. But on moving my husband's overcoat I caught sight of a large pocketbook that contained valuable papers and some money. This I quickly se-

cured, and managed to keep it during all my captivity. I caught up my baby boy, five months old, and placed him on one arm, and took Little Crow's gun in the other hand. My daughter also carried a gun. We hurriedly wended our way to the house of the sick neighbor, and thence went to the house of Mr. Earle.

There I found my twelve-year-old son Millard, who had been herding sheep. Having learned of the trouble with the Indians, he had driven the sheep up and put them in the yard. Eugene, my oldest son, had gone out on the prairie to bring in our colts, to keep them from the Indians, because they were collecting all the horses in the neighborhood to ride, as they said, in hunting Ojibways, that being the excuse they gave for this bold robbery. He found that the Indians had already got the colts and were breaking them to ride, having them in a slough, where they could easily handle them. Consequently he came back to the house of Mr. Earle. On his way back he met Mr. Weichman, a neighbor just from the Agency, who told him that the Indians were killing all the white people there.

At the house of Mr. Earle twenty-seven neighbors were assembled, men, women and children. Teams of horses were soon hitched to wagons, and we started on our perilous journey.

The Indians, anticipating our flight and knowing the direction we should be likely to take, had secreted themselves in ambush on either side of the road in the tall grass. On our arrival in the ambush, twenty or thirty Indians in their war paint rose to their feet; they did not shoot, but surrounded us, took our horses by the bits, and commanded us to surrender to them all our teams, wagons, and everything except the clothing we had on. A parley with them in behalf of the sick woman was had by one of our number who could speak the Sioux language. The Indians finally consented that we might go, if we would leave all the teams, wagons, etc., except one team and a light wagon in which Mrs. Henderson and her two children had been placed on a feather bed.

We felt a little more hopeful at getting such easy terms of escape, but our hopes were of short duration; for they soon

became dissatisfied with the agreement they had made and gave notice that they must have our last team, and we were forced to stop and comply with their demand. The team was given up, and the Indians said we might go. Several men took hold of the wagon, and we again started, feeling that there was still a little chance of escape. We had gone only a short distance when we were made fully aware of the treachery that predominates in the Indian character. They commenced shooting at the men drawing the wagon. Mr. Henderson and Mr. Wedge, in compliance with Mrs. Henderson's wishes, held up a pillowslip as a flag of truce; but the Indians kept on firing. The pillowslip was soon riddled. Mr. Henderson's fingers on one hand were shot off, and Mr. Wedge was killed.

Then commenced a flight, a run for life, on the open prairie, by men, women, and children, unarmed and defenceless, before the cruel savages armed with guns, tomahawks, and scalping knives. Imagine, if you can, the awful sight here presented to my view, both before and after being captured,—strong men making desperate efforts to save themselves and their little ones from the scalping knives of their merciless foes, who were in hot pursuit, shooting at them rapidly as they ran. Before the Indians passed me, the bullets were continually whizzing by my head. Those who could escape, and their murderous enemies, were soon out of my sight. In one instance, a little boy was shot and killed in his father's arms.

Woe and despair now seized all of us who were made captives. The bravest among us lost courage, being so helpless, defenceless, and unprepared for this act of savage warfare. With blanched faces we beheld the horrible scene and clasped our helpless little children closer to us. Then fearful thoughts of torture crowded into our minds, as Mrs. Henderson and her two children were taken rudely from the bed in the wagon, thrown violently on the ground, and covered with the bed, to which a torch was applied. The blaze grew larger and higher, and I could see no more! My courage sank as I wondered in a dazed, half insane manner, what would be our fate and that of other friends. The two little children, I was afterward told, had their heads crushed by blows struck with

violins belonging to the family of Mr. Earle.   The burial party
sent out by General Sibley from Fort Ridgely found the violins,
with the brains and hair of the poor little innocents still sticking to them, two weeks later.   Mr. Henderson was afterward
killed at the battle of Birch Coulie, September 2d.

Nine of our number were killed here in this flight, among
them being our oldest son, Eugene, then about sixteen years
old.   Eleven were taken prisoners, among these being myself,
my babe, and my daughter, fourteen years old.

Seven made their escape, my twelve-year-old son being
among them.   They started for Fort Ridgely, a distance of
twenty miles, thinking that there they would be safe; but, on
arriving near the fort, they could see so many Indians skulking around that they thought it extremely dangerous to make
any further effort to reach the fort.   They then decided to
go to Cedar Lake, a distance of thirty miles north.   Their boots
and shoes were filled with water in wading through sloughs
and became a great burden to them, so that they were compelled to take them off to expedite their flight.   Consequently,
in traveling through coarse wet grass, the flesh on their feet
and ankles was worn and lacerated until the bones were bare
in places.   They could get no food, and starvation stared at
them with its gnawing pangs.   They were hatless in the scorch-
ing sunshine, and were completely worn out by wading
through sloughs and hiding in the tall grass,—in fact, doing
anything to make their escape from the Indians.

When within ten or fifteen miles of Cedar Lake, the strongest man of the party was sent ahead for help, to get food
for those who were unable to walk much farther.   On reaching
a rise of ground he turned quickly, motioned to them, and then
threw himself in the tall grass.   The others of the party knew
that this meant danger and hid themselves as quickly as possible.   Soon sharp reports of guns came to their ears.   They
supposed, of course, that the young man was killed; but it was
not so.   These Indians, five in number, had been away on a
visit; and consequently they had not heard of the massacre.
They were returning to Little Crow's village.   The young man
was not seen by these Indians; but the others had been seen
before dropping in the grass.   They fired their guns for the

purpose of reloading, and soon tracked the party with whom my son was to their hiding places by their trail in the wet grass. My son noticed one of them skulking along on his trail, and watching him very intently. He supposed that the Indian would shoot him; so he turned his face away, and waited for the bullet that was to take his life. What a terrible moment it was to a lad of only twelve years!

But as no shot was fired, he turned his head to see what the Indian was doing. The Indian then asked him what was the matter. Fearing to tell the truth, he told him that the Ojibways were killing all the white people in their neighborhood, and also told how hungry they were.

The Indians gave them some cold boiled potatoes, turning them on the ground, and asked to trade for Little Crow's gun, which one of the party had received from me. Not daring to refuse, they gave them the gun, which was a very handsome one. The Indians now left them, and they managed to reach Cedar Lake, being the first to carry the news of the outbreak to that place. My son traveled from Cedar Lake to St. Peter without further hardship.

The day when the outbreak commenced my husband was on his return from Blue Earth county with Mr. and Mrs. Jacobson, parents of the sick Mrs. Henderson. Late in the afternoon, when within six miles of New Ulm, they met a large number of settlers, men, women, and children, fleeing for their lives, who told them that the Sioux Indians had commenced a desperate raid upon the settlers in the vicinity of New Ulm, that many of them had been killed, and that the Indians were then besieging the village; also that word from Renville county had been received, that all the settlers in the neighborhood of Beaver Creek and Birch Coulie were murdered, if they had failed to make their escape.

Having remained with the fleeing party until morning, my husband started on his return to the home of Mr. Jacobson, a distance of thirty miles. On his way back he saw farms deserted and cattle running at large in fields of shocked grain. At Madelia he found an assemblage of settlers contemplating the idea of making a stand against the Indians. They resolved not to be driven from their homes by the Sioux, thinking

26

that they could defend themselves by building breastworks of
logs which were at hand. Consequently my husband remained
with them one day, and assisted in the building of the fortifi-
cation, until reliable information came to them that there were
so many Indians engaged in the outbreak that it would be
impossible for them to make a successful stand. Therefore,
after taking Mr. and Mrs. Jacobson to their home, he started
for St. Peter, where he arrived on Saturday, the 23d day of
August.

There he met Millard, our twelve-year-old son, who narrated to him the dismal tidings of the outbreak; that his
mother, sister, and little baby brother, were taken off by the
Indians; and that Eugene was hit by a bullet in the leg while
running in advance of him. He told how Eugene ran about
a fourth of a mile after being wounded, then turned a little
to one side of the course they were running, and dropped into
a cluster of weeds. The Indians were soon upon him with
their scalping knives. In casting a look back he saw them
apparently in the act of taking his scalp.

My husband's team of horses and his carriage were pressed
into military service at St. Peter. He went with General Sibley's forces from St. Peter to Fort Ridgely, intending to go
with them on their expedition against the Indians. But it fell
to his lot to remain at the fort until after our release.

CAPTIVES TAKEN TO LITTLE CROW'S VILLAGE.

When I was captured, my captor seized me by the shoulders, turned me quickly around, and motioned for me to turn
back. At this I screamed, partly for the purpose of calling
Mr. Earle's attention to see that I was a prisoner, and he
looked around. This I did thinking that he might escape and
give the tidings to my relatives and friends.

Just before I was captured, my son Eugene, who was afterward killed, passed me and said, "Ma, run faster, or they will
catch you." This was the last time I heard him speak or saw
him, and he must have been killed soon afterward.

It was now near the middle of the day; the heat of the sun
was very intense; and we (the captives) were all suffering for
drink. I sat down a moment to rest, and then thought of my

dress, which had become very wet while wading through a slough; so I sucked some water from it, which relieved my thirst a little.

We captives and a few of the Indians walked back to the house of Mr. J. W. Earle. The Indians entered the house, and delighted themselves by breaking stoves and furniture of various kinds and throwing crockery through the windows. After they had completed the destruction of everything in the house which they did not wish to appropriate for their own use, we were put into wagons and ordered to be taken to Little Crow's village.

Members of families were separated and taken to different places, seemingly to add to our suffering by putting upon us the terrible agony of wondering where the other prisoners were and what was to be their fate. During this ride we passed several houses belonging to settlers who had been killed or had fled to save their lives. The Indians entered these houses and plundered them of many valuables, such as bedding and clothing. On our way to the Minnesota bottomland we had to descend a very steep bluff, where, by our request, the Indians gave us the privilege of walking down.

After reaching the foot of the bluff, our course was through underbrush of all kinds. The thought of torture was uppermost in my mind. I supposed that was why such a course was taken. There was no road at all, not even a track. We were compelled to make our way as best we could through grape vines, prickly ash, gooseberry bushes, and trees. After much difficulty in bending down small trees in order to let our wagons pass over them, we finally reached the Minnesota river with many rents in our clothing and numerous scratches on our arms.

When fording the river, we were all given a drink of river water, some sugar, and a piece of bread. The sugar and bread were taken from the house of one of my neighbors. Just as we were driving into the water, the wagon containing my daughter with other captives was disappearing beyond the top of the bluff on the other side of the river. I thought again, What will befall her?

We soon reached Little Crow's village, where we were kept about a week. The village numbered about sixty tepees, be-

sides Little Crow's dwelling, a frame building. Mrs. James Carrothers, Mrs. J. W. Earle and a little daughter, myself and babe, were taken to Little Crow's. On entering the house the object that first met my gaze was Little Crow, a large, tall Indian, walking the floor in a very haughty, dignified manner, as much as to say, "I am great!" However, his majesty condescended to salute us with "Ho," that being their usual word of greeting. The room was very large. The furniture consisted of only a few chairs, table, and camp kettles. A portion of the floor at one end of the room was raised about one foot, where they slept on blankets. His four wives, all sisters, were busily engaged packing away plunder which had been taken from stores and the houses of settlers. They gave us for our supper bread and tea. Soon after tea, Mrs. Carrothers and myself were escorted to a tepee where we remained until morning, when we were claimed by different Indians.

I have reason for believing that an emissary from the Confederate States had been among these Indians urging and encouraging them to their fierce outbreak and warfare against the innocent settlers. I heard Little Crow say, on the first day of my captivity, after he had been looking over some papers, that he was going to sell the Minnesota valley to the Southern States. An Indian told Mrs. James Carrothers, on the day of our capture, that they expected to sell Minnesota to the South. Mrs. Carrothers could speak the Sioux language.

It happened to be my lot in the distribution of the prisoners to be owned by Too-kon-we-chasta (meaning the "Stone Man") and his squaw. They called me their child, or "big papoose." Their owning me in this manner saved me probably from a worse fate than death; and although more than a third of a century has elapsed since that event, strange as it may appear to some, I cherish with kindest feelings the friendship of my Indian father and mother. Too-kon-we-chasta was employed by General Sibley as a scout on his expedition against the Indians in the summer of 1863. He now lives across the Minnesota river from Morton, in Redwood county, on a farm. He and his squaw called on me several times when we were living near Beaver Falls. They manifested a great deal of friendship. There is a wide difference in the moral character of Indians.

Before retiring for the night we were commanded to make ourselves squaw suits. The squaws told us how to make them, and mine was made according to their directions. Mrs. Carrothers failed to make hers as told, and consequently was ordered to rip it apart and make it over. I put mine on while she was making hers as first told. When finished she put it on. We thought our looks were extremely ludicrous. She cast a queer gaze at me, and then commenced laughing. I said to her that under the circumstances I could see nothing to laugh about. She replied that we might better laugh than cry, for we had been told that the Indians would have no tears, and that those who cried would be first to die.

I also had to lay aside my shoes and wear moccasins. The last I saw of my shoes, an Indian boy about a dozen years old was having great sport with them by tossing them with his feet to see how high he could send them.

On the third day of my captivity I was taken out by my squaw mother a short distance from our tepee, beside a cornfield fence, and was given to understand that I must remain there until she came for me. After being there a short time, an old squaw came to me, and, leaning against the fence, gazed at me some time before speaking. Finally she said in a low voice, "Me Winnebago; Sioux nepo papoose," and then left. I never learned why I was taken out there, but have thought since that the Indians had decided to kill my child, as "nepo papoose" means "kill a baby;" that my squaw mother took me there for the purpose of hiding my child from the Indians; and that being afraid to give the reason herself, she sent this old squaw from another tribe to tell me.

During this week of tepee life the ludicrous alternated with the sublime, the laughable with the heart-breaking and pathetic. We saw papooses of all sizes robed in rich laces and bedecked in many fantastic styles with silk fabrics, until one must laugh despite all their fearful surroundings. When the laugh died on our lips, the terrible thought crowded into our minds, Where did these things come from? What tales could they tell if power were given them to speak? Where are the butchered and mutilated forms that once wore them? My heart was crushed, my brain reeled, and I grew faint and sick

wondering, or rather trying not to wonder, what would be our own fate.

The Indians through plunder had on hand a good supply of provisions, consisting of flour, dried fruit, groceries of various kinds, and an abundance of fresh meat. Their manner of cooking was not very elaborate; an epicure would not have relished it as well as we did, until after being forced by the pain or weakness caused by the want of food. Hunger will make food cooked after the manner of the Indians palatable.

At times it seemed to me as though a hand had grasped my throat and was choking me every time I tried to swallow food, so great was the stricture brought about by the fearful tension on the nervous system. Truly and well has it been said that no bodily suffering, however great, is so keen as mental torture.

My squaw mother was our cook. She mixed bread in a six-quart pan by stirring flour into about two quarts of warm water, with one teacupful of tallow and a little saleratus, bringing it to the consistency of biscuit dough. She then took the dough out of the pan, turned it bottom side up on the ground, placed the dough on the pan, patted it flat with her hands, cut it in small pieces, and fried it in tallow. Potatoes they usually roasted in the hot embers of the camp fire. Their manner of broiling beefsteak was not much of a trick, but very remarkable for labor saving. They put the steak across two sticks over the blaze, without salting, and in a few minutes it was done. By so doing they did not have the trouble of cleaning a broiling pan. Tripe was an extremely favorite dish among them, and they were quite quick in its preparation. The intestines were taken between the thumb and finger, the contents were squeezed out, and then, without washing, the tripe was broiled and prepared in regular Indian epicurean style. Truly these noble red people can justly be called a labor-saving people, whatever other qualities they may lack.

They follow their white brothers in their love for tea and coffee, which they make very strong. They sometimes flavored their coffee with cinnamon. My share of coffee was always given me in a pint bowl with three tablespoonfuls of sugar in it. I ate some bread, which, with my tea and coffee, composed my bill of fare while with them. In fact, I think I could not

have eaten the most delicious meal ever prepared by civilized people while a prisoner among these savages, with my family killed or scattered as they were and my own fate still preying on my mind.

The Indians were all great lovers of jewelry, as every school child knows. Every captive was stripped of all jewelry and other valuables in her possession. The Sioux did not wear rings in their noses, like some tribes; but every other available place on the body was utilized to good advantage on which to display jewelry. The clocks that had been plundered from many a peaceful home were taken to pieces and made to do service in this line of decoration. The large wheels were used for earrings, and the smaller ones as bangles on bracelets and armlets.

They were also very proud of being able to carry a watch; but their clothing, being devoid of pockets, lacked the most essential convenience for this purpose. Consequently some of them would, in derision, fasten the chain around the ankle and let the watch drag on the ground.

You may think it strange that I took any notice of these little incidents. However trifling it may have been for me to observe their antics, it certainly had the effect partially to relieve me of the great weight that pressed so heavily on my mind. I looked at my poor little starving babe, and saw that he was growing thinner every day from pure starvation. I thought of my husband and children, whose fate I might never know. Had I given way to all the terrors of my situation, I should not have been spared to meet my family or had any chance of escape, but should have met instant death at the hands of my cruel captors. My will sustained me and forced me to take note of these insignificant things, so that I might not sink or give up to the dreadful reality I was passing through. I said to one of my neighbor captives, when we were first made prisoners, that I felt just like singing, so near did I in my excitement border on insanity. I have thought since many times that, had I given up to the impulse and sung, it would have been a wild song and I should have certainly crossed the border of insanity and entered its confines. Even now, after thirty-six years, I look back and shudder, and my heart nearly stops beating, when these awful things present

themselves fully to my mind. The wonder to me is how I ever endured it all.

The warriors were away all the time we were in Little Crow's village. They came back in time to escort us when we moved. They told us they had burned Fort Ridgely and New Ulm, and would soon have all the palefaces in the state killed. This was said, no doubt, to make our trials more painful, and that we might realize the full extent of their power.

All the time I remained in Little Crow's village my bed, shawl, and sunbonnet, covering for myself and babe, both night and day, consisted of only one poor old cotton sheet; and on our first move I gave it to an Indian to carry while we forded the Redwood river. Indian-like, he kept it. So my squaw mother gave me an old, dirty, strong-scented blanket, which I was compelled to wear around me in squaw fashion.

On the fourth day of my captivity, the squaws went out on the slough and came back with their arms full of wet grass, which was scattered over the ground inside the tepee to keep us out of the mud caused by the heavy rains. Every night when I lay down on this wet grass to sleep, I would think that perhaps I should not be able to get up again; and sometimes I became almost enough discouraged to wish that I would never be able to rise again, so terrible was my experience.

I was frequently sent by the squaws to the Minnesota river, a quarter of a mile distant, to bring water for tepee use. At one time I passed several tepees where Indians and half-breeds camped. On my return they set up a frightful whoop and yell, which nearly stunned me with fear. However, I kept on my way, drew my old sheet closer around me, and hurried back as fast as possible. As I entered our tepee, I drew a long breath of relief. I was not sent there for water again.

My sunbonnet was taken from me when I was first captured. The Indians used it for a kinnikinick bag. Kinnikinick is a species of shrub from which they scrape the bark to smoke with their Indian tobacco. They have some very long pipes. While smoking they let the bowl of the pipe rest on the ground. When this long pipe was first lighted, the custom among them was to pass it around, each Indian and squaw in the company taking two or three puffs. I never saw a

squaw smoke except when this long pipe was passed around. The pipe was not presented to me to take a puff. I believe this pipe was known as the pipe of peace.

ON THE MARCH WESTWARD.

A week having elapsed since we were taken to Little Crow's village, and the warriors having all returned, an aged Indian marched through the village calling out "Puckachee! Puckachee!" before every tepee; and then the squaws immediately commenced taking down the tepees. We understood that the crier had given command for a move, but whither we did not know. Their manner of moving was very ingenious. Every tepee has six poles, about fifteen feet long, which were fastened by strips of rawhide placed around the pony's neck and breast, three poles on each side of the pony, with the small ends on the ground. A stick was tied to the poles behind the pony to keep them together and spread in the shape of a V; and on the stick and poles bundles of various kinds, kettles, and even papooses were fastened when occasion required. It is astonishing to see the amount of service these natives will get out of one tepee and an Indian pony.

After getting the wagons and the pole and pony conveyances loaded, and everything else in readiness, our procession was ordered to "puckachee;" and away we went, one hundred and seven white prisoners and about the same number of halfbreeds who called themselves prisoners (they may have been prisoners in one sense of the word), eight hundred warriors, their families, and luggage of various kinds. We had a train three miles long. On either side of our procession were mounted warriors, bedecked with war paint, feathers, and ribbons; and they presented a very gay appearance, galloping back and forth on each side of this long train. Their orders were to shoot any white prisoner that ventured to pass through their ranks. This was done, of course, to intimidate the prisoners. I shall never forget the varied sights this motley procession presented to my view,—the warrior in his glory, feasting over the fact that he had killed or captured so many of his white enemies and thereby gotten his revenge for the great wrongs he had suffered from them; and the innocent victims, the prisoners, so woe-begone, so heart-broken, so grotesque and awk-

ward in their Indian dress, paying the awful penalty that the
red man imagined the white man owed him, for an Indian cares
not whether it is the perpetrator of a wrong or not, if he finds
some white victim whereon to wreak his revenge.

Our ears were almost deafened by the barking of dogs, the
lowing of cattle, the "Puckachee! Whoa! Gee!" of the Indians
in driving their teams of oxen, the neighing of horses, the
braying of mules, the rattle of heavy wagons. In fact, to me it
seemed like a huge chaotic mass of living beings making desperate efforts to escape some great calamity.

On we went with the utmost speed, the Indians seeming
to be in great glee. We crossed the Redwood river about one
mile from its entrance into the Minnesota river. The stream,
swollen by recent heavy rains and having a strong current, was
difficult and even dangerous to ford. Mrs. Earle, her daughter,
and myself, locked arms while crossing. Mrs. Earle's feet were
once taken from under her, and she would have gone down
stream had it not been for the aid received from us. A squaw
carried my babe across. Every Indian and squaw seemed to
be in a great rush to cross first. They dashed pellmell into
the water, regardless of their chances to land their teams.

On this march I had to walk and carry my child. I carried him on my arms, which was very disgusting to the squaws.
They frequently took him from my arms and placed him on
my back, squaw-fashion, but he always managed somehow to
slip down and I had him in my arms again. Before noon I
became so tired that I sat down to rest beside the road. The
squaws, in passing me, would say "Puckachee!" But I remained sitting about ten minutes, I should think, when an old
Indian came to me and took hold of my hand to help me up.
I shook my head. He then had the train halt, or a part of it,
a short time. I afterward learned that a council was held,
the object being to come to some agreement as to how they
would deal with me. Some thought best to kill me and my
child; others thought not. The final conclusion was to take
my child, place him on a loaded wagon, and start the train.
Then, if I did not "puckachee," they would kill me and the
baby also. They started, after putting the child on a wagon,
and I followed, taking hold of the end-board of the wagon.

which proved to be a great help to me to the end of our day's march. We followed up the Minnesota river valley until we came to Rice creek, reaching that point about sundown, having traveled nearly eighteen miles.

Our tepees were soon pitched, and everything quickly settled into the usual routine of tepee life. Then I wandered and searched around among the tepees to see if I could find my daughter and other friends who helped to make this long train.

After a short walk among the Indians and tepees, I was completely overjoyed at meeting my daughter, whom I had not seen since we forded the Minnesota river on the day we were made captives. It was like seeing one risen from the dead to meet her. She was as happy as myself. And oh! how pleased we were that so far we had been spared not only from death, but, worse than that, the Indian's lust. Killing beef cattle, cooking, and eating, seemed to be done in great glee in this camp.

The fourth day of our stay here the command "Puckachee!" was sent along as before, and our gigantic motley cavalcade, with its strange confusion, was soon on the move westward again. We passed Yellow Medicine village, near which the Upper Sioux Agency was located. As we came in sight of it, we could see the barracks burning, also the mills situated at this point where we crossed the Yellow Medicine river. John Other Day, who was a friend to the whites and was the means of saving sixty-two lives, had his house burned to the ground.

We stopped after traveling a distance of ten miles, and remained there eight or ten days. That part of the train where I was, pitched their tepees beside a mossy slough, from which we obtained water for tepee use. The first few days the water covered the moss and could be dipped with a cup. The cattle were allowed to stand in it, and dozens of little Indians were playing in it every day; consequently the water soon became somewhat unpalatable to the fastidious. However, we continued to use it. After remaining there three or four days, the water sank below the moss. To get it then we had to go out on the moss and stand a few minutes, when the water would collect about our feet. It is astonishing how some persons will become reconciled to such things when forced upon them.

A papoose was very sick here, but nothing was given it to
relieve the little sufferer. It died about sundown. They made
no demonstrations of grief when it died, nor mourned in the
least; but after an hour or two the warriors returned, and I
suppose that when notified they must have given the mourn-
ing signal. A dismal wailing was then begun and was continued about a half hour. It stopped just as suddenly as it
began, and not another sound was heard. I did not know
when or where the remains were deposited, so stealthy were
they in their movements.

The death of this baby caused me to think of the probable
death of my own. The little fellow was a mere skeleton. I
was only able to get a small quantity of milk for him once in
two days. This was all that kept him from starving. To
hold him and watch him, knowing that he was gradually pin-
ing away, was what I hope no mother will ever be called upon
to witness.

The usual manner of the wild Sioux in disposing of their
dead was to wrap the body in blankets and place it on a scaffold made of poles not more than four or five feet from the
ground. If it was in a wooded country, the scaffold was constructed of poles placed in the branches of low trees. During
one or two years the scaffold and wrap containing the corpse
were kept in order. Offerings of food were often made to the
ghost which was supposed to linger near until the memory of
great grief became dim. Afterward no more care or attention
was given to the remains. In time of war, when any of their
number were killed in battle or otherwise, they were, if possible, removed and secreted from the enemy. They were very
superstitious. They believed that if their killed fell into the
hands of their enemy, they would be made slaves in the future
life. Famous chiefs, and warriors who had gained great no-
toriety in war exploits, were sometimes buried sitting astride
a live pony. They were buried on top of the ground by placing layer after layer of prairie sod around and over them until
they were entirely covered. This grave or mound thereafter
remained intact; nothing was allowed to destroy it.

It was no uncommon occurrence to see the Indians, just
before going out on a raid or to battle, decorating themselves

with feathers, ribbons, and paint. The most hideous looking object I ever beheld was a large, tall Indian, who had be-smeared his face all over with vermillion red, and then had painted a stripe of green around each eye and his mouth, thickly dotting these stripes with bright yellow paint. Others would paint their faces red, and then apply a bright coat of yellow, which gave it a sunset hue, after which a blue flower was usually painted on each cheek. Some of them would daub their faces with something that looked like dark blue clay, and then would make zigzag streaks down their faces with their fingers, leaving a stripe of clay and,—well, a streak of Indian.

The squaws seemed to take great pride in ornamenting their head and hair. They usually parted their hair in the middle of the forehead, plaited it in two braids, and tied the ends firmly with buckskin strings, on which were strung three large glass beads at the end of each string. Then they painted a bright red streak over the head where the hair was parted. I saw one squaw with five holes in the rim of each ear, from which hung five brass chains dangling on her shoulders, with a dollar gold piece fastened to each chain.

After the warriors had completed the work of painting to their liking, they gathered in small squads, seemingly for con-sultation. They presented a very frightful appearance. Soon they began to gather in larger parties and start off in different directions, for the purpose, as I supposed, of victimizing some innocent settler. Many cattle were now being brought into camp, but no captives; which led me to believe that they massacred indiscriminately men, women, and children, and that proved to have been the case. The squaws seemed at all times to be highly elated over the good success the Indians had in bringing into camp beef cattle; "ta-ton-koes," they called them. They were also well pleased with the false reports which the Indians made in stating that they had killed or driven nearly all the white people from Minnesota.

To save labor in harvesting and hauling corn and potatoes into camp, we made many short moves from one enclosure to another. Cattle, horses, and ponies, were turned loose in the fields of grain. As soon as the supply was exhausted, we

moved on. At the end of one remove, I saw an old squaw with a very nice black silk shawl, which she had worn over her head, squaw-fashion, while on the move, climb over a rail fence and throw the shawl on the ground in the potato field. Then with all her might she commenced digging or scratching out potatoes with her hands, throwing them on the shawl until she had gathered nearly a half bushel, after which she gathered up the corners of the shawl, threw them over her shoulder, and hurried away to the campfire.

For one reason we were always glad to move; it furnished us a clean camp ground for a few days. But oh! the thought that I was a prisoner in the hands of savage Indians, moving on farther and farther from relatives, friends, and civilization, into the far Northwestern wilds, inhabited only by cruel savages who live in tepees, and cold weather coming on! I met an old Frenchman who had married a squaw and had lived with the Indians a long time. He could speak a little English. Judge what my feelings must have been when he said to me, "I 'spect you'll all die when cold weather comes," meaning the white captives.

Many times have I reluctantly retired for the night on the cold damp ground with my child on my arm, unable to sleep, thinking of friends and home. If by chance my eyes were closed in sleep, I would sometimes dream of seeing Indians perpetrating some act of cruelty on innocent white captives. Occasionally I would dream of having made my escape from my captors, and was safe among my relatives and friends in a civilized country. But on awaking from my slumbers, oh! the anguish of mind, the heart-crushing pangs of grief, to again fully realize that I was a prisoner still among the Indians, not knowing how soon I would be subjected to the cruelties of these revengeful savages!

In order to make myself as agreeable as possible to them, I feigned cheerfulness, and took particular notice of their papooses, hoping that by so doing I would receive better treatment from them, which I think had the desired effect. Once I was unable to suppress my feelings while in the presence of my Indian father, who was quick to observe my gushing tears and heart throbs, which must have excited his sympathy for

me. He said, through an interpreter, that he would give me bread and let me go; "but," said he, "the warriors will find you and kill you,"—as much as to say, "You had better remain with us." This was after we had gone so far from white settlements that it would have been impossible for me to make my way on foot and alone through the Indian country.

While in the camp beside the mossy slough, Little Crow and twenty or thirty of his chief warriors had a war council and dog feast. They occupied a place on the prairie a short distance outside of the camp ground, where they seated themselves on the ground in a circle around a large kettle, hung over a fire, in which the carcass of a fat dog was being boiled. The United States flag was gracefully waving over their detestable heads. What a contrast between this exhibition of hostile Indians and the gathering of loyal citizens of the United States under the stars and stripes, celebrating our nation's birthday!

These dusky savages seemed to have parliamentary rules of their own. One would rise, with stolid dignity, and deliver his harangue, after which they one by one would dip their ladles into the kettle of dog soup, until each had served himself to soup. Then came another speech and another dip by all. Thus they alternated until all or nearly all had their say and had their appetite satisfied with canine soup. Dog soup by them is considered to be a superb and honored dish. None but Indians of high rank were allowed to partake.

Dog beef was sometimes cooked by hanging the dog in a horizontal position by both fore and hind legs under a pole over a fire, without being dressed, except that the entrails were removed. When dogs are cooked in this manner, all are allowed to partake.

These natives generally used their fingers in conveying food to their mouths. If their meat was too hard to crush with their teeth, or too tough to tear with their fingers and teeth, they would firmly hold the meat in their teeth and one hand, and, with a sharp knife in the other hand, cut the meat between the teeth and fingers.

On the eighth or tenth day of our stay here the word "Puck-achee!" greeted our ears; and everything was soon in readiness

for a move, but it was a very short one. We stopped beside a small stream called Hazel Run. Beside this stream had been built residences for missionaries, which were burned to the ground soon after our tepees were pitched.

After remaining here two or three days, we were given orders as before to move on, and went only three or four miles. On the way we passed several small lakes, and our train was stopped long enough near one of them to allow the squaws to do some washing. This was the first washing that had been done since my stay with them. The squaws' mode of washing their wardrobes was to walk into water two or three feet deep, then quickly lower and raise themselves, and at the same time rub with their hands. Their wet clothing was allowed to remain on them to dry. The squaws, in washing their faces, would take water in their mouths, spurt it into their hands and rub it over their faces, but used no towel.

Here the squaws began to pay much attention to my poor starving babe. They would put their hands on his head and say, over and over, "Washta, washta do," meaning "good, very good."

When we stopped to pitch the tepees again, the Indians had what they called a horse dance. I did not learn whether it celebrated any particular event, or was merely for amusement. Before they commenced it, they decked their ponies with cedar boughs, and the warriors with feathers and ribbons. Then each warrior mounted his pony and paraded around in a meaningless manner, as it seemed to me.

Soon after this horse dance, my squaw mother came to me in a very excited manner, took hold of me and fairly dragged me into the tepee, telling me that the Sissetons were coming to carry me off. She hastily threw an old blanket over me, and there I remained with my babe in my arms for hours. I finally fell asleep and must have slept quite a while. Soon after waking I was given to understand that I might go out. I learned that there were about a hundred and twenty-five of the Sisseton tribe with us. They remained three days, and left camp taking nothing but a few ponies with them.

While in this camp my daughter came to me, crying as though her heart would break, and told me an Indian was

coming that night to claim her for his wife. I did not know what would be best to do. After thinking the matter over, I concluded to consult with a half-breed we called "Black Robinson" in regard to the trouble. After hearing what I had to say, he remarked, "An Indian is nothing but a hog, anyway. I will see what can be done about it." I returned and told my daughter what he said, and she returned to her tepee home, leaving me to worry over the great danger that threatened her. Time and time again I thought, Will this terrible calamity that has come to us ever end? Fortunately, we heard no more of this trouble.

While walking out one afternoon, my attention was called to the way in which the squaws sometimes put their papooses to sleep. They were fastened on a board about eight inches wide, with a footrest, and ornamented with net work at the head, made of willow twigs. They were wrapped to the board, with their arms straight down by their sides and their feet on the footrest, by winding strips of cloth around them. They cry and shake their heads a few minutes before going to sleep. In warm weather, unless it was storming, they were placed outside to sleep, in nearly an erect position.

The Indians and squaws had rules of etiquette which they strictly observed, and would frequently admonish me concerning them. They would tell me how to sit on the ground; how to stand; and how to go in and out the tepee door, which was very low. I think they must have considered me a dull scholar, for I could not conform, or would not, to all their notions of gentility. The Indians would frequently have a hearty laugh to see me go in and out the tepee door. They said I went in just like a frog. The tepees were of uniform size, about twelve feet in diameter on the ground, with a door about three feet high, that is, merely a parting of the tent cloth or hides, of which latter the tepees were usually made.

One dark and dreary rainy day I was put into a tepee made of buffalo hides. The perfume of the hides was not very pleasant to the smell; however, it accorded well with my other surroundings. Why I was put into this tepee I know not, unless it was to be entertained by a Sioux quartette. I had only been in there a short time when four warriors came in,

27

dressed in blankets, with their faces shockingly painted with
war paint and their heads decorated with long feathers.
Surely they presented a fearful sight.   Each had a stick about
two feet long.   They paid no attention to me, but seated themselves, Indian style, on the ground in a circle in front of me,
and beat time by striking on the ground with their sticks, at
the same time singing, or saying, "Ki-o-wah-nay, ki-o-wah-nay,
ki-o-wah-nay, yaw-ah——ah."   After repeating this three
times, they would give a loud whoop and a sharp yell.   This
performance was continued three or four hours.   There was
no variation in the modulation of their voices during all this
time.   The horrors of this experience I can never forget.   It
seemed as though my reason would be dethroned under this
terrible, monotonous chant.   When they stopped and in single
file walked out of the tepee, I clasped my hand to my whirling
brain and wondered if a more dreary or greater mental suffering could or would ever befall me.

CAMP RELEASE.

A few short removes now brought us to what proved to be
the end of our journey, Camp Release.   As soon as the tepees
were set the squaws and Indians commenced running bullets.
They had bar lead, bullet moulds, and a ladle to melt lead in.
They also had a large amount of powder which they had plundered, so they were well prepared to make some defense.
They gave us to understand that they expected to have a battle in a short time with the white soldiers.   Also they gave
us the cheering information that, if the white soldiers made
an attack on them, we, the prisoners, would be placed in front
of them, so that our rescuers' bullets would strike us and
thereby give them a chance to escape in case of their defeat.
We were now allowed to visit our friends a little while every
day, and it was understood among us that if such proved to be
the case we would lie flat on the ground and take our chances.
The expected battle was fought on the 23d day of September at Wood Lake, eighteen miles distant from our camp, the
Indians making the attack on General Sibley's forces.   A day
or two before the battle there was a disagreement among the

Indians. Some of them, I think, were in favor of surrendering to Sibley. But a large majority were opposed to it, consequently a removal of the hostile Indians farther west took place; how far, I did not know. The captives they had were nearly all left with those who wished to surrender.

We could distinctly hear the report of muskets during this battle. We were now in the greatest danger of all our captivity; for, with defeat of the Indians, they were likely to return and slay all the white captives and perhaps some of the half-breeds. The latter appeared to be somewhat alarmed, and consequently we were all put to work by "Black Robinson," throwing up breastworks. I was not a soldier, but soldier never worked with better will than I did to get those fortifications completed. I used a shovel; my squaw mother used an old tin pan. The remains of those breastworks are still visible, I am told. When I worked on them I had no idea that I should ever take any pride in the remembrance of my labor on them, but I do, although at the time I felt as though it would be as well, were I digging my own "narrow house." We cannot afford to part with the remembrance of any incidents of our lives, even though they were heavily burdened with suffering and sorrow.

We were also made to construct breastworks inside the tepee. We sank a hole in the ground about eight feet in diameter and two feet deep, and placed the earth around the pit, thereby increasing the depth to about four feet. In this den eleven of us spent three nights. While the battle was raging, the squaws went out with one-horse wagons to take ammunition to the warriors and to bring in the dead and wounded Indians. Once when they returned one squaw was giving vent to her feelings by chanting, or singing, "Yah! ho! ho!" On making inquiry, I was told that her husband had been killed. On the next two days after the battle we were almost constantly looking and longing to see the soldiers make their appearance on the distant prairie. The hostile Indians had returned to their camp before sunset on the day of the battle, and it was evident to us by their appearance that they had met with defeat. But each day the sun went down, night came on, and our expectation and ardent desires were not realized. Therefore we were compelled through fear once more

to enter our own tepee and the dismal hole in the ground before mentioned, to spend the night, with fearful forebodings that the hostile Sioux might return and kill us before morning. Our tepees were guarded during the night by Indians who pretended to be friendly, but I could not sleep.

Morning came with bright sunshine on the day of our deliverance, the 26th of September. Being so anxious to be delivered from our present surroundings, we could not refrain from gazing, as we had done on the two former days, nearly all the time in the direction of the battle ground, to see who should get the first view of our expected rescuers. About ten o'clock in the morning, to our great joy and admiration, the glimmer of the soldiers' bayonets was first seen and pointed out to us by the Indians, before we could see the men. As they came nearer and nearer, our hearts beat quicker and quicker at the increased prospect of our speedy release.

When they had come within about a half mile of our camp, the Indians sent a number of us to the Minnesota river for water, telling us the palefaces would be thirsty. They thought, as did the captives, that the soldiers would come right among us and camp near by; but they marched past about a half mile, where they pitched their tents. A flag of truce was flying over every tepee. After the soldiers had passed by, some of the Indians came in laughing, saying the white soldiers were such old men that they had lost all their teeth. They had an idea that all of our young men were engaged in our civil war. The papooses were skirling around with a flag of truce, shouting "Sibilee, Sibilee!" as though they thought it great sport.

While the soldiers were pitching their tents, the general sent orders for us to remain in the tepees until he came for us. This was a very hard command for us to obey, now that an opportunity came for us to flee from our captors.

The tepees were set in a circle. After about one and a half hours, General Sibley marched his command inside of this circle. The general now held a consultation with some of the Indians, after which the soldiers were formed into a hollow square. The captives were then taken into this square by the Indian who claimed to have protected them during their captivity, including also those captives who had been left with

them by the hostile Indians. Some had only one or two to deliver up; others had eight or ten. Those who had the largest number to deliver brought them forward in a haughty manner. My Indian father had seven captives to give up.

After all the white captives were delivered to the general in military style, the order was given to move to the soldiers' tents. I am sure every captive there offered up fervent and grateful thanksgiving that the hour of release had come. Right well did this Camp Release come by its title. I believe every adult captive has a warm place in her memory for this spot of prairie land, where so many destinies hung by a thread, with the balance ready to go for or against us. Every Indian, after having delivered his last captive, walked directly out of this hollow square, and was conducted by a soldier to where he, I supposed, was kept under guard.

This giving up or release of the captives was one of the most impressive scenes that it has ever been my lot to witness. Many of my fellow captives were shedding tears of joy as they were being delivered up. After reaching the tents prepared for us, many commenced laughing; oh! such joyful peals from some, and from others came a jerking, hysterical laugh. Others were rapidly talking and gesticulating with friends whom they had just met, as if fairly insane with delight in meeting relatives and friends and to be freed from their savage captors. And again there were others clapping their hands and whirling around in wild delight over the happy good fortune that had come to us.

As for myself, I could only remain silent, as if an inspiration had come to me from the great beyond. I gazed at this assembly of released captives while in their manifestations of joy and happiness, tinctured with grief from the loss of dear friends and relatives, and in quiet satisfaction drew the fresh free air into my lungs and thought what contentment and peace freedom brings to one who has been a captive among the wild savages of the Northwest. None but those who have passed through the terrible experience can ever know the varied feelings and emotion which the deliverance produced.

We still wore our squaw suits. Some of us were given quarters in what were called or known as Sibley tents, and

others in smaller tents. It was now about four o'clock in the afternoon, and by reason of our not having had dinner, the soldiers treated us to a lunch, consisting of light biscuit and apple sauce. It was not served after modern style. We simply gathered around two large dishpans containing our lunch, and each helped herself. When supper time came the soldiers brought into our tent, prepared to be served, an abundance of rice, hardtack, coffee and meat. My lunch was the most delicious repast I ever enjoyed, it being the first white cooking I had tasted since I ate breakfast in my own home the day I was captured; but my appetite for supper entirely failed me in consequence of having had the late lunch, and because of the excitement produced by our release. After the first day of our release, a campfire was provided us and we had the privilege of doing our own cooking. A guard was placed around our tents and campfire, the object, I suppose, being to keep away all would-be intruders.

My mind was now involuntarily absorbed in the strange sights of the afternoon. I could scarcely think a moment in regard to the condition or whereabouts of my family. I had not learned whether they all succeeded in making their escape or were all killed and scalped by the Indians.

We remained with the soldiers ten days for the purpose of giving our testimony against the Indians. The soldiers were very kind to us, they were always careful to provide campfires for us, and seemed at all times to take delight in making us feel at home, or at least among civilized people. Three different times during our stay with them they serenaded us with songs. As the sweet sounds of civilization greeted my ear, the great contrast between freedom and captivity among savages grew more prominent. I shall always hold these brave soldiers in most grateful remembrance.

RETURN THROUGH ST. PETER AND ST. PAUL TO WISCONSIN.

In the forenoon of our last day with the soldiers, Mrs. David Carrothers, Mrs. Earle, and myself, were out consulting with a soldier (Mrs. Carrothers' brother) on the chances or prospect of our getting to St. Peter. After having talked the

matter over, and when we were returning to our tent, I caught sight of my husband, of whom I had not known whether he was dead or alive, accompanied by J. W. Earle. I leave you to imagine our feelings at this meeting,—words would be inadequate.

Mr. Earle and my husband, having learned of the release of their families, had engaged Mr. William Mills, then of St. Peter, to go with a four-horse team with them to Camp Release, a distance of about 120 miles, for the purpose of bringing their families to St. Peter. They arrived at Camp Release about ten o'clock in the forenoon of the fifth day of October. Soon after dinner we started with our husbands, children, and Mr. Mills, for St. Peter, without an escort.

Whether or not our husbands were proud of us in our squaw dress we did not stop to question, for we were so glad to get started for civilization that we did not take a second thought as to our clothing, but rode triumphantly into St. Peter in squaw costume. Danger was thick around us on our journey. Consequently Mr. Mills hurried his team, forded the Redwood river soon after dark in the same place where we crossed when going west with the Indians, and stopped for the night in a small Indian log hut.

The three men stood on guard until two o'clock, when, fearing the presence of stray Indians, we became uneasy and concluded to journey on in the night. We arrived at the Lower Sioux Agency about sunrise, or where the village and the agency buildings had been located. All had been destroyed by fire. Here we visited the garden that had belonged to Dr. Humphrey, who was killed, and also all the members of his family, while trying to make their escape, excepting one son. We found some onions and tomatoes, and boiled a few; with the government rations, they made quite a good breakfast.

While there I could almost see where our house was located on Beaver creek, and had a pretty fair view of the prairie over which we were so frightfully chased by hostile Sioux Indians. The sight brought back vivid remembrance in my mind of just what transpired there on the 18th day of August. Before my mental eye was unrolled a panorama of fearful deeds

perpetrated by the wild men of the Northwest, shockingly painted, and having their heads decorated with feathers according to their rank; also the cruelties committed on innocent white people on that memorable day. I could see the Indians as they surrounded us with their guns presented at the men, demanding of them a surrender of all their teams, etc., to them. I could see men, women, boys and girls, in almost every direction in alarmed haste, closely pursued by Indians shooting at them. I could see one man fall here, another there, and to all appearance Indians in the act of taking off their scalps. I could see two men holding up a flag of truce over a wagon in which a sick woman and her two children lay on a bed. I saw again the blaze and smoke arising from the burning bed, where Mrs. Henderson and her two children were put to death in a shocking manner. I saw my son as he passed me in great haste when he said to me, "Ma! run faster, or they will catch you." Poor fellow; his remains were never found. Then, after the first fright was over, and the men and boys and their pursuers were out of sight, I could see myself with other captives walking back into captivity among a barbarous people, escorted by our cruel captors.

We still journeyed on the south side of the Minnesota river until we reached the ferry near Fort Ridgely, where we crossed the river, arriving at the fort about noon. On the road between the agency and the fort, we saw the body of a man who had recently been killed, of which we notified the military officials, who soon sent a burial party.

We took dinner at the fort, and then traveled on until sunset, and stopped with a German over night. I think this was the first house we passed where people lived. During the night rain came down in torrents, which made the roads very bad. Still we traveled on in the morning, and arrived at St. Peter just in the shade of evening. In the outskirts of the village we were halted by the picket's "Who goes there?" Our answer was satisfactory, and we were then allowed to go on, and at nine o'clock were being hospitably entertained by a Mrs. Fisher. Here we exchanged our squaw outfit for new calico dresses, and really began to feel as though we were white folks again.

My babe's weight was now just eight pounds, and he was a little past seven months old. I found my twelve-year-old son here safe and well. Our family was now all together, except our oldest son, whose life was taken to satisfy the revenge of the Sioux warrior. My mind was now at rest, at least as to the whereabouts of my family, and we could begin to plan as to what we should do. We were among strangers and had but very little money. Our horses, cattle, sheep, farming implements, household furniture, etc., to the value of nearly three thousand dollars, had been all taken or destroyed by the Indians.

One afternoon, while my husband and I were conferring together about what was best for us to do, we were agreeably surprised by meeting an old neighbor just from our Wisconsin home, who had volunteered to carry financial aid to us, which had been donated by the neighbors. This aid was gratefully received and was a surprise to us. We now could buy some necessary articles of clothing and pay our fare back to Wisconsin.

After remaining in St. Peter about two weeks, we took a steamboat for St. Paul. While there, at the Merchants' Hotel, a gentleman (a stranger to us) called to talk with Mrs. Earle and myself about our captivity. After a short conversation, he excused himself for a few minutes, and on his return gave each of us fifteen dollars. The landlady was very kind to us, and gave me many useful articles of clothing, which, as we were very destitute, were more than acceptable. We remained in St. Paul three or four days, waiting for a boat to take us to La Crosse. There were no charges made against us for the hotel bill.

It was near the middle of November when we took the boat for La Crosse, where we arrived at noon. Here we went aboard the cars for our old home in Columbia county, Wisconsin. On our arrival at the depot at Pardeeville, the platform was thronged with relatives and friends to greet us, as restored to them from a worse fate than death.

We remained there until the following March, when we returned to Rochester, Minnesota. The Indians having been

subdued and peace restored, we ventured back in the fall of
1865 to our Renville county home, from which we were so
suddenly driven by the Indians, and we have ever since continued to live in this county. ·

The day of retributive justice came to some of the bloodthirsty savages. Little Crow, while on a horse-stealing expedition on the frontier, accompanied by his son and other Indians,
was shot and killed by a Mr. Lampson, on July 3d, 1863, six
miles north of Hutchinson. A military commission was established at Camp Release, in which over three hundred murderous Indians were recommended to be hanged; but the final decision of President Lincoln was that only thirty-eight of them
should be executed. The day of execution was ordered to be
Friday, the 26th day of December, 1862, at Mankato.

The gallows was built in the shape of a rectangle. Ten Indians were on each of two sides, and nine on each of the other
two sides. The trap for the whole was sprung at the same
instant, and thirty-eight bloody Indian villains were dangling
at the ends of as many ropes. The trap was sprung by William J. Duly of Lake Shetek, Murray county, who had three
children killed and his wife and two children captured, they
being at that time in the possession of Little Crow on the
Missouri river.

SNANA.

NARRATION OF A FRIENDLY SIOUX.*

BY SNANA, THE RESCUER OF MARY SCHWANDT.

As I was asked to write my experience of the outbreak of 1862, I must begin from my earliest days of my life as much as I can remember.

My mother's aunt was married to a white man, and her name was Gray Cloud; so her daughters were half-breeds. As I was related to those folks, I lived with one and another from time to time. These two daughters' names are Mary Brown and Jennie Robertson. At the time I lived with Mary Brown, there was a schoolhouse near, in which I was a day scholar for two years. There were three other Indian girls besides myself. When these two years of my schooling had expired, I began to board with the family of Dr. Thomas S. Williamson, where the schoolhouse was located. We were taught by Dr. Williamson's sister, whose name was Jane Williamson.

Before we boarded at Dr. Williamson's, it was very difficult for us to go to school at this special period of time, for the Indians said that we would spend money for doing this; and they tried to discourage us by scolding, and pretended to pun-

*The following notes, contributed by Mr. Robert I. Holcombe, of St. Paul, in explanation of some parts of this narration, may be helpful to the reader. With a few slight changes, the story is here given as Snana wrote it.

Mahkpia-hoto-win, in translation Gray Cloud, was a noted Sioux woman of early times who lived on the well known island of the Mississippi below St. Paul, which still bears her English name. She was first married to a white trader named Anderson, by whom she had two children, Angus and Jennie. The latter became the wife of Andrew Robertson, who became prominent in Indian affairs in Minnesota.

After Anderson's death, which occurred in Canada, Gray Cloud was married to Hazen P. Mooer, another white trader, who was a Massachusetts man by birth. By the latter marriage she had two children, Mary and Jane Ann, of whom the latter died unmarried. Mary was married to John Brown, a brother of Major Joseph R. Brown, and is still living at Inver Grove, near St. Paul.

Snana (pronounced Snah-nah) was born at Mendota in 1839. Her name means tinkling. Her mother was Wamnuka, which means a small ovate bead, called by the traders a barleycorn. She was a member of the Kaposia band of Sioux, whose village was on the west side of the Mississippi about four miles below St. Paul.

Dr. Williamson established a mission school at Kaposia in November 1846. Snana entered this school when she was about ten years old, and continued as a pupil there during three years.

She was married to Wakeah Washta (Good Thunder) when she was only fifteen years of age, and soon after accompanied her husband and the other members of the Kaposia band to the reservation on the upper Minnesota

ish us, and tried every way to stop us. It was three years altogether in regard to my schooling, as day scholar and boarding at the schoolhouse. By the teaching and helping of the kind family of Dr. Williamson, we had a very good opportunity, and made use of those three years. I got so that I could read the fourth reader by the time I left the school.

It was then my mother came and I went home with her to the Indian village. She dressed me up in Indian costume, but as I had been living among the white people mostly I was bashful to go out in Indian style, and for some days I stayed inside the tent where many people could not see me. But after years of living among them and being dressed in my own people's costume, I never forgot what I learned towards the white people's ways, their language, their civilization, and so forth. Although dressed in Indian costume, I thought of myself as a white lady in my mind and in my thoughts.

river set apart for the Indians by the treaties of Mendota and Traverse des Sioux in 1851. She and her husband were Christian Indians, and for some years lived in a log house and "in civilization" at the Lower or Redwood Agency, on the south side of the Minnesota, two miles southeast from where the village of Morton now stands.

The Lower Agency was the scene of the outbreak of the Sioux on the morning of August 18th, 1862. The Christian Indians were of course opposed to the uprising and the war; but in time they all, or very nearly all, were swept into it, some by inclination, and others by the force of public sentiment and through fear and coercion. Good Thunder and his wife, and the other Indians who were "in civilization" at the Lower Agency, were obliged to leave their houses, remove a few miles westward to Little Crow's village, and take up new abodes there in tepees.

It was on the fourth day of the outbreak when Snana purchased Mary Schwandt from her captor. This act, which doubtless saved the life of an innocent young girl, was wholly Snana's; her husband was away from home at the time.

Mary Schwandt was then fourteen years old. Her story of her captivity is published in the sixth volume of these Historical Collections (pages 461-474).

After Snana had restored Mary Schwandt to the whites at Camp Release, she and her husband came down with other Indians to Fort Snelling, where they were encamped for some time. Here, in the following winter, her two children died; and soon after their death she went to Faribault, and lived there for some years.

Later she removed to Santee Agency, Nebraska, where she was again married, this time to another man of her race whose Indian name was Mazazezee (Brass), his English name being Charles Brass. He was for several years a scout in the United States military service, and died from injuries received while scouting under Generals Terry and Custer. Snana (or Mrs. Maggie Brass, this being her English name) was afterward employed in the Government school at Santee Agency, and has lived on the farm allotted to her there. Her son, William Brass, has received an education in the Government school at Genoa, Nebraska. She also has two adopted daughters, both Indians.

Her name appears, with the few others, upon the monument erected by the Minnesota Valley Historical Society, at Morton, in commemoration of the services of the Indians who saved the lives of white persons and were true in their fidelity to the whites throughout the great Sioux War in Minnesota in 1862.

The spelling of the foregoing Dakota (Sioux) proper names conforms with their pronunciation, giving to the letters their usual English sounds. It therefore differs somewhat from the system used by Rev. Stephen R. Riggs in his Dictionary of the Dakota Language, which gives mostly the French sounds for vowels and employs ten peculiarly marked consonants, such as cannot be supplied by our English fonts of type. A final syllable, win, is often added in a Dakota name, as that of Gray Cloud, to indicate that it is a feminine name.

An Indian man whose name was Good Thunder then offered some special things to my mother for me to be his wife, which was, as we may say, legal marriage among the Indians. But I insisted that, if I were to marry, I would marry legally in church; so we did, and were married in the Protestant Episcopal church.

Some years after we got married, we were the first ones to enter the Christian life, which was in 1861. We were confirmed in the same church.   On account of our becoming Christians we were ridiculed by the Indians who were not yet taught the gospel of Jesus and who could not yet understand what Christianity meant.

I want everybody to understand that what little education I have was taught me by the kind family of Dr. Williamson. It has been of very great use to me all through my life; and it led me from the darkness of superstition to the light of Christianity in those dark days among my people.

Then came the dreadful outbreak of 1862. About eight days before the massacre, my oldest daughter had died, and hence my heart was still aching when the outbreak occurred. Two of my uncles went out to see the outbreak, and I told them that if they should happen to see any girl I wished them not to hurt her but bring her to me that I might keep her for a length of time. One evening one of my uncles came to me and said that he had not found any girl, but that there was a young man who brought a nice looking girl.   I asked my mother to go and bring this girl to me; and my uncle, having heard of our conversation, advised my mother that she ought to take something along with her in order to buy this girl. Hence I told her to take my pony with her, which she did.

When she brought this girl, whose name was Mary Schwandt, she was much larger than the one I had lost, who was only seven years old; but my heart was so sad that I was willing to take any girl at that time.   The reason why I wished to keep this girl was to have her in place of the one I lost.   So I loved her and pitied her, and she was dear to me just the same as my own daughter.

During the outbreak, when some of the Indians got killed, they began to kill some of the captives. At such times I always hid my dear captive white girl.   At one time the Indians

reported that one of the captives was shot down, and also that another one, at Shakopee's camp, had her throat cut; and I thought to myself that if they would kill my girl they must kill me first. Though I had two of my own children at that time with me, I thought of this girl just as much as of the others.

I made her dress in Indian style, thinking that the Indians would not touch her when dressed in Indian costume. I always went with her wherever she went, both in daytime and night. Good Thunder never helped me in any way to take care of this girl, but he always went with the men wherever they went. Only my mother helped me to take care of her; especially whenever she would wash, she always provided the soap and towel.

The soldiers seemed not to come near to us, but instead of that they could be heard at a distance beating the drum day after day, which I did not understand. Of course we who had captives wished the soldiers to come to us or to kill all the bad Indians.

Once, when the soldiers came near us, all the bad Indians were trying to skip from the country, mean and angry; but at this time I dug a hole inside my tent and put some poles across, and then spread my blankets over and sat on top of them, as if nothing unusual had happened. But who do you suppose were inside the hole? My dear captive girl, Mary Schwandt, and my own two little children. When the soldiers camped beside us, my heart was full of joy.

General Sibley was in command of the army, and he advised us to camp inside of his circle, which we did. He was so kind that he provided for us some food just the same as the soldiers had; and I thought that this was something new to me in the midst of my late troubles. When I turned this dear child over to the soldiers my heart ached again; but afterward I knew that I had done something which was right.

From that day I never saw her nor knew where she was for thirty-two years, until the autumn of 1894; when I learned that she lives in St. Paul, being the wife of Mr. William Schmidt. Soon I went to visit her, and I was respected and treated well. It was just as if I went to visit my own child.

THE SIOUX OUTBREAK IN THE YEAR 1862, WITH NOTES OF MISSIONARY WORK AMONG THE SIOUX.*

BY REV. MOSES N. ADAMS.

With the rapid and marvelous increase of the white population coming by immigration into Minnesota during the ten or twenty years previous to the Sioux outbreak of August, 1862, there was at the same time the concentration, more and more, of the native Sioux or Dakota Indians, on well defined and smaller reservations.

To this end, new treaties were made by the United States government, providing for the sale of their best and most desirable lands; and new, if not better provision was made by treaty stipulations to induce the lower bands of Sioux on the Mississippi and Minnesota rivers to remove from the lands which they so long had occupied and from the graves of their fathers, and once more to pitch their tents westward, towards the setting sun. This change was the result of the treaty of 1851, at Traverse des Sioux, Minnesota.

Although this movement was not without valuable considerations, it was not altogether satisfactory to the Indians. This, together with the remembrance of former treaties and their failure to realize the stipulated benefits thereof, and their oft repeated wrongs, whether real or only imaginary, all combined to make them feel uncomfortable and restive.

One thing, however, is certain, that the United States government desired to deal fairly with them, as its wards, and had provided well for them. If the treaty stipulations had been honestly and faithfully carried out, the Sioux or Dakotas

---

*Read at the monthly meeting of the Executive Council, October 9, 1899.

would have been satisfied for the time, and possibly the outbreak would have been forestalled, Minnesota saved from so
great a sacrifice of life and property, and the national government from a vast amount of trouble and expense.

CAUSES OF THE OUTBREAK.

Many attempts have been made to give the causes of that
Sioux outbreak in 1862. Whatever were the grievances of the
Sioux, although many and great, there was no justifiable cause
for that uprising and indiscriminate massacre of the innocent
white settlers, men, women and children, without mercy. Yet
we cannot afford to ignore the fact that there was much at
that time, as there had been for years before in the management of Indian affairs, that was exasperating to the Indians
and increasingly provoking and vexatious to them.

It had been previously announced to them, in 1861, in council at Yellow Medicine Agency, Minnesota, that "the Great
Father (the President) at Washington was to make them all
very glad."

They had already received their annuities for that year,
but were told that the government would give them a further
bo nt in the autumn. Some of the Indians were pleased
with this offer, but others demurred and complained to the
general superintendent, asking him, "Where is the promised
extra gift to come from?" The superintendent could not or
would not tell them, only that "it was to be great and make
them very glad."

By such words the four thousand upper Sioux were encouraged to expect great things. In the autumn of that year
1861 the Sissetons from Lake Traverse came down to the
Yellow Medicine Agency, confidently expecting that the promised goods for them would be there; but the low water of the
Mississippi and Minnesota rivers delayed the arrival of the
goods; and the Indians were very greatly disappointed. They
waited there, however, and had to be fed by the agent. When
finally the goods came the deep snows and cold winds of
winter had also come, and the proper season for hunting was
past and gone.

After all, the promised "great gift" was only $10,000, instead of $20,000 that had been expected. When distributed among so many it would be only about two dollars and fifty cents to each one of them. Many of the Indians, in the meantime, would have earned from fifty to a hundred dollars by hunting. To say the least, that was a great mistake; for more than four thousand disappointed and chagrined Indians had to be fed all that long and severe winter by the Indian agent.

The lower Sioux Indians were so greatly displeased that they positively refused to receive their share of the $10,000 worth of goods until they could ascertain whence they came.

Soon, however, on a change of administration, it appeared, and it was noised abroad, that an effort was made by the administration to change the money annuity into goods, and that there had been sent $70,000 which would be due the next summer. The knowledge of this new departure greatly exasperated the annuity Sioux, and no doubt had much to do with bringing on the outbreak and massacre of 1862.

Furthermore, there were in the country sympathizers with the Southern Rebellion, who, taking advantage of these unfortunate circumstances and of the national troubles, worked upon the fears and hopes of the dissatisfied and restive Sioux to make them more and more uncomfortable and unreconciled to the state of things. In their party strife and overt disloyalty to the Union, they no doubt carried the matter further than they thought to do; and so they kindled a fire, wild and destructive, which they could not control or extinguish.

As a matter of fact, the Indians had learned that nearly all the white men capable of bearing arms had gone south into the Union army; and they were told that, bad as it was then with them, it would soon be worse, and that the United States government would fail and become bankrupt, and consequently would be unable to make any more payments of annuities to them. In view of all this, the Sioux decided that this was their opportunity to arise and exterminate the whites in Minnesota and to re-possess themselves of the lands, together with all the improvements. Hence there ensued one of the most terrible and disastrous Indian wars in modern times.

28

LITTLE CROW, CONSPIRATOR AND LEADER.

It was on Sunday, August 17th, 1862, when a small party of Sioux, belonging to Little Crow's band, while out ostensibly hunting and fishing at Acton, in Meeker county, Minnesota, obtained from a white man some spirituous liquor, became intoxicated and murdered a white man and a part of his family, which act precipitated the Sioux War. Hence, on the return of the murderers to the Yellow Medicine Reservation, on the Minnesota river, and, on their reporting to their chief, Little Crow, what they had done at Acton the day before, in the murder of the whites, Little Crow said that it was sooner than he had intended, but, now that it was already begun and blood was spilled, the war must go on. Forthwith he called everybody "to arms," and to fight the white people. He sent his swift messengers to all the different bands of Sioux, not only in Minnesota, but also to all those beyond the Missouri river, in Nebraska, and in what is now Montana and North and South Dakota, calling them all to join in the uprising and the massacre of the white settlers wherever found.

It was a well known and acknowledged fact that Little Crow, only a very short time before this outbreak occurred, had in secret council tampered with more than one of the neighboring tribes of Indians, with the view of securing them as his allies in the contemplated war and massacre of the whites. Only a few days before the outbreak, both the Ojibways and the Winnebagoes, by their representative head men and chiefs respectively, were for several days and nights consecutively in council with Little Crow and his warriors, on the Yellow Medicine reservation. They had little more than reached their homes when the Sioux precipitated that war, which began August 18th at the Lower Agency and thence spread, fearfully desolating and depopulating all that region of the state of Minnesota.

Little Crow not only summoned the Sioux or Dakotas to join in fighting and murdering the white people, after the most despotic manner of the Indians, but he conscripted by a savage and cruel conscription that meant death to every one who should persistently refuse to join the hostile party and go with them on the war-path. His fighting force was va-

riously estimated at from four to six thousand warriors, all of them well armed and equipped, and most of them mounted after the Indian fashion.

THE MASSACRE.

The first attack, in force, began at the Lower Sioux Agency, on the Yellow Medicine reservation, about twelve miles above Fort Ridgely, where the hostile Sioux murdered or frightened away the whites, robbed and plundered the homes, warehouses and stores, and then burned these buildings. This they did all the way up on both sides of the Minnesota river as far as Lac qui Parle. No one residing outside of that terror-stricken portion of Minnesota could form any adequate idea of the fearful and dreadful state of things in all that region.

Even some of the loyal and friendly Indians themselves were terrified and frightened away with their families, as in the case of Marpiya Wicasta (Cloud Man), Wamdiokiya (Eagle Help), and Enoch Marpiya-hdi-na-pe (Cloud in Sight), who, with their families, seeing the terrible disaster coming, and not being able to avert it nor willing to connive at the horrible massacre of the white people, fled north to the British possessions, and for the time being took refuge in the province of Manitoba, until the storm was past and peace restored.

The first two of these men were two of the wisest and most progressive men of the Hazelwood Republic, and were the original leaders and founders of that settlement; and the last one named was an educated Indian, having been our teacher in the Sioux language at Lac qui Parle from 1848 to 1853, and the acting secretary of the Hazelwood Republic in 1862.

The settlers at that season of the year were generally engaged in harvesting their crops, all unarmed and totally unprepared for that awful crisis, when they were suddenly stricken with terror indescribable. Many of them were shot down in their fields and dooryards. Their families were horribly murdered or taken captives by the hostile Indian warriors, and some of them suffered worse than death.

Sudden and unexpected as was the outbreak, yet some of the white people, and some of the friendly and loyal Indians, were enabled to make their escape from the impending fury of

I was personally acquainted with some of the unfortunate victims of the Sioux War, but can mention only a few of them here.

Amos W. Huggins, the eldest son of Alexander G. Huggins, one of the oldest missionaries laboring among the Sioux for the American Board of Commissioners of Foreign Missions, was a Government teacher at Lac qui Parle at the time of the outbreak, and was shot down in sight of his house and almost in the immediate presence of his wife and their little children. Another good man, Philander Prescott, the United States interpreter at the Yellow Medicine Agency, who for almost a lifetime had been a faithful friend and a generous benefactor of the Sioux, seeing the dreadful storm coming, fled for his life, and was overtaken by a hostile Sioux and shot down, without mercy, at a point nearly opposite Fort Ridgely.

Similarly Dr. Philander P. Humphrey and his family, who at that time were at the Lower Sioux Agency, lost their lives. Dr. Humphrey was the Government physician for the Indians there. His family consisted of his wife and three children, the eldest of whom was Johnnie, then nine years old.

Early on Monday morning, August 18th, the first day of the outbreak, the family heard the firing of guns, and caught some glimpses of wild Indians running here and there about the Agency buildings. Finally they became alarmed, and to their surprise they found that already their neighbors were all gone, and had taken away with them their teams and wagons. Although Mrs. Humphrey was sick and in bed, at the earnest request of her husband, she arose, and, leaning on his strong arm, set out on foot, with their three children. They had left their own horse and carriage, only a short time before the outbreak, at St. Peter, where they had been visiting their friends.

They walked down the hill, crossed the river at the ferry, and wended their way along the Fort Ridgely road about four miles, to what was known as "the Magner place." Mrs. Humphrey there became faint and almost exhausted, so that they halted for a rest. Finding no water in the pail at the Magner house, Johnnie, their son, took the water pail, and ran down to the spring, in the ravine near-by, to bring some fresh water for his sick mother. While he was at the spring, the hostile

Sioux came and attacked the others of the family at the house, shot and killed Dr. Humphrey, and, in their haste, severed the head from the body, scalped it, and left it about fifty yards distant in the bushes. It was afterward found there by us, on the expedition sent up from Fort Ridgely to reconnoiter and to bury the dead.

It is not certainly known what the hostile Indians did with the remainder of the family. The probability is, that, seeing the fatal result of the attack, in the death of her husband, Mrs. Humphrey took refuge, with her two youngest children in the vacant Magner house, a primitive log cabin, bolted the door, and there perished with the children, the house being burned by the Sioux. Their remains were afterwards found by us in the ashes of that burned building.

Johnnie Humphrey, hearing the reports of the guns and the noise of the hostile Indians in the murder of his father, did not venture to return to the house, but, having met Mr. Magner, the owner of the house, who was in concealment near the spring, was persuaded by him to flee for his life, with him, and try to reach Fort Ridgely. They escaped and made their way, with great peril and difficulty, through the almost impenetrable brush, until they met Captain Marsh and his men, on their way from Fort Ridgely to the Lower Agency.

At Captain Marsh's request, Johnnie returned with the military force. When they arrived at the Magner place, they saw the decapitated body of Dr. Humphrey in the yard, and found the house all on fire. Without stopping to bury the dead, they hastened on, thinking that Mrs. Humphrey and the children had been taken captive by some wild, marauding, drunken Indians, and, if so, that they would overtake them and rescue them. Onward they went, down the hill, and along the narrow wagon-road, toward the ferry, near the Lower Agency, when suddenly Little Crow, from the bluff on the opposite side of the Minnesota river, gave the signal, and from three to five hundred Sioux warriors, lying there in ambush at the roadside, fired upon that little detachment of soldiers. Twenty-seven of them instantly fell dead, at the first volley of the Indians. Captain Marsh ordered the survivors to break ranks and escape for their lives, and nine or ten of them, together with little Johnnie Humphrey, escaped alive and finally reached Fort Ridgely.

Captain Marsh himself escaped and ran down along the river, to a point at some distance below the ferry, where he probably swam across to the opposite side, and there drowned in the Minnesota river, where his body was afterward found, with no visible marks of violence on it, and with his uniform and side arms all intact. The bodies of his men who fell at or near the ferry were dreadfully hacked and mutilated after they had fallen. So we found them, and sorrowfully interred them, on Sunday, August 31st.

EVENTS OF THE FOLLOWING TWELVE DAYS.

Very soon after the outbreak, word came down to us, at St. Peter, that all the missionaries and their families, teachers, visiting friends, and employees at Hazelwood, Yellow Medicine. and the Lower Agency, were murdered by the Indians, and that the buildings were burned. It was also rumored that Fort Ridgely, Fort Abercrombie, New Ulm and Hutchinson were attacked, and partly destroyed by fire, and that many of the white people were murdered, and many others taken captive. Still there was much uncertainty about what it meant, and by whom it had been done. In the meantime, cries for help were wafted on every breeze that swept over the prairies from that direction. Day and night, almost an unbroken line of refugees came, wending their way into St. Peter, for safety, with a large overflow who hastened on to St. Paul and other cities.

Few, if any, of them could give us any definite and satisfactory account of what was the real trouble, or what the Indians were actually doing, only that "the Indians were killing the whites and burning their houses and homes."

It should be borne in mind that at that time almost all our able-bodied men at St. Peter and vicinity, as also at other places in Minnesota, had gone into the Union army and were at the South, in the Union service. Those remaining and capable of bearing arms, however, volunteered and went up to New Ulm, to help defend and save that place.

Hon. Charles E. Flandrau, then a citizen of St. Peter, went up to New Ulm, in command of the volunteer forces, chiefly representing Nicollet, Le Sueur, and Blue Earth counties. During the severest fight, which lasted two days, August 23rd

and 24th, fourteen of our men were killed, and from fifty to eighty wounded, and the hostile Indians were defeated, this being one of the most important battles of the Sioux War.

The next day after the battle, a council of the surviving soldiers of the command and the citizens of New Ulm was held, and, in view of the facts that the provisions and ammunition were becoming scarce and the sanitary conditions of the place were unsafe, it was decided that the command should evacuate, and that the citizens of New Ulm should leave with them and try to reach Mankato for safety. Accordingly, a train of about a hundred and fifty wagons, loaded with women and children, and with some fifty or eighty wounded men, was taken down by the way of the ford of the Big Cottonwood river, and through Butternut Valley and South Bend, to Mankato, with no serious casualty occurring during that entire march of thirty miles from New Ulm.

At about that time, I had the honor (no one else being available and willing) to volunteer my services and carry an important public document which purported to be from Gov. Alexander Ramsey, of St. Paul, addressed to the "Commander of the Volunteer Forces at Mankato, Minnesota." It was a dark, rainy night when I left St. Peter with that war message, but by Divine grace I made the journey safely to Mankato, delivered the message, and returned home safely to St. Peter. Afterwards, I was credibly informed that two hostile Indian spies were down that night at the Kasota ferry, and that they saw me drive off of the ferry-boat on my return. My good horse gave me notice at the time, by his usual sign, that Indians were near us. But, as I had only one horse, and as there were two of them, they did not molest me, hoping to do better and secure two horses at some other time and place less exposed.

Those same Indian spies, however, came down, and looked St. Peter over, with its throngs of refugees, who filled the houses from cellar to attic, and who crowded the streets with their wagons and teams, all of whom they mistook for soldiers. On their return, they reported to Little Crow that "the town of St. Peter was full of soldiers, armed and equipped for the war." This mistake probably saved St. Peter from an attack by the Indians.

At our own house, then crowded full of refugees, I stood on guard for several nights in succession, with no adequate means of defense or protection. But I greatly desired to do something more and better, and, if possible, something more consistent with my calling; and especially I wished to arrange my affairs so that I might go up to and beyond Fort Ridgely, and assist in recovering and burying the remains of the murdered friends and citizens, many of whom were our personal acquaintances. Mrs. Adams and I therefore decided to leave our house of refugees. Mrs. Adams and Ella, our daughter, would go down to St. Paul for the time, and I would go to the front as soon as possible. Accordingly I took my family down to Shakopee, and from there sent them on down to St. Paul by the steamer Antelope.

Then I returned and overtook a part of the Sixth Regiment of Minnesota Volunteers, at Belle Plaine, en route for Ft. Ridgely by way of St. Peter. I subjected my horse and buggy to the use of the regiment as an ambulance, and I volunteered to go along as chaplain, until a more permanent one should be appointed. On reaching St. Peter, there was a delay, occasioned by having to wait for necessary supplies of arms and ammunition; although everybody was in a hurry, urging an "onward march to the front, to chastise the murderers of our people."

At length, so much of the Sixth Regiment as was there marched out from St. Peter westward for Fort Ridgely, and, by invitation of Captain Grant, I was his guest on that expedition. We camped that night only about eight miles from St. Peter. The next day we resumed our march along the old Lac Qui Parle road, a clearly marked "seven path road," worn through the turf of the prairies.

All the way up to Fort Ridgely, a distance of forty-five miles, the country was practically desolated. Many of the houses and barns had been consumed by fire, and we found the remains of some of the owners, where they were murdered in their dooryards and in their fields, where some of them had fallen beside the last sheaf of grain, raked up and ready to bind, when the fatal, deadly shot struck them down. In some of the houses, we found the table still standing, as if the fam-

ily had been surprised and taken captive, or frightened away, while about to partake of their breakfast or dinner.

As we drew near to Fort Ridgely, on the upland prairie, we found the remains of a murdered colored man. His body had been badly mutilated. An empty bandbox and the scattered contents were all that was left of his outfit, apparently that of a barber.

As we passed on down the hill, into that deep ravine at the fort, we reached the place where my dear friend and brother, Eliphalet Richardson, of Glencoe, fell into the hands of the hostile Sioux and was shot, as he was riding along that road toward Fort Ridgely to ascertain, if possible, what all the rumors of Indian hostilities meant. Simultaneously, both Mr. Richardson and his horse were fatally shot. He fell dead there, and his horse ran off to the left some fifty or sixty yards, where he fell and was found dead.

Poor Mr. Richardson! He was a brave, noble and self-sacrificing, good man. When his brother was about ready to go over to Fort Ridgely on that trip, to bring news to the terrified people of Glencoe and vicinity, he said, "No, my brother! You have a wife and little children to mourn your death, but I have none to mourn for me, if anything should happen to me while over there." So saying, he seized the reins, sprang into the saddle, and rode away into the very jaws of death, not knowing fully of the terrible state of affairs, nor of the danger and sudden death that awaited him there.

After our arrival at Fort Ridgely, and that of other parts of the Sixth Regiment, there was some delay, occasioned by the want of a sufficient force to warrant a division of it, leaving men enough to hold the fort and protect the refugees then there, and at the same time to take forward an adequate fighting force to meet and chastise the hostile Indians.

At that very time, while we were waiting, there were also at Fort Ridgely nearly one hundred mounted men, on some of the very best horses in Minnesota. These citizens were armed and equipped, ready, as they said "to make a dash on the Indians, and punish the murderers;" but they positively and persistently refused to enlist in the United States army service, or to commit themselves for any definite period of time in the con-

templated expedition against the hostile Sioux. And on Saturday morning before we left there, to reconnoiter and bury the dead, that splendid company of men with their horses left Fort Ridgely for their homes. No one of us was glad to see them leave us then and there. General Sibley was deeply moved with sorrow at their conduct and departure, and so expressed himself. I said to General Sibley, "Why did you let them go?" He replied, "Only because I could not help it. If I had attempted to hold them, there would have been a mutiny on their part. So I had to let them go home."

After their departure, General Sibley gathered up what was left of men and horses that were available for public service. It was ascertained that there were only some fifty or sixty in all. Some of these had saddles and bridles, arms and ammunition, all right; but quite a number of them had only the merest excuses for these things, so necessary for good and efficient cavalry service. Manifestly, many of the horses had never been broken to the saddle, and some of them were not even bridle-wise, nor at all used to the noise of fire-arms and standing the fire, as in cavalry service. However, they were the best available there for the contemplated expedition.

RECONNOISSANCE AND BURIAL OF THE DEAD.

Finally, on Saturday afternoon, General Sibley gave orders that on Sunday morning, August 31st, Company A of the Sixth Regiment, commanded by Capt. Hiram P. Grant, together with as many mounted men as were available, should leave Fort Ridgely and proceed to reconnoiter and bury the dead; that on Sunday night they should encamp at the mouth of Birch Coulie, nearly opposite the Lower Agency; that on Monday they should finish burying the dead, and go into camp on Monday night at the Birch Coulie crossing of the old Lac Qui Parle road; and that the infantry and mounted forces should keep close together for mutual support and protection. Accordingly, on the Sabbath morning, the detachment marched out in the direction of the Lower Sioux Agency.

After we left Fort Ridgely, the mounted force, headed by Maj. Joseph R. Brown, reconnoitered on both sides of the road leading to the Lower Sioux Agency, until they reached the thick growth of bushes and briers, when their horses refused

to proceed, and they wheeled into the narrow wagon road. Thence they went before the infantry and the transportation teams, in the line of march, pretty much all the rest of the way.

Before we quite reached the "Magner place," about eight miles from the fort, we found and interred the bodies of the murdered citizens. On reaching the site of Mr. Magner's log cabin, which had been burned, we found the headless body of Dr. Humphrey, lying where he fell, in the front yard. By making diligent and thorough search, we found the remains of Mrs. Humphrey and of their two children, at least so much as were not consumed by fire, in the cellar, in the ashes of the burned house. Having brought an impromptu coffin, obtained from the post quartermaster at Fort Ridgely for the purpose before leaving there, we gathered up the remains of this little family and placed them all in that large plain coffin and buried them near where we found them.

We proceeded down the hill, and buried the remains of a number of murdered white people at the roadside, usually near where we found them.

At length, we reached the point, near the Lower Agency ferry, where we found the remains of the twenty-seven men of Captain Marsh's company, who fell dead by the fatal shots of three to five hundred of Little Crow's warriors, who, from their ambuscade in the brush, fired upon them with terribly disastrous results. Many of these, our fallen soldiers, we found lying there with their faces to the ground, their bodies riddled with bullets and their backs hacked with knives and tomahawks, presenting a shocking and mournful sight, long to be remembered. There we buried them. That Sabbath day, by us who were on that burying expedition, was one never to be forgotten, as a day of solemn funeral services of the most sad and sorrowful character.

Our reconnoitering party failed to find the remains of Captain Marsh, who was in command of the little force that was surprised and so nearly all murdered by such an overwhelming number of Sioux warriors. His body, however, was afterwards found and recovered by his brother, being taken from the Minnesota river, in which he had perished by drowning. It was removed to Elliota, Minn., for interment.

That Sunday night, we went into camp opposite the Lower Sioux Agency, at the mouth of Birch Coulie, a very much exposed place. Had the hostile Sioux known it, they might have successfully attacked us from at least three sides of our encampment, in that little oaf-stubble field all aglow with our camp fires. Fortunately, however, they were not there to molest us that night.

Nothing of special interest occurred, except that, about midnight, the lieutenant of Captain Grant's company, who was the officer of the day, came into the captain's tent and reported that one of the guard, on duty, was found delinquent of the password for the night. Captain Grant replied, "Lieutenant, that does not accord well with your first report, that you had the best guard mounted that ever was on duty in the Minnesota valley.'" "Oh no! Captain, but all is right now," was the lieutenant's reply.

The next morning we finished burying the dead in that vicinity. For the same purpose, a small party crossed the Minnesota river, with Mr. Nathan Myrick, and recovered the body of his brother, Mr. Andrew Myrick, and that of Mr. J. W. Lynd. They were murdered at the Lower Sioux Agency, among the first victims of the outbreak.

BATTLE OF BIRCH COULIE.

In the meantime, others, chiefly of the cavalry or mounted men, reconnoitered. A few of them ventured as far up as the Redwood crossing, and there recrossed the Minnesota river, and returned, late in the evening of that day, to Captain Grant's camp, three miles from the mouth of the Birch Coulie, at the crossing of the old Lac Qui Parle road. They reported that they saw no Indians in all that region reconnoitered by them. But the hostile Sioux saw them, and their spies followed them down from the Redwood crossing, saw them ride into that encampment for the night, and then returned and reported to Little Crow.

Thereupon, the entire force of the hostile Sioux marched down that night, and before daylight the next morning attacked Captain Grant and his command in that encampment with most disastrous results, killing twenty-three and wounding sixty of our soldiers and citizens. Ninety-two horses were

shot and killed or mortally wounded, including all the transportation teams and nearly all the cavalry horses in that expedition.

The dead horses, however, proved helpful to the survivors in the camp, who promptly utilized them in constructing impromptu barricades or breastworks, behind which they were enabled to withstand the attack, holding the camp against the firing of the Sioux, until they were relieved. But the defence was not without loss of some more of their bravest and best comrades, such as Mr. Holbrook of Belle Plaine and Mr. Dickinson of Henderson, both of whom I had known for many years before that terrible battle.

Fortunately for myself and horse, on the afternoon of Monday, the day before that disaster occurred at Birch Coulie, having finished the burial of the dead up to the mouth of the coulie and in its vicinity, with the leave of Captain Grant, I returned with my horse and buggy to Fort Ridgely, and, as directed by Captain Grant, reported to General Sibley, commander in chief of the Minnesota volunteers.

The next morning, very early, even before it was daylight, after my return to the fort, we heard the firing of guns, but such was the confused sound and strange reverberation that it seemed almost impossible for any of us, even the most expert men present, including General Sibley and his staff officers, to determine certainly from what direction the reports of musketry came, whether from Captain Grant's camp at Birch Coulie crossing, or from New Ulm, down the Minnesota river.

Finally, General Sibley decided to send up a detachment of soldiers, with orders to go with all possible speed directly to Captain Grant's camp. It was almost noon, however, when all was ready and the relief detachment marched out in that direction, and so nearly was it dark that evening when they neared Captain Grant's camp, about fifteen miles distant from Fort Ridgely, that they could not in the twilight distinctly and certainly see whether it was his camp or that of the hostile Sioux. So they waited there until the early dawn of the next morning, when they marched into that almost annihilated encampment, strewn with the bodies of our soldiers, and surrounded, as it was, with the dead horses, riddled wagons, and

impromptu earthworks. Then they understood why they could
not in the dim twilight, of the evening before, recognize the
encampment as that of our soldiers.

The following citizens of St. Paul were killed in the Birch
Coulie battle, namely, Robert Baxter, Fred S. Beneken, Wil-
liam M. Cobb, John Colledge, George Colter, Robert Gibbons,
William Irvine, William Russell, Benjamin S. Terry, and H.
Walters. Their bodies were recovered and brought to this city
for interment.

Having returned to Fort Ridgely and reported to General
Sibley, and having accomplished, as I thought, about all that
I could well do as a volunteer chaplain in the public service,
and learning that Rev. S. R. Riggs was under appointment as
chaplain and designated as interpreter of the Sioux language
for that expedition, and that he would soon be there to accompany General Sibley's command, I obtained leave from him and
returned home.

SUMMARY OF LOSSES BY THE MASSACRE AND WAR.

Various estimates have been made of the number of white
people killed by the hostile Sioux in 1862. The most probable
number, all told, was not far from five hundred, including the
soldiers who fell in the battles at the Lower Agency, New
Ulm, Birch Coulie and Wood Lake. That entire portion of the
upper Minnesota valley, including the whole or large parts of
some fifteen or twenty counties of our state, was fearfully desolated, and for the time almost entirely depopulated. Nor has
it yet, in 1899, fully recovered.

The mission stations, the United States Indian agencies,
churches and schools, were all broken up, the buildings were
burned, and the people were either murdered or frightened
away. Some of the women and children were taken captive by
the hostile Sioux, and while in captivity were in constant fear
of death.

AID BY FRIENDLY DAKOTAS.

Very few, if any, of the Christian Sioux, who were then
connected with the Presbyterian mission churches among
them, were found guilty of participating in that outbreak and
the murder of the white settlers in Minnesota. And it is worthy of record here that all the white people who were rescued

and saved alive were directly or indirectly saved by the Christian Indians, who in so doing greatly jeopardized their own lives and those of their families. That so many white people were enabled to escape was, indeed, as if by a special Divine providence and merciful dispensation of God, which to us seemed almost as miraculous as the deliverance of the apostle Peter from prison more than eighteen hundred years ago.

Among the loyal and friendly Dakotas, who were most active and efficient, and who were distinguished for their zeal and helpfulness in behalf of the imperilled and defenceless white people during that dreadful ordeal, I may mention the following names, with brief recital of their heroic aid.

Paul Maza-ku-ta-ma-ne and Antoine Renville were the first to notify Dr. S. R. Riggs and his family, and others then at Hazelwood mission station, and begged them to "hasten and escape." At midnight these two friendly Sioux guided and otherwise assisted them in their flight through the tall, wet grass, to the Minnesota river; took them in canoes, and piloted their wagons and teams to an island; and there left them for a time in that somewhat concealed place for safety.

Thence these refugees from Hazelwood and its vicinity were led in their escape by Chaskedan (Robert Hopkins), an elder in Dr. Williamson's mission church, who kindly drove Dr. Williamson's team and guided the escaping party successfully out through the lines of the mounted hostile Indians, although they were vigilantly patrolling all that region and were conscripting every Sioux into the war against the whites. Chaskedan is the same full-blooded Indian who, when a boy, with his father, near Lac Qui Parle, several years before the outbreak, had saved Mr. Joseph A. Wheelock from drowning in the Chippewa river.

Simon Anawag-ma-ne, another good man, when Dr. Williamson's team had been taken away before he decided to leave, brought his own ox team and strong wagon, and gave them to the doctor, thus enabling him and his family to escape from the impending danger and make their way to St. Peter. Anawag-ma-ne was the same brave and kind man who afterwards befriended Mrs. Newman and her captive children while in camp, and, at an opportune time, brought them down in his one-horse wagon, through the lines of the hostile Sioux, in safety to Fort Ridgely.

Enoch Marpiya-hdi-na-pe (Cloud in Sight), another full-blood Dakota Indian, who was in sympathy with the whites, very early in that momentous crisis warned Dr. Williamson of the uprising and the murderous designs of the Indians, and of the fearful possibility that he and other friendly Indians might not much longer be able to protect him and his family and save them alive. He entreated Dr. Williamson to leave and try to reach a place of safety before it would be too late, thus leading him to escape with the Hazelwood party.

Lorenzo Lawrence, also a full-blood Dakota, in the midst of that fiery trial, left Hazelwood with canoes lashed together side by side, and hiding by day and paddling the canoes by night, brought down a precious cargo, comprising Mrs. De Camp and her three children and Mrs. Robideau and five children, together with his own wife and five children, sixteen in all, and landed them safely at Fort Ridgely. When Mrs. De Camp's little child fell overboard in the darkness of the night, Lorenzo plunged into the river and rescued and restored it to its mother's arms; and this was characteristic of that good man, whom I knew from 1848 to the day of his death.

Wakan-ma-ne (Walking Spirit), very early after the outbreak occurred, like a tender and compassionate father, took charge of Mrs. Amos W. Huggins and her two little children, after her husband was killed, August 19th, at Lac Qui Parle. He protected them from the hostile Sioux, gave them food and shelter, and faithfully delivered them in safety to General Sibley at Camp Release. Amanda, Wakan-ma-ne's wife, in her sympathy and kind care of Mrs. Huggins and her little children, walked down thirty miles and back to obtain flour and make wheat bread for them, during their captivity, the mother and children not being able to eat the corn used in the tent life of the Dakotas.

There were also a number of other good Christian Indian women who joined heartily and faithfully in befriending and helping the white people. Among them was Zoe, who very considerately and in the nick of time carried the forgotten bag of bread from the mission home over to Mrs. Riggs, while as yet the party were in their hiding place on the island opposite the Hazelwood mission station. In like manner Winyan, a

devoted Christian woman, early notified the whites of the reported trouble and of their peril, and in many ways did all she could to help them make their escape.

Mrs. Bird, Mrs. Antoine Renville, and Mrs. John B. Renville, Christian Dakota women of influence and of sympathy with the white people, made great sacrifices and took great risks in helping them to escape in safety from death; and meantime they did all they could to quell the outbreak and protect the captives.

Rev. John B. Renville and his brothers, Antoine and Michael, and others associated with them at the Hazelwood Republic, formed a nucleus and did stalwart service in quelling the outbreak, in rescuing and saving the prisoners from death, and in aid of their final release. .

Last, but by no means least, was John Otherday (Angpetu Tokecha), a Dakota who had married a white woman. He lived at Yellow Medicine Agency, and had renounced the heathenism of the Sioux and abandoned the war-path. On profession of his faith in Christ, he had been received into Dr. Williamson's church, of which he was then a member. Hearing of the trouble at the Lower Sioux Agency, and knowing that it was not in his power to stop it, nor, indeed, to protect and defend his white friends from its fearful march and fatal results, he thought that the best thing he could then do, in the circumstances, was to try to save the white people by aiding their escape. Accordingly, he gathered some sixty-two white people, including forty-two women and children, and on August 19th took up the line of march, crossing the Minnesota river, and, under his guidance, the party made their way out over the prairies, by way of Hutchinson and Henderson, to Shakopee and St. Paul, in safety. On his arrival at St. Paul, John Otherday publicly said, "This deliverance I attribute to the mercy of the Great Spirit," meaning that it was the gospel of Christ which had led him to befriend and guide that company in the midst of so great peril, bringing them safely to their friends, with so much joy and thankfulness.

CHRISTIAN MISSIONS AND THEIR RESULTS.

The wonderful changes in the Sioux or Dakota people within the last half century, and the truly marvelous results of

29

the efforts made for their intellectual, moral and spiritual improvement, should not be overlooked by us in our review of the Sioux outbreak and war.

Long before the outbreak, the Sioux were known for their bravery, and distinguished for their warlike disposition. So fierce and cruel were they in their hostility and bloodthirsty warfare, that they were commonly styled "the bloody Sioux." Yet they were very much like all other heathen people, without the gospel of Christ and the blessings of Christian civilization.

Providentially and geographically, the Sioux and other Indians of our country were at our very doors, and therefore they had special claims on us, the people of the United States, for our sympathy and helping hand. To this end and on this line, much had been done for the Sioux people, both by the United States government and by the Christian churches and their boards for home and foreign missions, to educate, train, and instruct them in the new and better ways of Christian civilization and Christianity. Great sacrifices were made, in this Christian and truly philanthropic work, in behalf of these aborigines of our country. For many years "the good seed of the kingdom" was sown, and many prayers and entreaties to God were offered in their behalf; much money was expended for them; and many precious elect lives were laid on the altar of consecrated service for them.

It was my privilege, coming here for mission work at Lac Qui Parle in 1848, to be associated with some of these pioneer missionaries, namely, Rev. T. S. Williamson, M. D., and his son, Rev. John P. Williamson; Rev. S. R. Riggs and his sons; Revs. Samuel and Gideon H. Pond; Rev. Robert Hopkins; Rev. Joshua Potter; Rev. John F. Aiton; and Rev. Joseph W. Hancock. Many of these have ceased from their labors and entered into their rest, "and their works do follow them."

Before the Sioux outbreak and massacre of the whites, and at that time, the medicine men and warriors of the Sioux nation said that, in the contemplated war with the white people, they would surely succeed. They stipulated that, if they should not overcome and destroy the whites, then the "Taku Wakan" of the Sioux or Dakotas is false and must be re-

nounced by them, and the white people's God would be the true God and their God. Accordingly it was believed that the gods of the Sioux nation fought. When they were defeated, it was seen that the brightest and mightiest of the stars in the entire Dakota mythology, as known to them, had fought, but were overcome. It was therefore acknowledged that the "Taku Wakan" of their fathers was false, unworthy to be trusted, and had failed them in the day of battle, as at Wood Lake, when Little Crow and Little Six, and the hostile Sioux gen-erally, were driven back, and fled to the broad plains beyond, defeated and utterly routed.

After the decisive battle of Wood Lake, there was a won-derfully great change in the Sioux nation. Their heathen gods had utterly failed them. Great multitudes of them turned to God; and ever since that time there has been an open door for the preaching and teaching of the gospel of Christ among the Dakotas, as never before.

What now are the facts and figures showing the results of missionary work among the Dakotas, since the reconstruction and new order of things, for their uplifting and salvation? Only a few of them can here be mentioned.

Without boasting or making any invidious comparisons, or in the least depreciating the labors and results of others among the Sioux (or Dakotas, as they themselves prefer to be called), I would state that the Presbyterian Church alone, and its missionary boards, have, according to the last reports, pub-lished in the Minutes of the General Assembly of May, 1898, the following interesting statistics of their work and member-ship: 19 native Dakota ordained ministers; 4 candidates, and 1 licentiate; 23 organized Presbyterian churches, with 69 rul-ing elders, ordained to the work, and 27 deacons, elect and set apart to the office; 1,334 church members, in good and regular standing; and 600 Sunday school scholars. Within the pre-ceding year, $448 were contributed for miscellaneous pur-poses; $1,774 for home missions; $65 for foreign missions; $1,976 for their own church expenses, and $105 as their share of the General Assembly fund. Besides, they also made very commendable contributions to each of the other Boards of the General Assembly of the Presbyterian Church. Most of these

Dakota churches now have neat and comfortable houses of worship of their own, all paid for on or before the day of dedication.

The Dakota people also have schoolhouses on their respective reservations; and some of them have boarding schools for manual training. They are interested in the education and training of their children and youth; and many of the parents, whom I have known, make great sacrifices in order to keep their children in school so long as to become well educated and fitted for usefulness in life.

In connection with their churches, they have pretty much all the usual voluntary societies and associations, as of Christian Endeavor, etc., each in its place, doing a good work.

In view of what God has done among the Sioux or Dakotas, and what he is now doing, for their enlightenment, uplifting and salvation, through all the agencies of Christian mission work among them, we may well exclaim, "Behold what God hath wrought! It is marvelous in our eyes!"

Nathaniel P. Langford

THE LOUISIANA PURCHASE AND PRECEDING SPANISH INTRIGUES FOR DISMEMBERMENT OF THE UNION.*

BY NATHANIEL PITT LANGFORD.

"The Mississippi river," says George Bancroft, "is the guardian and the pledge of the union of the States of America. Had they been confined to the eastern slope of the Alleghanies, there would have been no geographical unity between them; and the thread of connection between lands that merely fringed the Atlantic must soon have been sundered. The father of rivers gathers his waters from all the clouds that break between the Alleghanies and the farthest ranges of the Rocky Mountains. The ridges of the eastern chain bow their heads at the north and the south, so that long before science became the companion of man, Nature herself pointed out to the barbarous races how short portages join his tributary waters to those of the Atlantic coast. At the other side his mightiest arm interlocks with the arms of the Oregon and the Colorado; and, by the conformation of the earth itself, marshals highways to the Pacific. From his remotest springs he refuses to suffer his waters to be divided; but as he bears them all to the bosom of the ocean, the myriads of flags that wave above his head are all the ensigns of one people. States larger than kingdoms flourish where he passes, and beneath his step cities start into being, more marvellous in their reality than the fabled creations of enchantment. His magnificent valley, lying in the best part of the temperate zone, salubrious and wonderfully fertile, is the chosen muster-ground of the various elements of human culture brought together by men summoned from all the civilized nations of the earth, and joined in the bonds of common citizenship by the strong invincible

*Read at the monthly meeting of the Executive Council, February 13, 1899.

attraction of republican freedom. Now that science has come to be the household friend of trade and commerce and travel, and that Nature has lent to wealth and intellect the use of her constant forces, the hills, once walls of division, are scaled or pierced or levelled, and the two oceans, between which the republic has unassailably intrenched itself against the outward world, are bound together across the continent by friendly links of iron. From the grandeur of destiny, foretold by the possession of that river and the lands drained by its waters, the Bourbons of Spain, hoping to act in concert with Great Britain as well as France, would have excluded the United States, totally and forever."

In the early days of our republic, the great national artery so justly eulogized by our leading historian, was the fruitful cause of the most dangerous intrigues, aimed at the perpetuity of our Union. The inhabitants of the Ohio and Mississippi valleys, cut off by the Appalachian range from all commercial intercourse with the Atlantic seaboard, were necessarily dependent upon the Mississippi for access to the markets of the world. The mouth of that river was, as to them, the threshold of subsistence. Extensive possessions, richness of soil, and immensity of production were of little value without the means which this great channel alone afforded for the establishment of commercial relations with other nations. The most prolific, as well as most unbounded region of varied agricultural production in the world was comparatively valueless without this single convenience.

At the time whereof I now speak, the mouth of the Mississippi and the country adjacent was owned and controlled by Spain, then a powerful nation, jealous of her possessions in America, and unfriendly to the young republic which had suddenly sprung into existence on the northern borders of her empire. She had assented to the stipulation in the treaty between Great Britain, the United States, and herself in 1783 in which the independence of our country was recognized, that the navigation of the Mississippi from its source to its mouth should be and should forever remain free and open to the subjects of Great Britain and the citizens of the United States. This privilege, sufficient for ordinary purposes in time of peace, was liable at any moment and on almost any pretence, as we

shall hereafter see, to be absolutely denied, or to be hampered with oppressive duties, or to be used for purposes dangerous to the very existence of our government.

FORESIGHT OF WASHINGTON.

The first individual to see the evils which might flow from a dependence upon this outlet to the ocean by the people living west of the Alleghanies, was Washington himself. He had carefully noted the flow of the rivers beyond the Alleghanies, and the portages between them and the rivers flowing down their eastern slope, at the time of his first visit into that region before the Revolution, and was only hindered from forming a company to unite them by an artificial channel, by the occurrence of the Revolution itself. The year after peace was declared he again visited the country bordering the upper waters of the Ohio, and at this time regarded the improvement not only of immense importance in its commercial aspect to the States of Maryland and Virginia, but as one of the necessities of the general government. "He had noticed," says Washington Irving, "that the flanks and rear of the United States were possessed by foreign and formidable powers, who might lure the Western people into a trade and alliance with them. The Western States, he observed, stood as it were on a pivot, so that the touch of a feather might turn them any way. They had looked down the Mississippi and been tempted in that direction by the facilities of sending everything down the stream, whereas they had no means of coming to the Atlantic sea-board but by long land transportation and rugged roads. The jealous and untoward disposition of the Spaniard, it was true, almost barred the use of the Mississippi; but they might change their policy and invite trade in that direction. The retention by the British Government, also, of the posts of Detroit, Niagara, and Oswego, though contrary to the spirit of the treaty, shut up the channel of trade in that quarter."

Washington's views were laid before the legislature of Virginia, and were received with such favor that he was induced to repair to Richmond to give them his personal support. His suggestions and representations during this visit gave the first impulse to the great system of internal improvements since pursued throughout the United States.

DISSATISFACTION OF WESTERN SETTLERS.

While Washington was urging upon the people of Virginia the importance of a water communication between the head waters of the Potomac and the Ohio, and had succeeded so far as to effect the organization of two companies under the patronage of the Governments of Maryland and Virginia, the people of the Western States, dissatisfied with the tax imposed upon them to pay the interest on the debt of the country to France, were many of them abandoning their dwellings and marching towards the Mississippi, "in order to unite with a certain number of disbanded soldiers who were anxious to possess themselves of a considerable portion of the territory watered by that river." Their object was to establish a government under the name of The Western Independence, and deny the authority of the American Congress, as McGillivray says in a letter to the governor of Pensacola.

This Alexander McGillivray, the head chief of the Talapouches, or Creeks, was a half-breed, the son of Lachland McGillivray, a Scotchman, and a Creek woman. He was educated in Scotland. Pickett, the historian of Alabama, calls him the Talleyrand of Alabama; and Gayarre, in an extended eulogy, says of him: "The individual who, Proteus-like, could in turn,—nay more, who could at the same time, be a British colonel, a Spanish and an American general, a polished gentleman, a Greek and Latin scholar, and a wild Indian chief with the frightful tomahawk at his belt and the war paint on his body, a shrewd politician, a keen-sighted merchant, a skillful speculator, the emperor of the Creeks and Seminoles, the able negotiator in person with Washington and other great men, the writer of papers which would challenge the admiration of the most fastidious,—he who could be a Mason among the Christians, and a pagan prophet in the woods; he who could have presents, titles, decorations, showered at the same time upon him from England, Spain and the United States, and who could so long arrest their encroachments against himself and his nation by playing them like puppets against each other, must be allowed to tower far above the common herd of men." McGillivray died 17th February, 1793. He was buried with Masonic honors, in

the garden of William Panton, in Pensacola. His death spread desolation among his people.

PROPHECIES OF NAVARRO

Martin Navarro, the Spanish intendant at New Orleans, united with remarkable sagacity and foresight a jealousy of the American population of the Western States, amounting almost to mania. His policy in regulating commercial intercourse with all neighbors was in the largest degree conciliatory and generous. From the hour of its birth, he predicted with singular accuracy the power and growth of the American republic. In 1786, speaking of the commercial relations between the province of Louisiana and the numerous Indian tribes which owned the territory bordering upon the Mississippi river, he says:—

"Nothing can be more proper than that the goods they want should be sold them at an equitable price, in order to afford them inducements and facilities for their hunting pursuits, and in order to put it within their means to clothe themselves on fair terms. Otherwise they would prefer trading with the Americans, with whom they would in the end form alliances which cannot but turn out to be fatal to this province."

The surplus productions of the Western settlements at this time had grown into a very considerable commerce, which, having no other outlet than the Mississippi, was sent down that river to New Orleans where it was subjected to unjust and oppressive duties. The flatboat-men complained of the seizures, confiscations, extortions and imprisonments which in almost every instance were visited upon them by the Spanish authorities. Infuriated by the frequency and flagrant character of these outrages, and denying the right of Spain under the treaty of 1783 in any way to restrict the free navigation of the river, the Western people began seriously to contemplate an open invasion of Louisiana, and a forcible seizure of the port of New Orleans. They laid their grievances before Congress and petitioned that body to renew negotiations with Spain, and secure for them such commercial privileges as were necessary to the very existence of their settlements.

Navarro seconded these views, and writing to his Government says: "The powerful enemies we have to fear in this

province are not the English, but the Americans, whom we must oppose by active and sufficient measures." He then, by a variety of reasons, urges that a restriction of commercial franchises will only increase the embarrassment of Spain. "The only way," he says, "to check them, is with a proportionate population, and it is not by imposing commercial restrictions that this population is to be acquired, but by granting a prudent extension and freedom of trade."

By granting the Americans special privileges, donating lands to them and affording them other subsidies, Navarro hoped to lure them from their allegiance to our Government. Very many, yielding to these inducements, moved their families into the Spanish province and became willing subjects of His Catholic Majesty. The majority of those who remained. owing to the repeated failures and rebuffs they had suffered in their efforts to obtain free commercial privileges, were forced at length to consider the idea of forming a new and independent republic of their own. Their separation by distance and mountain barriers from the Atlantic states rendered all commercial intercourse impracticable between the two portions of the country. They were surrounded by savages against whose murderous attacks their Government was unable to afford them adequate protection, and their commerce was burdened with oppressive and ruinous duties before it could gain access to the markets of the world. Besides these considerations, they were oppressed with heavy taxation to pay the interest on the great war debt to France. These reasons, to any one who can identify himself with the period of our history now under review, would certainly seem sufficient to overcome a patriotism which had always been measured by the amount of sacrifice it was capable of making without any return. Our Government, still under the old confederacy and no longer bound by the cohesive elements of the war, was ready to fall to pieces because of its inherent weakness. The majority of the people, both east and west, had little confidence in its stability. The leading patriots of the Revolution, alarmed at the frequent and threatening demonstrations of revolt made in all parts of the country, were at a loss to know how to avoid a final disruption.

"What, then," says Washington in a letter to John Jay, "is to be done? Things cannot go on in the same strain forever. It is much to be feared, as you observe, that the better kind of people, being disgusted with the circumstances, will have their minds prepared for any revolution whatever. We are apt to run from one extreme to another. * * * * * * I am told that even respectable characters speak of a monarchical government without horror. From thinking proceeds speaking;—then acting is often but a single step. But how irrevocable and tremendous! What a triumph for our enemies to verify their predictions! What a triumph for the advocates of despotism to find that we are incapable of governing ourselves, and that systems founded on the basis of equal liberty are merely ideal and fallacious."

It was when the country was in this condition, that the idea of a separate independence took form among the people west of the Alleghanies. Want of unanimity in the adoption of a basis for the new republic only prevented its organization; for as soon as the question came under serious consideration, no less than five parties appeared, each claiming its plan to be the only one suited to the purposes in view. Judge Martin, in his history of Louisiana, says:

«The first party was for being independent of the United States, and for the formation of a new republic unconnected with the old one, and resting on a basis of its own and a close alliance with Spain.

"Another party was willing that the country should become a part of the province of Louisiana, and submit to the admission of the laws of Spain.

«A third desired a war with Spain and the seizure of New Orleans.

«A fourth plan was to prevail on Congress, by a show of preparation for war, to extort from the cabinet of Madrid what it persisted in refusing.

«The last, as unnatural as the second, was to solicit France to procure a retrocession of Louisiana, and to extend her protection to Kentucky."

Encouraged in their designs to lure the Western people into Louisiana by this public evidence of their disaffection

toward their own country, the Spanish authorities from this
moment conceived the idea of working a dismemberment of
our confederacy and attaching the vast country west of the
Alleghanies to the other Hispano-American possessions. Separate plans for effecting this object were formed by Miro, the
governor of Louisiana, and Gardoquoi, the Spanish minister
at Philadelphia. These officials were jealous of each other,
and though partners in design, frequently clashed in their
measures.

GEN. WILKINSON'S INTRIGUES.

In June, 1787, General James Wilkinson, an officer of the
Revolution who had emigrated to the West a few months before, descended the Mississippi to New Orleans, with a cargo
of flour, tobacco, butter and bacon. His boat having been
seized, Wilkinson, after a protracted interview with Governor
Miro, parted from him with an order for its release and permission to sell his cargo free of duty. This arch-intriguer was
permitted, during the entire period that his negotiations with
Miro were in progress, to enjoy all the privileges of the New
Orleans market free of duty. He sold large cargoes of tobacco,
flour and butter to the Spanish authorities on different occasions, and received from Miro, at various times, very large sums
of money to aid him in the work of dismemberment. We learn
that at one time he sought to become a Spanish subject, but
was dissuaded by Miro, who, while he loved the treason, hated
the traitor. At another time, in the midst of his intrigues he
besought Miro to obtain for him a portion of the country to
which he could flee to escape the vengeance which would pur-
sue him in case his diabolical acts should be discovered by
Washington. He remained in New Orleans until September.
During that period, at Miro's request, he furnished him with
his views in writing of the political interests of Spain and the
Western people. This document strongly advocated the free
navigation of the Mississippi, and was sent to Madrid for
the perusal of the king. But it was intended simply as a
blind, to conceal the inception of an intrigue between Miro and
Wilkinson for the separation of the Western settlements from
the Union, and their adherence to Spain. It was soon ascertained that, coincident with the submission of this document,

Wilkinson presented another to Miro, containing different representations, but which was not made public.

In the meantime, Gardoquoi, acting without Miro's compliance, had invited the people of Kentucky and the region bordering the Cumberland river to establish themselves under the protection of Spain in West Florida and the Florida district of lower Louisiana, offering as inducements that they might hold slaves, stock, provisions for two years, farming utensils and implements, without paying any duty whatever, and enjoy their own religion. Allured by these promises, many Americans removed to Louisiana and became Spanish subjects. To encourage this work of emigration, Gardoquoi made a concession of a vast tract of land, seventy miles below the mouth of the Ohio, to Col. George Morgan, upon his proposition to settle it with a large number of immigrants. In pursuance of this purpose, Morgan afterwards laid the foundations of a city there, which, in compliment to Spain, he called New Madrid.

Gardoquoi, fearful lest his plans might be disturbed by Miro, sent an agent to New Orleans to obtain for them the support of that functionary. Miro was deeply embroiled in the intrigue with Wilkinson;—an enterprise, which, if successful, would prove vastly more important than that of Gardoquoi. Concealing his purpose from the latter, Miro, upon one pretext and another, avoided committing himself to plans which, if prosecuted, were certain to clash with his own. In January, 1788, he wrote to Valdes, the minister for the department of the Indies:—

"I have been reflecting for many days whether it would not be proper to communicate to D'Arges (Gardoquoi's agent) Wilkinson's plans, and to Wilkinson the mission of D'Arges, in order to unite them and dispose them to work in concert. * * * The delivering up of Kentucky into His Majesty's hands, which is the main object to which Wilkinson has promised to devote himself entirely, would forever constitute this province a rampart for the protection of New Spain."

In the course of this intrigue, Gardoquoi's agent stipulated to lead fifteen hundred and eighty-two Kentucky families into the Natchez district. Miro ordered Grandpre, the governor of Natchez, to make concessions of land to each family on its

arrival, and require them to take the following oath: "We the undersigned do swear, on the Holy Evangelists, entire fealty, vassalage and lealty to His Catholic Majesty, wishing voluntarily to live under his laws, promising not to act either directly or indirectly against his real interest, and to give immediate information to our commandants of all that may come to our knowledge of whatever nature it may be, if prejudicial to the welfare of Spain in general and to that of this province in particular, in defence of which we hold ourselves ready to take up arms on the first summons of our chiefs, and particularly in the defence of this district against whatever forces may come from the upper part of the river Mississippi, or from the interior of the continent."

"Whilst presenting to them these considerations," writes Miro, "you will carefully observe the manner in which they shall receive them, and the expression of their faces. Of this you will give me precise information, every time that you send me the original oaths taken."

In furtherance of his enterprise, Wilkinson spent several months in the Atlantic States after leaving New Orleans. He wrote to Miro in cipher, on his return to the West, that all his predictions were verifying themselves. "Not a measure," he says, "is taken on both sides of the mountains which does not conspire to favor ours." About the same time he wrote to Gardoquoi in order to allay his suspicions. Receiving from Miro no immediate reply to his letter, he sent a cargo of produce down the river in charge of Major Isaac Dunn, whom he accredited to Miro as a fit auxiliary in the execution of their political designs. Dunn assured the Spanish governor that Kentucky would separate entirely from the Federal Union the next year.

While these schemes were in progress, the settlers in the district of Cumberland, reduced to extremities by the frequent and bloody invasions of the Indians south of them, sent delegates to Alexander McGillivray, head chief of the tribes, to declare their willingness to throw themselves into the arms of His Catholic Majesty, as subjects. They said that Congress could neither protect their persons nor property, nor favor their commerce, and that they were desirous to free themselves from all allegiance to a power incapable of affording the smallest benefit in return.

SPANISH INQUISITION.

One of the difficult questions for the Spanish authorities to settle with the people they expected to lure to their embrace was that of religion. Spain was not only Catholic, but she had not abandoned the Inquisition, as a means of torturing the rest of the world into a confession of that faith. Gardoquoi had promised all immigrants into Louisiana freedom of religious opinion. Miro, willing to make some concessions, would not concede entire freedom. Just at the time that a promise had been made of a large emigration from the western settlements, Miro received a letter from the Reverend Capuchin Antonio de Sedella, informing him that he had been appointed commissary of the Inquisition, and that, in order to carry his instructions into perfect execution, he might soon, at some late hour of the night, deem it necessary to require some guards to assist him in his operations. A few hours afterwards while this inquisitor was reposing, he was roused by an alarm. Starting up he met an officer and a file of grenadiers, who, he supposed, had come to obey his orders. "My friends," said he, "I thank you and his excellency for the readiness of this compliance with my request. But I have no use for your services, and you shall be warned in time when you are wanted. Retire, then, with the blessing of God." The surprise of the Holy Father may be conceived when told that he was under arrest. "What!" he exclaimed, "will you dare lay hands on a commissary of the Holy Inquisition?"

"I dare obey orders," was the stern reply,—and Father de Sedella was immediately conducted on board a vessel which sailed the next day for Cadiz.

Miro, writing to one of the members of the cabinet of Madrid concerning this unceremonious removal, says: "The mere name of the Inquisition, uttered in New Orleans, would be sufficient, not only to check immigration, which is successfully progressing, but would also be capable of driving away those who have recently come, and I even fear that in spite of my having sent out of the country Father de Sedella, the most fatal consequences may ensue from the mere suspicion of the cause of his dismissal." This was the first and last attempt of the Spaniards to plant the Inquisition in North America.

In the midst of these intrigues and schemes, Navarro, the talented intendant, was recalled by his Government and returned to Spain. The two offices of governor and intendant thus became united in Miro. In his last official dispatch, Navarro expressed his views of the province with considerable detail. He depicted the dangers which Spain had to fear from the United States,—predicting that the "newborn giant would not be satisfied until he extended his domains across the continent and bathed his vigorous young limbs in the placid waters of the Pacific." A severance of the Union was, in his opinion, the only way this could be prevented. This was not difficult if the present circumstances were turned to advantage. "Grant," said he, "every sort of commercial privilege to the masses in the Western region, and shower pensions and honors on the leaders."

While actively engaged in the prosecution of his intrigue with Miro, we learn from a letter written to that official in February, 1789, that in October of the previous year Wilkinson met with Col. Connelly, a British officer, who, he says, "had travelled through the woods to the mouth of the river Big Miami, from which he came down the Ohio in a boat." He claimed to be an emissary of Lord Dorchester, the governor-general of Canada. Ignorant of Wilkinson's secret negotiations with Miro, he met him by invitation at his house, and upon Wilkinson's assurance of regard for the interests of His Britannic Majesty, Connelly unfolded to him the object of his mission. He informed Wilkinson that Great Britain was desirous of assisting the Western settlers in their efforts to open the navigation of the Mississippi. She would join them to dispossess Spain of Louisiana, and as the forces in Canada were too small to supply detachments for the purpose, Lord Dorchester would, in place thereof, supply our men with all the implements of war, and with money, clothing, etc., to equip an army of ten thousand men.

Wilkinson, in his letter to Miro, says: "After having pumped out of him all that I wished to know, I began to weaken his hopes by observing that the feelings of animosity engendered by the late Revolution were so recent in the hearts of the Americans that I considered it impossible to entice them into an alliance with Great Britain; that in this district, par-

ticularly in that part of it where the inhabitants had suffered
so much from the barbarous hostilities of the Indians, which
were attributed to British influence, the resentment of every
individual was much more intense and implacable. In order
to justify this opinion of mine, I employed a hunter who feigned
attempting his life. The pretext assumed by the hunter was
the avenging the death of his son, murdered by the Indians at
the supposed instigation of the English. As I hold the commission of a civil judge, it was of course to be my duty to protect him against the pretended murderer, whom I caused to be
arrested and held in custody. I availed myself of this circumstance to communicate to Connelly my fear of not being able
to answer for the security of his person, and I expressed my
doubts whether he could escape with his life. It alarmed him
so much that he begged me to give him an escort to conduct
him out of the territory, which I readily assented to, and on
the 20th of November he recrossed the Ohio on his way back
to Detroit."

Such was the influence of Wilkinson with the people of the
districts of Kentucky and Cumberland, that between the years
1786 and 1792 he thwarted them four times in their designs to
invade Louisiana, after preparations had been made for that
purpose. His object was to unite the Western settlements
with Spain,—not to maintain the integrity of the Federal
Union.

STATE OF FRANKLAND.

Circumstances which had occurred several years before
this time gave birth to another intrigue of remarkable character, which culminated in the fall of 1788. The western portion of North Carolina, known as the Washington District,
in 1784 declared itself independent and organized a government under the name of the State of Frankland. The name
was afterward changed to Franklin.

At that time North Carolina was a turbulent state, and
there was little cohesion between the eastern and western
portions. The desire of the western portion to form a separate
state government was aimed at the parent state rather than
the United States. The parent state did not oppose the secession, for the reason that it had been severely taxed to pay

30

the Indian war debts incurred in protecting the western frontier. On the other hand, the inhabitants of the western portion complained that the jurisdiction of the courts was not extended over them, so as to protect them from the incursions of the outlaws from adjoining states.

In the year 1784 the legislature of North Carolina ceded what is now the State of Tennessee to the United States, coupled with the condition that within two years it should formally accept the gift; and further, that until the expiration of that period, North Carolina should exercise sovereignty over it. On August 23, 1784, a constitutional convention was called at Jonesboro, of which John Sevier was president. A difference of opinion arose among the members as to whether their declaration of independence should go into effect at once, or at a future day;—but a vote being taken, two-thirds of the members declared for immediate secession. The same question divided the members when they met in November to frame a constitution, and the convention dissolved in utter confusion. In the meantime the State of North Carolina became alarmed at the attitude of the secessionists, and repealed its act of cession, which had not at that time been accepted by the United States, and Governor Sevier advised his followers to abandon the scheme for the organization of the new state. But his adherents would not recede. They met on December 14, 1784, at Jonesboro and adopted a constitution, subject to its ratification by a future convention, which was to meet at Greenville in November, 1785. In March, 1785, the two houses of the Legislature met and elected John Sevier Governor of the new state, and organized courts, and passed general laws. Among these acts of the Legislature was one authorizing the payment of taxes and of salaries to be made in various articles of merchandise. Among the articles in which taxes were payable were the following: Beaver, otter and deer skins, which were rated at six shillings each; raccoon and fox skins, rated at one shilling three pence each; beeswax, at one shilling per pound; rye whiskey, at three shillings six pence per gallon; peach brandy, at three shillings per gallon. The salaries of all officers were to be paid wholly in skins. The following is a copy of one of the acts of the Legislature:—

"Be it enacted by the general assembly of the State of Franklin, and it is hereby enacted by authority of the same,

.that from and after the first day of January next the salaries
of this commonwealth shall be as follows, to-wit:

His Excellency, the Governor, per annum, 100 deer skins.

His Honor, the Chief Justice, 500 deer skins.

The Secretary to His Excellency, the Governor, 500 raccoon
skins.

County Clerk, 300 beaver skins.

Clerk of the House of Commons, 200 raccoon skins.

Members of the Assembly, per diem, three raccoon skins.

Justice's fee for serving a warrant, one mink skin."

Among the names proposed for the new state was that of
Frankland, or the "Land of freemen;" but by a very small
majority it was decided to call it Franklin in honor of Benjamin
Franklin. Franklin, however, did not know that the
new state had been named for him until eighteen months after
its organization. Seemingly this name was given for the purpose
of securing the friendship of Franklin for the new state;—
but the wily statesman, while expressing his appreciation of
the honor conferred upon him, was loth to avow himself on the
side of the secessionists, and advised them to submit their
claims to Congress for adjustment. He pointed out to them
the excellence of a system of paternal government which provided
for a Congress which could act as a judge in such matters.

Governor Sevier apprised Governor Alexander Martin of
North Carolina that the inhabitants of the counties west of
the mountains had declared themselves independent and had
formed a separate State. Governor Martin replied that he
could not consent to such an irregular mode of separation, and
intimated that the Congress of the United States would interfere
to prevent it.

The convention which was expected to ratify a constitution
met at Greenville on November 14, 1785. A new constitution
was presented, which, after an angry discussion, was
rejected, and one similar to that of North Carolina was
adopted. The rejected constitution was a curious document.
Full religious liberty was established, so far as it related to
forms of worship, but no one was allowed to hold office unless
he believed in Heaven, Hell, and the Trinity. Neither could
sabbath breakers, immoral men, clergymen, doctors, nor

lawyers hold office. Five days after the adoption of the constitution, the Legislature of North Carolina assembled at New-
bern, and granted amnesty and full pardon to all who were
engaged in revolt against the authority of the State;—and
many men of influence returned to their allegiance, and resist-
ance to the authority of the state of Franklin assumed a more
determined form. Congress finally interfered, put an end to
the new State, and restored the country to North Carolina. Indignant at the interposition, the secessionists persisted in their
designs, and through their displaced governor, Sevier, on the
12th of September, 1788, informed the Spanish minister, Gardoquoi, that they were unanimous in their vehement desire to
form an alliance and treaty of commerce with Spain and put
themselves under her protection. The settlers of the district
of Cumberland river, who were also under the jurisdiction of
North Carolina, gave the name of Miro to a district they had
formed, as evidence of their partiality for the Spanish government. The promise of protection which the inhabitants of
the two districts received from Gardoquoi was so modified by
Miro that the scheme, though prosecuted for a time with
great vigor, finally failed from inability on the part of the secessionists to comply with the conditions of recognition.

A company composed of Alexander Moultrie, Isaac Huger,
Major William Snipes, Colonel Washington, and other distinguished South Carolinians was formed at Charleston in
1789, which purchased from the State of Georgia fifty-two
thousand nine hundred (52,900) square miles of territory extending from the Yazoo to the banks of the Mississippi near
Natchez. The Choctaws, Chickasaws, and Spain claimed a
portion of this territory. The ulterior designs of the company
in the purchase and settlement of the country were carefully
concealed for some time. Wilkinson, who was still engaged
in the effort to dismember the Union, having heard of this purchase, lost no time in communicating his views to the company and expressing a desire to coöperate with them as their
agent. At the same time he addressed a letter to Miro, in
which, after telling him that he had applied to the company
for an agency, he says:—

"If I succeed, I am persuaded that I shall experience no
difficulty in adding their establishment to the domains of His

Majesty, and this they will soon discover to be to their interest.
* * * * You will have the opportunity to modify the plan
of the company as your judgment and prudence will suggest
and the interest of the King may require. I will keep you informed of every movement which I shall observe, and it will
be completely in your power to break up the projected settlement, by inciting the Choctaws to incommode the colonists,
who will thus be forced to move off and to establish themselves
under your government."

Wilkinson's application for an agency was declined because of the appointment of Dr. O'Fallon before it was received. He wrote to Miro on the subject of the company's
purposes. After speaking of the dissatisfaction of the members of the company with the Federal Government, he states
that he has induced them to become subjects of Spain, "under
the appearance of a free and independent state, forming a rampart for the adjoining Spanish territories, and establishing
with them an eternal reciprocal alliance offensive and defen-
sive. This," he continues, "for a beginning, when once secured with the greatest secrecy; will serve, I am fully persuaded, as an example to be followed by the settlements on the
western side of the mountains, which will separate from the
Atlantic portion of the Confederacy, because, on account of
the advantages which they will expect from the privilege of
trading with our colony under the protection of Spain, they
will unite with it in the same manner and as closely as are the
Atlantic States with France, receiving from it every assistance
in war and relying on its power in the moment of danger."

In a letter written to Miro on the 20th of June, Wilkinson
fully endorses the plans of the company. Miro submits to the
Court at Madrid the documents unfolding these plans, accompanied by a dispatch in which he sums up the advantages and
disadvantages of "taking a foreign state to board with us."
When near the conclusion, he explains how he has excited the
hostility and secured the opposition of all the Indian tribes to
the Americans. "I have recommended them," says he, "to remain quiet, and told them if these people presented themselves
with a view to settle on their lands, then to make no concessions, and to warn them off, but to attack them in case they
refused to withdraw; and I have promised that I would supply
them with powder and ball to defend their legitimate rights."

INVASION OF LOUISIANA THREATENED.

Both Louisiana and the United States became at this time apprehensive that an invasion of the former would be attempted by the British from Canada. Such an event would impose upon our Government the necessity of determining a course proper to be pursued should a passage be asked by Great Britain for her troops through our territory, or should that passage be made without permission. The opportunity was deemed favorable to the prosecution of our claim to the navigation of the Mississippi, and negotiations were opened with Spain for the purchase of the Island of New Orleans and the Floridas,—but Spain declined our offer of friendship, the only consideration we were then able to give, and the project failed. Miro's administration terminated in 1791. He was succeeded by the Baron de Carondelet.

Such was the confidence inspired in the Government by the adoption of the Constitution and the firm and watchful administration of Washington, that not only in the Eastern States but in the Western districts also, all intrigues, cabals, and schemes of dismemberment, during the first three years of Carondelet's administration had seemingly expired. A brighter era had dawned upon the country; hope had taken the place of doubt in the minds of the people, and the old patriotism which had borne us through the Revolution reinstated loyalty in the bosoms of thousands whose thoughts had been for years ripening for revolt. But the danger was not all over. Some discontented and some ambitious spirits yet remained in the West. Great Britain cast a greedy eye occasionally at the mouth of the Mississippi, and poor torn, bleeding France, which had just murdered her king, sent a sufficient number of her maniac population to our shores to keep the spirit of misrule in action.

Early in the year 1794 a society of French Jacobins, established in Philadelphia, sent to Louisiana a circular which was widely distributed among the French population of the province, appealing to them to take up arms and cast off the Spanish yoke. The alarm which this gave the Baron de Carondelet was increased by a knowledge of the efforts put forth by Genet, the French minister to the United States, to organize and lead an expedition of French and Americans against Louisiana.

Armed bands had assembled upon the Georgia frontier to join it, and French emissaries were everywhere stirring up the Western people to aid in the invasion. New Orleans was strongly fortified, and the grim visage of war was again wrinkled for the conflict.

TREATY OF MADRID.

Fear of English invasion over, Carondelet addressed himself with great vigor to the unfinished schemes of Miro for dismembering the Union and winning over the Western settlements to Spain. Meantime, the negotiations so long pending between our Government and Spain culminated on the 20th of October, 1795, in the Treaty of Madrid. By this treaty a boundary line was established between the United States and the Floridas. Spain also conceded to our people the free navigation of the Mississippi from its source to the sea, and agreed to permit them, "for the term of three years, to use the port of New Orleans as a place of deposit for their produce and merchandise, and export the same free from duty or charge, except a reasonable consideration to be paid for storage and other incidental expenses; that the term of three years may, by subsequent negotiation be extended, or, instead of that town, some other point in the island of New Orleans shall be designated as a place of deposit for the American trade."

It was believed by the provincial authorities that this treaty was formed for the purpose of propitiating the neutrality of our Government in the event of a war, at that time imminent, between Great Britain and Spain. They had no faith in its permanency, or that its provisions would be observed by Spain after her European embarrassments had been settled. Instead of arresting, it had the effect to stimulate the efforts of Carondelet in his favorite plan for the acquisition of the Western settlements. He made proposals to Sebastian, Innis, and other early associates of Wilkinson, and through his emissaries approached Wilkinson himself with promises;—but it was too late. The Union had become consolidated. The wise counsels of Washington allayed discontent, and the successful campaign of Wayne had given assurance of protection. Wilkinson and his associates, foiled in the designs formed and conducted under more favorable auspices, whatever their aspirations might have been, were too sagacious to revive an

enterprise which neither policy nor necessity could excuse, and which a vigilant government was sure to punish. After a few more struggles the Spanish authorities, on the 26th of May, 1798, surrendered to Wilkinson (who, by the death of Wayne, had been promoted) the territory claimed by the Treaty of Madrid, and the Spanish power in America from that moment began to decline.

Morales, the Spanish intendant, construing the letter of the treaty strictly, on the 17th of July, 1799, chose to consider that three years had elapsed since its ratification, and, for the purpose of crippling the commerce of the Western people, issued an order prohibiting the use of New Orleans as a place of deposit by them, without designating, in accordance with the treaty, any other suitable point. This measure aroused the indignation of the West. An expedition against New Orleans was openly contemplated. President Adams ordered three regiments of regulars to the Ohio, with instructions to have in readiness a sufficient number of boats to convey the troops to New Orleans. Twelve new regiments were added to the army, and an invasion seemed inevitable, and would most certainly have been attempted, had not indications of a popular determination to elect Mr. Jefferson to the Presidency caused the postponement of a project which could not be completed before the close of Mr. Adams' administration.

No public documents of the period, accessible to me, speak of the suspension by the Spaniards of this prohibitory order, but from the fact that it was renewed afterwards, there can be no doubt that terms of accommodation satisfactory to the Western people were for the time agreed upon.

TREATY OF ST. ILDEPHONSO.

Napoleon, at this time First Consul, cast a longing eye at the mouth of the Mississippi. His ministers had been instructed to obtain all possible information concerning Louisiana. Monsieur de Pontalba, who had passed an official residence of many years in Louisiana, prepared at their request a very remarkable memoir on the history and resources of that province, which was presented to the French Directory on the 15th of September, 1800. On the 1st of October following, a treaty between France and Spain was concluded at

St. Ildephonso, of which the third article is in the following words:—

"His Catholic Majesty promises and engages to retrocede to the French Republic, six months after the full and entire execution of the above conditions and stipulations relative to His Royal Highness the Duke of Parma, the colony or province of Louisiana, with the same extent that it now has in the hands of Spain, and that it had when France possessed it, and such as it ought to be after the treaties subsequently entered into between Spain and the other States."

France being at war with England when this treaty was concluded, it was, at the request of Napoleon, carefully concealed, lest England, then mistress of the seas, should take the country from her, as she doubtless would have done, had Napoleon taken possession of the province.

Spain inserted in this treaty a condition that she should have the preference, in case France, in her turn, should be disposed again to cede the territory. Great embarrassments resulted from this stipulation.

The retrocession of Louisiana to France was not suspected by our Government until March, 1801, six months after the treaty of St. Ildephonso was concluded. It was then brought to the notice of Mr. Madison, the secretary of state, by Mr. Rufus King, our minister at the court of St. James, who wrote on March 29, 1801:—

"The cession of Tuscany to the infant Duke of Parma, by the treaty between France and Austria, adds very great credit to the opinion which at this time prevails both at Paris and London, that Spain has in return actually ceded Louisiana and the Floridas to France. I am apprehensive that this cession is intended to have, and may actually produce, effects injurious to the Union and consequent happiness of the people of the United States."

Mr. Madison seems to have shared the general incredulity of England and other powers regarding the event, for he took no notice of the intimation conveyed by Mr. King's dispatch, until it was partially confirmed by another from the same source on the 1st of June thereafter. In the first letter on the subject Mr. King had deemed it of sufficient importance to recommend the appointment of a minister to represent the interests of our government near the court of France. In

the last he related the substance of a conversation between himself and Lord Hawkesbury relative to Louisiana, in which that nobleman said that he had from different quarters received information of the cession to France, and very unreservedly expressed the reluctance with which they should be led to acquiesce in a measure that might be followed by the most important consequences:—that the acquisition might enable France to extend her influence and perhaps her dominion up the Mississippi and through the lakes, even to Canada. To this, Mr. King replied: "We are content that the Floridas remain in the hands of Spain, but should be unwilling to see them transferred, except to ourselves."

CLAIM OF OUR GOVERNMENT.

Our government took the alarm instantly. The negotiations it had effected with Spain, though still embarrassed with some offensive conditions, had produced a state of comparative quiescence in the West; all dangerous intrigues were at an end, and a further settlement had been projected which would harmonize all opposing interests and forever secure to our Western possessions the uninterrupted enjoyment of free navigation of the Mississippi to the ocean. Such an arrangement with France was deemed impossible. In the hands of Napoleon, Louisiana would be at once transformed into a powerful empire, and the Mississippi would be used as a highway to transport troops on errands of meditated invasion all over the continent of North America. In her eager desire to regain the Canadian possessions taken from her by Great Britain, France would march her armies through our territories and inevitably embroil us in a war which would prove in the end fatal to the liberties we had just established. Heavy duties would necessarily be imposed upon our Western population, and all the prejudices now so fortunately allayed would be revived against the Government because of its powerlessness to relieve them.

Mr. Madison addressed a dispatch to Mr. Pinckney, our minister at Madrid, requesting him to ascertain whether a treaty had been made, and if so, the extent of the cession made by it. The Government appointed Mr. Robert R. Livingston minister to France.

In November, 1801, Mr. King succeeded in procuring a copy of the secret treaty, and forwarded it to Mr. Madison. In the midst of the alarm occasioned by this intelligence, the war between France and England was terminated, and articles of peace signed on the 1st of October, 1801, and France commenced secret preparations to avail herself of the treaty and take early possession of Louisiana. In the meantime Mr. Livingston had arrived in Paris. On the 12th of December, in a dispatch to Mr. Madison, he informed him that he had hinted to one of the ministers that a cession of Louisiana would afford them the means of paying their debts,—to which the minister replied: "None but spendthrifts satisfy their debts by selling their lands," adding, however, after a short pause, "but it is not ours to give."

TALLEYRAND'S DIPLOMACY.

Talleyrand was the Minister of Exterior Relations. In all his interviews with Mr. Livingston relative to the purchase of Louisiana he fully exemplified one of the maxims of his life, that "speech was given to man to enable him to disguise his thoughts." All of Mr. Livingston's inquiries respecting the treaty were met with studied reserve, duplicity, or positive denial. Often when he sought an interview the minister was preoccupied or absent. He not only failed to obtain information of the extent of the cession and whether it included the Floridas, but so undemonstrative were the communications of the minister upon the subject, that often he left him doubtful of the intention of France to comply with the terms of the treaty at all. His dispatches to Mr. Madison, while they show no lack of exertion or expedient on his part to obtain the desired information, bear evidence of the subtlety, cunning, and artifice of one of the greatest masters of statecraft the world has yet produced. At one time he expresses his concern at the reserve of the French Government, and importunes Talleyrand to inform him whether East and West Florida or either of them are included in the treaty, and afford him such assurances, with respect to the limits of their territory and the navigation of the Mississippi heretofore agreed upon between Spain and the United States, as may prove satisfactory to the latter.

"If," he continues in the same note, "the territories of East and West Florida be included within the limits of the cession obtained by France, the undersigned desires to be informed how far it would be practicable to make such arrangements between their respective governments, as would at the same time aid the financial operations of France and remove by a strong natural boundary all future causes of discontent between her and the United States."

Six days afterwards he writes to Mr. Madison that he has received no reply to the above note. A month later in a dispatch he says: "They have as yet not thought it proper to give me any explanations." One month afterwards he writes: "The business most interesting to us, that of Louisiana, still remains in the state it was. The minister will give no answer to any inquiries I make on the subject. He will not say what their boundaries are, what are their intentions, and when they are to take possession."

Meantime the treaty of Amiens opened the ocean to Bonaparte's contemplated expedition to Louisiana. The anxiety of our government was greatly increased. Mr. Madison, in a dispatch full of complaint at the ominous silence of the French minister, among other intimations, conveys the following:—

"Since the receipt of your last communication, no hope remains but from the accumulating difficulties of going through with the undertaking, and from the conviction you may be able to impress that it must have an instant and powerful effect in changing the relations between France and the United States."

Fears were entertained that the British Government might have acquiesced in the treaty, so as to impair the stipulations, concerning the free navigation of the Mississippi, but these were dissipated by the assurance of Lord Hawkesbury, in reply to a letter addressed to him on the subject by Mr. King, that "His Majesty had not in any manner directly or indirectly acquiesced in or sanctioned the cession."

TEDIOUS DELAY.

Nearly one month after this last dispatch to Mr. Madison, Mr. Livingston again informs him that the French Government still continues to hold the same conduct with respect

to his inquiries in relation to the designs on Louisiana, but assures him that nothing shall be done to impair the friendly relations between America and France. Eight days after this dispatch was written, he writes again that he has acquired information on which he can depend, in relation to the intention of the French Government. "Bernadotte," says he, "is to command, Collot second in command, Adet is to be prefect;" but the expedition is delayed until about September, on account of some difficulty which Mr. Livingston conceives to have "arisen from the different apprehensions of France and Spain relative to the meaning of the term Louisiana, which has been understood by France to include the Floridas, but probably by Spain to have been confined to the strict meaning of the term."

On the 30th of July, 1802, Mr. Livingston informs Mr. Madison that he is preparing a lengthy memorial on the subject of the mutual interest of France and the United States relative to Louisiana; and that he has received the explicit assurance of the Spanish ambassador that the Floridas are not included in the cession.

On the 10th of August following he again writes the secretary that he has put his essay in such hands as he thinks will best serve our purposes. "Talleyrand," he says, "has promised to give it an attentive perusal; after which, when I find how it works, I will come forward with some proposition. I am very much at a loss, however, as to what terms you would consider it allowable to offer, if they can be brought to a sale of the Floridas, either with or without New Orleans, which last place will be of little consequence if we possess the Floridas, because a much better passage may be found on the east side of the river."

Mr. Livingston now followed up his interrupted negotiations with activity. He made several propositions for the purchase of Louisiana, but was informed by the minister that all offers were premature. "There never," says Mr. Livingston in a dispatch to the secretary of state, "was a Government in which less could be done by negotiation than here. There is no people, no legislature, no counsellors. One man is everything. He seldom asks advice, and never hears it unasked. His ministers are mere clerks; and his legislature

and counsellors parade officers. Though the sense of every reflecting man about him is against this wild expedition, no one dares to tell him so. Were it not for the uneasiness it excites at home, it would give me none; for I am persuaded that the whole will end in a relinquishment of the country, and transfer of the capital to the United States."

Soon after this, Mr. Livingston had an interview with Joseph Bonaparte, who promised to deliver to Napoleon any communication Livingston could make. "You must not, however," he said, "suppose my power to serve you greater than it actually is. My brother is his own counsellor, but we are good brothers. He hears me with pleasure, and as I have access to him at all times, I have an opportunity of turning his attention to a particular subject that might otherwise be passed over." He informed Mr. Livingston that he had read his notes and conversed upon the subject with Napoleon, who told him that he had nothing more at heart than to be upon the best terms with the United States.

On the 11th of November Mr. Livingston wrote a hurried letter to Mr. Madison, informing him that orders had been given for the immediate embarkation of two demi-brigades for Louisiana, and that they would sail from Holland in about twenty days. The sum voted for this service was two and one-half millions of francs. "No prudence," he concludes, "will, I fear, prevent hostilities ere long, and perhaps the sooner their plans develop themselves the better."

RIGHT OF DEPOSIT PROHIBITED.

This was the condition of affairs when the Western people, beginning to feel the effect of a proclamation suspending their right of deposit in New Orleans, were importuning our Government for relief. Some idea may be formed of the excitement which this act had produced, on reading the following, which is one of many similar appeals addressed to Congress by them:—

"The Mississippi is ours by the law of nature; it belongs to us by our numbers, and by the labor which we have bestowed on those spots which, before our arrival, were desert and barren. Our innumerable rivers swell it, and flow with it into the Gulf of Mexico. Its mouth is the only issue which

nature has given to our waters, and we wish to use it for our vessels. No power in the world shall deprive us of this right. We do not prevent the Spaniards and the French from ascending the river to our towns and villages. We wish in our turn, without any interruption, to descend it to its mouth, to ascend it again, and exercise our privilege of trading on it, and navigating it at our pleasure. If our most entire liberty in this matter is disputed, nothing shall prevent our taking possession of the capital, and when we are once masters of it we shall know how to maintain ourselves there. If Congress refuses us effectual protection, if it forsakes us, we will adopt the measures which our safety requires, even if they endanger the peace of the Union and our connection with the other states. No protection, no allegiance."

Perhaps at no period in the history of our Government was the Union in more immediate danger of dissolution. Had our citizens been fully apprised of our relations with France and the neglect with which our embassador was treated, nothing could have prevented an immediate secession of the people west of the Alleghanies. Mr. Madison saw the gathering of the storm, and on the 27th of November, a few days before Congress assembled, addressed an earnest dispatch to the American minister at Madrid. "You are aware," said he, "of the sensibility of our western citizens to such an occurrence. This sensibility is justified by the interest they have at stake. The Mississippi to them is everything. It is the Hudson, the Delaware, the Potomac, and all the navigable rivers of the Atlantic States, formed into one stream.* * * Whilst you presume, therefore, in your representations to the Spanish Government, that the conduct of its officer is no less contrary to its intentions than it is to its good faith, you will take care to express the strongest confidence that the breach of the treaty will be repaired in every way which justice and regard for a friendly neighborhood may require."

Congress met, and President Jefferson, in a message on Louisiana, said: "The cession of the Spanish province of Louisiana to France which took place in the course of the late war, will, if carried into effect, make a change in the aspect of our foreign relations which will doubtless have just weight in any deliberations of the legislature connected with

that subject." That body replied, that, relying with perfect confidence on the wisdom and vigilance of the Executive, they would wait the issue of such measures as that department of the Government should have pursued for asserting the rights of the United States,—holding it to be their duty at the same time to express their unalterable determination to maintain the boundaries and the rights of navigation and commerce through the river Mississippi, as established by existing treaties.

MONROE APPOINTED MINISTER EXTRAORDINARY.

Party spirit at that time was but another name for party animosity. The Federalists, anxious to regain the power that they had lost by the election of· Jefferson, seized upon the subject of Mr. Livingston's mission and the proclamation of prohibition by the Spanish intendant, and held them up before the people as the necessary and inevitable product of Democratic principles. They were determined if possible to force the country into a war of invasion against New Orleans and the country including the mouth of the Mississippi,—a measure in which the Western people would generally co-operate. The administration, on the other hand, still adhered to the policy of negotiation,—and foreseeing that it must be expeditious to avoid the inevitable destruction of the party, and deprive the Federals of the prestige which their vigorous measures were acquiring for them, President Jefferson, on the 10th of January, 1803, wrote to Mr. Monroe:—

"I have but a moment to inform you that the fever into which the Western world is thrown by the affair of New Orleans, stimulated by the mercantile and generally the Federal interest, threatens to overbear our peace. In this situation we are obliged to call on you for a temporary sacrifice of yourself, to prevent this greatest of evils in the present prosperous tide of affairs. I shall to-morrow nominate you to the Senate for an extraordinary mission to France, and the circumstances are such as to render it impossible to decline; because the whole public hope will be rested on you."

The Senate confirmed the nomination. Mr. Jefferson again wrote to Mr. Monroe, urging him not to decline. "I know nothing," he says, "which would produce such a shock, for on the event of this mission depend the future destinies of

this republic. If we cannot by a purchase of the country insure to ourselves a course of perpetual peace and friendship with all nations, then, as war cannot be far distant, it behooves us immediately to be preparing for that course, without, however, hastening it; and it may be necessary (on your failure on the Continent) to cross the Channel." We shall see later the significance of this suggestion that he cross the Channel into England.

The session of Congress had advanced to the middle of February before any remedial measures were proposed for the action of the Spanish intendant at New Orleans. Every fresh dispatch from Mr. Livingston was a repetition of the old story of neglect and silence. Meantime the Federal leaders, incited by the continued and growing disaffection of the Western people, as manifested by their inflammable appeals to Congress, had resolved upon recommending immediate hostilities as the last resort of the Government. The memorable debate which involved a consideration of this question was opened by Mr. Ross, of Pennsylvania, on the 14th of February, in a speech of remarkable force. The infraction of the treaty of Madrid in 1795, by which the right of deposit had been solemnly acknowledged, was claimed to be a sufficient justification for a resort to arms. In the further progress of this argument the speaker considered the opportunity as too favorable to be lost, because success would be more assured if a war was prosecuted while the Spaniards held possession of the country than it would be after it had passed under the dominion of France. With New Orleans in our possession, we could dictate the terms of a treaty that would forever secure our citizens from further molestation. These views were enforced by urgent appeals to the patriotism of the people, and the sternest denunciation of the tardy policy of the administration. At the close of his speech Mr. Ross presented a series of resolutions declaring the right of the people to the free navigation of the Mississippi and a convenient place of deposit for their produce and merchandise in the island of New Orleans. The President would have been authorized by the passage of these resolutions to take possession of such place or places in the island or adjacent territories as he might deem fit, and to call into actual service fifty thousand

31

militia to coöperate with the regular military and naval forces in the work of invasion. They also provided for an appropriation of five millions of dollars to defray the expenses of the war.

A long and exhaustive debate followed, in which the speeches on both sides were marked by distinguished ability and eloquence,—those of Mr. Clinton against, and of Mr. Morris in favor of the resolutions, being among the ablest ever before or since delivered on the floor of Congress. Milder measures were finally substituted, authorizing the enrolment of an army of eighty thousand men at the pleasure of the President, and Congress adjourned.

Meantime Mr. Livingston reported some little progress in the work of negotiation, and had addressed a memorial to Bonaparte complaining of the conduct of the Spanish intendant. Just at this time hostilities were again about to be renewed between England and France. Mr. Addington, the British minister, in a conversation with Mr. King upon the subject, observed that in case of war it would be one of the first steps of Great Britain to occupy New Orleans. On the 11th of April, in an interview with Talleyrand, that minister desired to know of Mr. Livingston if our Government wished to purchase the whole of Lousiana. On receiving a negative reply, he remarked that if they gave New Orleans, the rest would be of little value. "Tell me," he continued, "what you will give for the whole?" At the close of the dispatch conveying this information to Mr. Madison, Mr. Livingston appends a postscript saying: "Orders are given this day to stop the sailing of vessels from the French ports; war is inevitable; my conjecture as to their determination to sell is well founded. Mr. Monroe has just arrived."

BONAPARTE'S PROPOSITION.

Fear that Great Britain would make an early attack upon New Orleans, now that war between England and France was certain, favored the efforts of Mr. Livingston for an early purchase, and increased the anxiety of France to dispose of the entire province. Indeed, in a consultation held with Decres and Marbois on the 10th of April, Napoleon fully resolved to sell the whole of Louisiana. The little coquetry that followed between Talleyrand, Marbois and Livingston,

was simply to obtain as large a price as possible. Napoleon then said, "I know the full value of Louisiana, and I have been desirous of repairing the fault of the French negotiator, who abandoned it in 1762. A few lines of treaty have restored it to me, and I have scarcely recovered it when I must expect to lose it. But if it escapes from me, it shall one day cost dearer to those who oblige me to strip myself of it, than to those to whom I wish to deliver it. The English have successively taken from France, Canada, Cape Breton, New Foundland, Nova Scotia, and the richest portions of Asia. They are engaged in exciting trouble in St. Domingo. They shall not have the Mississippi, which they covet. Louisiana is nothing in comparison with their conquests in all parts of the globe, and yet the jealousy they feel at the restoration of this colony to the sovereignty of France acquaints me with their wish to take possession of it, and it is thus they will begin the war."

The morning after this conference he summoned his ministers, and terminated a long interview in the following words:—"Irresolution and deliberation are no longer in season. I renounce Louisiana. It is not only New Orleans I will cede,—it is the whole colony without any reservation. I know the price of what I abandon, and have sufficiently proved the importance that I attach to this province,—since my first diplomatic act with Spain had for its object its recovery. I renounce it with the greatest regret. To attempt obstinately to retain it would be folly. I direct you to negotiate this affair with the envoys of the United States. Do not even await the arrival of Mr. Monroe;—have an interview this very day with Mr. Livingston. But I require a great deal of money for this war, and I would not like to commence it with new contributions. * * * * I will be moderate in consideration of the necessity in which I am of making a sale. But keep this to yourself. I want fifty millions, and for less than that sum I will not treat; I would rather make a desperate attempt to keep these fine countries. To-morrow you shall have full powers."

LOUISIANA PURCHASE TREATY SIGNED.

On the 30th of April, 1803, the treaty of cession was signed. Louisiana was transferred to the United States, on

condition that our government should consent to pay to France eighty millions of francs. Of this amount, twenty millions should be assigned to the payment of what was due by France to the citizens of the United States. Article 3rd of the treaty was prepared by Napoleon himself. It reads:—
"The inhabitants of the ceded territory shall be incorporated in the Union of the United States, and admitted, as soon as possible according to the principles of the Federal Constitution, to the enjoyment of all the rights, advantages and immunities of citizens of the United States, and in the meantime they shall be maintained and protected in the free enjoyment of their liberty, property, and the religion which they profess."

After the treaty was signed, the ministers rose and shook hands, and Mr. Livingston, expressing the satisfaction which they felt, said: "We have lived long, but this is the noblest work of our whole lives. The treaty which we have just signed has not been obtained by art or dictated by force:— equally advantageous to the two contracting parties, it will change vast solitudes into flourishing districts. From this day the United States takes its place among the powers of the first rank;—the English lose all exclusive influence in the affairs of America. Thus one of the principal causes of European rivalries and animosities is about to cease. However, if wars are inevitable, France will hereafter have in the New World a natural friend, that must increase in strength from year to year, and one which cannot fail to become powerful and respected in every sea. The United States will re-establish the maritime rights of all the world, which are now usurped by a single nation. These treaties will thus be a guarantee of peace and concord among commercial states. The instruments which we have just signed will cause no tears to be shed; they prepare ages of happiness for innumerable generations of human creatures. The Mississippi and Missouri will see them succeed one another and multiply, truly worthy of the regard and care of Providence, in the bosom of equality, under just laws, freed from the errors of superstition and the scourge of bad government."

When Napoleon was informed of the conclusion of the treaty, he uttered the following sententious prophecy: "This

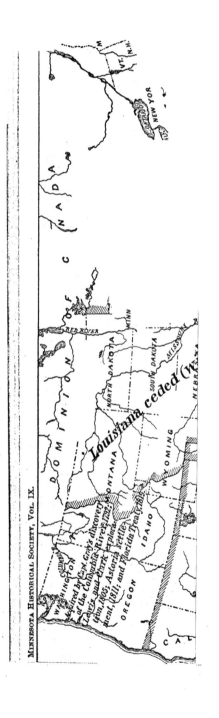

Plate XVII.

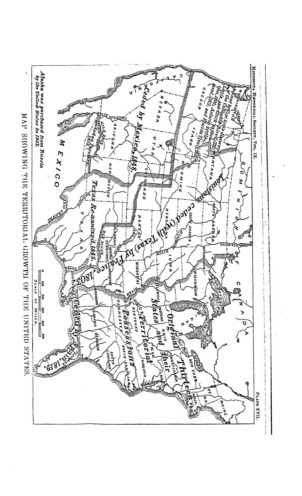

MAP SHOWING THE TERRITORIAL GROWTH OF THE UNITED STATES.

accession of territory strengthens forever the power of the United States;—and I have just given to England a maritime rival that will sooner or later humble her pride."

Neither of the contracting parties to this treaty was able to define the boundaries of the vast territory of which it was the subject. They were known to be immense, and in his message to Congress announcing the purchase, Mr. Jefferson says:—

"Whilst the property and sovereignty of the Mississippi and its waters secure an independent outlet for the produce of the Western States and an uncontrolled navigation through their whole course, free from collision with other powers and the dangers to our peace from that source, the fertility of the country, its climate and extent, promise in due season important aids to our treasury, an ample provision for our posterity, and a wider spread for the blessings of freedom and equal laws."

Up to this time Spain had continued in actual and uninterrupted possession of the territory;—and, pending the ratification of the treaty, the Spanish minister served notice upon our Government that the treaty with France would be void, on the ground that France had agreed that Spain should have the preference, in case France should again cede Louisiana. President Jefferson replied that these were private questions between France and Spain;—that the United States derived its title from Napoleon, and did not doubt his guarantee of it;—and after farther unavailing protest, Spain reluctantly abandoned her claim to the territory.

TEXAS INCLUDED IN THE LOUISIANA PURCHASE.

Was Texas, as re-annexed to the United States in 1845, a part of the original Louisiana Purchase? If so, under what circumstances did it pass from our possession, so that its recovery resulted in the war with Mexico? If we did not acquire it in that purchase, why did we cede it to Spain in 1819, in exchange for the Floridas?

The United States claimed that the territory ceded to her by France, extended to the Rio Bravo river, now called the Rio Grande del Norte. The attitude of France was in support of our government in this contention, she basing her own claim to the territory prior to the date of its cession by her to Spain

in 1762, upon its occupancy by LaSalle, who, with sixty men, descended the Mississippi in 1682, and took possession, in the name of Louis XIV., of all the country drained by the tributaries of the Mississippi on the west,—to which he gave the name Louisiana, and built Fort Prudhomme. Two years later he sailed from LaRochelle, France, with a company of two hundred and eighty men, and, having passed the mouth of the Mississippi through an error in the computation of longitude, he landed in the Bay of St. Bernard, or Matagorda Bay, built forts, and placed garrisons in them. LaSalle's explorations along the shore of the Gulf of Mexico extended no farther west than Matagorda Bay and the rivers which flow into it. France therefore could not make claim by virtue of LaSalle's "discovery and occupancy" alone, to any portion of the country lying south or west of the dividing ridge between the waters of Matagorda Bay and the Rio Grande. The territory north and east of these limits embraces about three-fifths of the state of Texas. In 1685, LaSalle was killed upon the soil of Texas.

In the year 1699, Louis XIV. sent D'Iberville to found a new colony, of which he was made Governor. D'Iberville took possession of the country from the mouth of the Mobile to the Bay of St. Bernard, in the name of France. Of this possession, Marbois, in his "History of Louisiana", says:—

The occupation was hardly contested by the Spaniards, and the relations of amity and common interest which were established at the beginning of the 18th century between the two kingdoms, *put an end to any claims on the part of the court of Madrid.* There was however no settlement of boundaries;—and it appears that, on the one side, the Spaniards were afraid that if they were accurately described, they would have to consent to some concessions;—and on the other, the French were unwilling to limit, by precise terms, their possible extension of territory.

Louis XIV., in 1712, also issued letters patent to Crozat, granting him the exclusive right, for twelve years, to trade in this colony, which included Texas. Marbois, in speaking of this privilege, says:—

The Government had only a very vague notion of what it was granting. * * * The limits of Louisiana were not afterwards much better defined;—but agreeably to the practice which certain maritime powers

had made a principle of the law of nations, the effect of the occupation of the mouths of rivers and streams extended to their sources.

Marbois says that according to old documents, the bishop-ric of Louisiana *extended to the Pacific ocean, and the limits of the diocese thus defined were secure from all dispute;*—but that the spiritual jurisdiction had no connection with the rights of sovereignty and property.

France continued in almost undisputed possession of the country for eighty years, or until her treaty of cession to Spain in 1762. France believed that the territory belonged to her prior to 1762, and there can exist little doubt that she in-tended to include it all in the cession to Spain in that year;— and it is equally evident that Spain relinquished her claim to all that she acquired from France under the terms of the treaty of St. Ildephonso, when she retroceded "Louisiana with the same extent that it now has in the hands of Spain, and that it had when France possessed it." Both France and Spain clearly understood that Louisiana extended on the west to the Rio Grande. The only question at issue was that relating to the eastern limit of Louisiana, and it was in reply to Living-ston's question, "What are the eastern bounds of Louisiana?" that Talleyrand replied, "I do not know. You must take it as we received it."

Upon the execution of the treaty of St. Ildephonso, the French General, Victor, was designated by Decres, Napoleon's Minister of Marine, to take possession of Louisiana. In the in-structions which he prepared for the guidance of Victor, Decres said:—

The extent of Louisiana is well determined on the south by the Gulf of Mexico. But bounded on the west by the river called the Rio Bravo, from its mouth to about the thirtieth parallel, the line of de-marcation stops after reaching this point, and there seems never to have been any agreement in regard to this part of the frontier. The farther we go northward the more undecided is the boundary. This part of America contains little more than uninhabited forests or Indian tribes, and the necessity of fixing a boundary has never yet been felt there.

These instructions, given immediately after the cession by Spain to France, and in anticipation of her taking possession

of the country, can leave little doubt that both France and Spain regarded the Rio Grande as the western boundary of Louisiana. Decres was the able coadjutor of Marbois in the negotiations with Livingston and Monroe for the purchase of Louisiana.

The Hon. Binger Hermann, commissioner of the General Land Office, in his admirable work "The Louisiana Purchase;" which comprises a concise history of our various acquisitions of territory during the past century, says:—

Our nation always claimed, as did France, that the Louisiana Purchase extended westward to the Rio Bravo, because of the settlement made by LaSalle, when, on his return from France, failing to find the mouth of the Mississippi, he landed on the coast of what is now Texas; therefore, the French always regarded the mouth of the Del Norte as the western limit of Louisiana on the Gulf coast. Popple, an eminent English geographer at that time, conceded this claim, and represented on his map the Del Norte as the western limit of Louisiana. The United States on this ground claimed Texas up to 1819, and then abandoned it when Spain ceded to us the two Floridas. It was said at the time that the Spaniards prided themselves on their diplomacy in saving Texas by surrendering Florida; indeed, there is much truth in this boast, when we know how intently resolved our people were to possess the Floridas, and hence we may well infer how ready they also were to relinquish very substantial claims in order to acquire the long envied Florida possessions;—this view is corroborated by reference to President Monroe's message to Congress, December 7, 1819, concerning the treaty with Spain in that year, wherein he says: "For territory ceded by Spain, other territory of great value (Texas) to which our claim was believed to be well founded, was ceded by the United States, and in a quarter more interesting to her." A quarter of a century later on there was still a vivid remembrance of our old claim to Texas under the Louisiana Purchase, and when, in 1844, the annexation of Texas was accomplished, President Tyler, in his message to the Senate announcing the negotiation of that treaty, said that in event of the approval of annexation, "the Government will have succeeded in reclaiming a territory which formerly constituted a portion, as is confidently believed, of its domain under treaty of cession of 1803, by France to the United States."

In the progress of the debate upon the annexation of Texas, Thomas H. Benton said:—

The oldest advocate for the recovery of Texas, I must be allowed to speak in just terms of the criminal politicians who prostituted the question of its recovery to their base purposes, and delayed its success by degrading and disgracing it. A western man, and coming from a

State more than any interested in the recovery of this country so un-accountably thrown away by the treaty of 1819, I must be allowed to feel indignant at seeing Atlantic politicians seizing upon it.

It will be borne in mind that in the speeches made in Congress at the time of the admission of Texas to the Union, the act was usually referred to not as the "annexation," but as the "re-annexation" of Texas.

When the cession by France to the United States, of the whole colony of Louisiana was agreed upon, Livingston and Monroe thought that the terms in the third article of the treaty, defining the extent of the territory, were too general, and insisted that the true extent of Louisiana be specifically defined. The French negotiator said that circumstances were too pressing to permit them to consult the Court of Madrid, and that Spain might wish to consult the viceroy of Mexico, thus prolonging the discussion, and that it would be better for the United States to abide by a general stipulation, as the country was still for the most part in possession of the Indians;—and reminded them that in granting Canada to the English in 1763, France only ceded the country it possessed without specifically defining its limits;—yet England, in consequence of that treaty, occupied territory as far west as the Northern Ocean. This reasoning seemed to satisfy Livingston and Monroe, and they made no more objections. Marbois, writing, a quarter of a century later, of this incident, says:—

If, in appearing to be resigned to these general terms through necessity, they considered them really preferable to more precise stipulations, it must be admitted that the event has justified their foresight.

When Napoleon's attention was directed to the obscurity and uncertainty of this stipulation, he said:—

If an obscurity does not already exist, it would perhaps be good policy to put one there.

While there undoubtedly did exist much obscurity in the minds of the negotiators of these several treaties concerning the western limit of the ceded territory, France was prepared to defend, and, had she not ceded it to the United States, would have successfully defended, by negotiation or conquest, her right to the territory as far west as the Rio Grande, against

any claim which Spain might have made. The territory with this extent, including the Texas re-annexation, was specifically known as Louisiana. It had been in the possession of France for eighty years prior to 1762;—and whatever France ceded to Spain at that time, she again ceded to the United States in 1803. It is evident, therefore, that the "Texas re-annexation" of 1845, was, in 1803, part of the Louisiana Purchase.

VIEWS OF CONGRESSMEN.

It is not surprising that the public men of that day should have feared the consequences of enlarging our republican domain. It looked to them like the renewal of the troubles which they had just escaped, by the purchase of New Orleans and the mouth of the Mississippi. It unsettled the ideas they had formed of a Constitutional Government. They could not see, as we can in this day of railroads and swift postal service, and of telegraphs, giving immediate information concerning the affairs of the nation, how such an immense territory was to be subordinated to the control of a single General Government. Hence we find such men as John Quincy Adams, Timothy Pickering, Rufus Griswold, James White, and Uriah Tracy, all men of enlarged, statesmanlike views, opposing the bill entitled "An Act authorizing the erection of a stock to the amount of eleven millions two hundred and fifty thousand dollars, for the purpose of carrying into effect the convention of the 30th of April, 1803, between the United States and the French Republic."

The speech of Mr. White against the passage of the bill is a fair reflex of the views entertained by the leading public men of that day. Speaking of the treaty, he says:—

I wish not to be understood as predicting that the French will not cede to us the actual and quiet possession of the territory. I hope to God they may, for possession of it we must have:—I mean of New Orleans and of such other portions on the Mississippi as may be necessary to secure to us forever the complete and uninterrupted navigation of that river. This I have ever been in favor of. I think it essential to the peace of the United States and the prosperity of our Western country. But as to Louisiana, this new, immense, unbounded world,—if it should be ever incorporated into this Union, which I have no idea can be done but by altering the Constitution, I believe it will be the greatest curse that could at present befall us;—it may be productive of innumerable evils, and especially of one that I fear even to look upon. Gentlemen on all sides, with very few exceptions, agree

that the settlement of the country will be highly injurious and dangerous to the United States; but as to what has been suggested of removing the Creeks and other nations of Indians from the eastern to the
western banks of the Mississippi, and making the fertile regions of
Louisiana a howling wilderness, never to be trodden by the foot of
civilized man, it is impracticable. * * * To every man acquainted
with the adventurous, roving, and enterprising temper of our people,
and with the manner in which our Western country has been settled,
such an idea must be chimerical. The inducements will be so strong,
that it will be impossible to restrain our citizens from crossing the
river. Louisiana must and will be settled, if we hold it, and with the
very population that would otherwise occupy part of our present territory. Thus our citizens will be removed to the immense distance
of two or three thousand miles from the capital of the Union, where
they will scarcely ever feel the rays of the General Government; their
affections will become alienated; they will gradually begin to view
us as strangers; they will form other commercial connections; and
our interests will become distinct.

These, with other causes that human wisdom may not now fore-
see, will in time effect a separation, and I fear our bounds will be
fixed nearer to our houses than the water of the Mississippi. We have
already territory enough, and when I contemplate the evils that may
arise to these States from this intended incorporation of Louisiana into
the Union, I would rather see it given to France, to Spain, or to any
other nation of the earth, upon the mere condition that no citizen of
the United States should ever settle within its limits, than to see the
territory sold for a hundred millions of dollars, and we retain the sovereignty. * * * And I do say that, under existing circumstances,
even supposing that this extent of territory was a desirable acquisition,
fifteen millions of dollars was a most enormous sum to give.

This "enormous sum" was less than three cents an acre
for this immense domain, which had, in 1890, as shown by the
U. S. census, a population of over 11,000,000 people, and to
say nothing of its yield of gold, silver, copper, coal and lumber,
whose agricultural products alone in 1896, amounted to $345,-
000,000.

The dread of the disastrous consequences which Mr. White
feared would follow the crossing of the Mississippi river for
the purposes of settlement, found expression at that time in
a resolution presented in Congress, declaring that any American citizen who should cross the Mississippi river for the purpose of settlement, should, by that act, forfeit all claim to the
protection of his Government.

We can to-day readily see that the questions which are now
engrossing the attention of the country concerning the acqui-

sition of new territory in the Philippines are not new questions. The history of one hundred years ago is to-day repeating itself in every essential feature. The arguments of to-day are those of a century ago. The question of the constitutional right of our Government to purchase Louisiana, and the larger question of the expediency of forming an Anglo-American alliance should France attempt openly to take possession of the vast region which she had acquired under the secret treaty with Spain, were, in their immediate results as well as in their distant consequences, fully discussed on the floor of Congress and in the diplomatic correspondence of President Jefferson. Some of the New England members of Congress, foreseeing that in a brief period of time many new States would be formed out of the Louisiana purchase, and deprecating a loss of the political supremacy of their own States in the national Legislature, were ready to dissolve the Union on this issue. Even after the Louisiana treaty was ratified by the payment of the purchase money and the country at large had begun to realize the value of its new possessions, there was seemingly no abatement of this feeling;—and eight years later, when the bill admitting Louisiana into the Union as a State was under discussion in the United States Senate, Josiah Quincy, then Senator from Massachusetts, uttered these words:—

I am compelled to declare it as my deliberate opinion, that if this bill passes, the bonds of this Union are virtually dissolved;—that the States which compose it are free from their moral obligations;—and that as it will be the right of all, so it will be the duty of some to prepare, definitely, for a separation;—amicably if they can, violently if they must.

At this point in the debate he was called to order by Mr. Poindexter, delegate in Congress for Mississippi (which was then a Territory), for the utterance of these words of treason against the United States Government.

Just fifty years later the conditions were changed, and it was Mississippi and not Massachusetts that sought to separate herself from the Union.

Following this remarkable declaration, Mr. Quincy said:—

I have already heard of six States, and some say there will be, at no great distance of time, more.

Were Mr. Quincy in the United States Senate to-day, he would be greeted by forty of his Senatorial colleagues, and

nearly one hundred members of the lower house of Congress, from twenty States in the Union formed out of the Louisiana purchase and other and later acquisitions of territory.

Mr. Tracy, after delivering an elaborate argument on the subject, in which he arrives at the conclusion that the purchase itself is constitutional, says:—

We can hold the territory;—but to admit the inhabitants into the Union, to make citizens of them, and to make States by treaty, we cannot constitutionally do;—and no subsequent act of legislation, or even ordinary amendment to our Constitution, can legalize such a measure. If done at all, they must be done by universal consent of all the States or partners of our political association;—and this universal consent I am positive can never be obtained to such a pernicious measure as the admission of Louisiana,—of a world,—and such a world,—into our Union. This would be absorbing the Northern States and rendering them as insignificant in the Union as they ought to be, if by their own consent the new measure should be adopted.

Senator Plumer of New Hampshire also said:—

Admit this Western world into the Union, and you destroy at once the weight and importance of the Eastern States, and compel them to establish a separate independent Empire.

These declarations indicate that local interests and jealousies measured, in a great degree, the patriotism of many of the statesmen of that day.

LETTERS OF JEFFERSON.

We frequently hear it alleged to-day that Thomas Jefferson stood upon the ground which is taken by many of his party at this time, that the United States had no constitutional power to purchase Louisiana. Jefferson, however, held that view in theory only. He was sufficiently sagacious to see that Louisiana would become essential to the United States in its future development, and, without awaiting the action of Congress, he made the purchase regardless of the constitutional inhibition which he declared existed. It was a sublime act of statesmanship;—a master stroke for which he is and ever will be more renowned than as the author of the Declaration of Independence. He acknowledged that he, as the Executive, had gone beyond the letter of the Constitution;—yet he used his utmost endeavor to have the treaty ratified promptly, and the purchase money provided with the least possible discussion

of the constitutionality of the purchase, which he regarded
as the crowning event of his administration, and for the consummation of which he was ready to proceed to any extreme.

On August 30, 1803, he wrote to Levi Lincoln:—

The less that is said about any constitutional difficulty, the better;
—and it will be desirable for Congress to do what is necessary, *in
silence.*

On Sept. 7, 1803, Jefferson wrote to Wilson C. Nicholas:—

Whatever Congress shall think it necessary to do should be done
with as little debate as possible, and particularly so far as respects
the constitutional difficulty. * * * * As the constitution expressly declares itself to be made for the United States, I cannot help believing
the intention was not to permit Congress to admit into the Union new
States to be formed out of the territory, for which, and under whose
authority alone they were then acting. * * * * I had rather ask
an enlargement of power from the Nation where it is found necessary,
than to assume it by a construction which would make our power
boundless. * * * * Let us go on then, perfecting it, by adding, by
way of amendment to the Constitution, those powers which time and
trial show are still wanting. * * * * I think it important, in the
present case, to set an example against broad construction, by appealing for new power to the people. If, however, our friends shall
think differently, certainly I shall acquiesce with satisfaction;—confid-
ing, that the good sense of our country will correct the evil of construction when it shall produce its ill effects.

On August 12, 1803, Jefferson wrote to Mr. Breckenridge:—

This treaty must of course be laid before both Houses. * * * *
They, I presume, will see their duty to the country in ratifying and
paying for it; * * * * but I suppose they must then appeal to the
Nation for an additional article to the Constitution, approving and con-
firming an act which the Nation had not previously authorized. The
Constitution has made no provision for our holding foreign territory,
still less for incorporating foreign nations into our Union. The Executive, in seizing the fugitive occurrence which so much advances the
good of his country, has done an act beyond the Constitution. The
Legislature, in casting behind them metaphysical subtleties, and risk-
ing themselves like faithful servants, must ratify and pay for it, and
throw themselves on their country for doing for them unauthorized,
what we know they would have done for themselves had they been
in a situation to do it. It is the case of a guardian investing the money
of his ward in purchasing an important adjacent territory, and saying
to him when of age, 'I did this for your good; I pretend to no right
to bind you; you may disavow me, and I must get out of the scrape
as I can; I thought it my duty to risk myself for you.' But we shall

not be disavowed by the Nation, and their act of indemnity will confirm and not weaken the Constitution, by more strongly marking out its lines.

Although Jefferson here acknowledges that he had gone beyond the letter of the Constitution, he evidently believed that he had not violated the spirit of Republican Government which was behind that instrument, nor the fundamental principles upon which it was based;—and he was willing to accept as its proper interpretation, that many of the powers of the Government under it are implied;—and that, as the people made the Constitution, they could also amend it whenever it became necessary to do so;—but that the purchase of new territory, not being in violation of the underlying spirit of the Constitution, could be made without any amendment to it.

OPINION OF CHIEF JUSTICE MARSHALL.

This view of Jefferson was upheld and confirmed twenty-five years later, by United States Chief Justice John Marshall. In the case of the American Insurance Company vs. David Canter, reported in 1st Peters, page 511, Chief Justice Marshall, in delivering the opinion of the court, in January, 1828, said:—

The Constitution confers absolutely on the Government of the Union, the powers of making war and making treaties;—consequently that Government possesses the power of acquiring territory either by conquest or by treaty. The usage of the world is, if a nation be not entirely subdued, to consider the holding of conquered territory as a mere military occupation until its fate shall be determined at the treaty of peace. If it be ceded by the treaty, the acquisition is confirmed, and the ceded territory becomes a part of the nation to which it is annexed;—either on the terms stipulated in the treaty of cession, or on such as its new master shall impose. On such transfer of territory it has never been held that the relations of the inhabitants with each other undergo any change. Their relations with their former sovereign are dissolved, and new relations are created between them and the government which has acquired their territory. *The same act which transfers their country transfers the allegiance of those who remain in it;* and the law, which may be denominated political, is necessarily changed.

The language of the learned Chief Justice clearly establishes the right of one nation to transfer to another, any territory, and the allegiance and loyalty of its inhabitants, with-

out their consent. It is also evident, from an examination of
that portion of the opinion of the court which is not quoted
above,. that the court believed that the Constitution and laws
of the United States did not extend by their own force over
territory so acquired, but that Congress alone could determine
all questions involved in their government.

Many of the most eminent jurists of our country believe
that the liberal powers which Chief Justice Marshall gave to
the Constitution during the thirty-four years that he inter-
preted it, were necessary to its durability, and that a strict adherence to its letter would have destroyed it. Judge Story
said:—

The Constitution, since its adoption, owes more to him than to any
other single mind for its true interpretation and vindication.

No amendment of the Constitution has ever been deemed
necessary to confirm the purchase of Louisiana, as the general
power of the government to acquire territory and also to govern any territory it chooses to acquire, cannot be enlarged or
strengthened by any such amendment. And as the Nation
did not disavow the President of the United States at the beginning of the nineteenth century in acquiring Louisiana, so it
will not disavow its President at its close, in acquiring the
Philippines.

ANGLO-AMERICAN ALLIANCE.

It is interesting to note the radical attitude of Jefferson at
this time, on the subject of forming an Anglo-American alliance, and the length to which he was willing to go in this respect in order to acquire Louisiana.

I have already adverted to Jefferson's letter to Monroe, in
which he wrote that if Louisiana could not be purchased from
Napoleon, it might be necessary for him (Monroe) to cross the
Channel into England. For what purpose did he think this
might become necessary? It was to form an alliance with
England, in case of a failure of the negotiations for the purchase of Louisiana. In a letter to Robert Livingston, dated
April 18, 1802, he boldly declared his policy in case of the refusal of France to sell Louisiana to the United States. On
that day he wrote to Livingston:—

The cession of Louisiana by Spain to France, works most sorely
on the United States. * * * * It completely reverses all the polit-

ical relations of the United States. * * * * There is on the globe one single spot, the possessor of which is our natural and habitual enemy. It is New Orleans, through which the produce of three-eighths of our territory must pass to market. * * * * France, placing herself in that door, assumes to us the attitude of defiance. Spain might have retained it quietly for years. Her pacific disposition, her feeble state, would induce her to increase our facilities there, so that her possession of the place would hardly be felt by us, and it would not be very long before some circumstance might arise which might make the cession of it to us the price of something of more worth to her. Not so can it ever be in the hands of France. The impetuosity of her temper, the energy and restlessness of her character, placed in a point of eternal friction with us, and our character, which, though quiet and loving peace and the pursuit of wealth, is high-minded, despising wealth in competition with insult or injury, enterprising and energetic as any nation on earth;—these circumstances render it impossible that France and the United States can continue long friends, when they meet in so irritable a position. They, as well as we, must be blind if they do not see this;—and we must be very improvident if we do not begin to make arrangements on that hypothesis. The day that France takes possession of New Orleans, fixes the sentence which is to restrain her forever within her low-water mark. *It seals the union of two nations, who, in conjunction, can maintain exclusive possession of the ocean. From that moment we must marry ourselves to the British fleet and Nation.* We must turn all our attention to a maritime force, for which our resources place us on very high ground;—and having formed and connected together a power which may render reinforcement of her settlements here impossible to France, make the first cannon which shall be fired in Europe the signal for the tearing up of any settlement she may have made, and *for holding the two continents of America in sequestration for the common purposes of the United British and American Nations.* * * * * In that case France will have held possession of New Orleans during the interval of a peace, long or short, at the end of which it will be wrested from her.

This letter to Chancellor Livingston was enclosed by Jefferson to M. Dupont de Nemours, an eminent and influential citizen of France, whose good offices in behalf of our government Jefferson sought, and to whom he wrote on April 25, 1802:—

You may be able to impress on the Government of France the inevitable consequences of their taking possession of Louisiana;—and though, as I here mention, the cession of New Orleans and the Floridas to us would be a palliation, yet I believe it would be no more, and that this measure will cost France, and perhaps not very long hence, a war which will annihilate her on the ocean and place that element under the despotism of two nations, which I am not reconciled to the more be-

cause my own would be one of them. Add to this the exclusive appropriation of both continents of America as a consequence.

These letters reveal the length to which Jefferson was willing to carry the Nation on this issue. It was not only Louisiana, but it was the whole of North America and South America that he proposed to hold jointly with England, under an alliance which would sweep France from the ocean, and place it—"that element," as he terms it,—under the control of America and England. The wildest imagination cannot carry us farther than this. All our present purposes of expansion, and all suggestions of the present concerning an Anglo-Saxon alliance, are dwarfed into insignificance when compared with this proposal of Jefferson.

Mr. Breckenridge did not share in the fears of his colleagues, concerning the purchase of Louisiana. In the stirring reply which he made to them, he asks:—

Is the Goddess of Liberty restrained by water-courses? Is she governed by geographical limits? Is her dominion on this continent confined to the east side of the Mississippi? So far from believing that a Republic ought to be confined within narrow limits, I believe on the contrary that the more extensive its dominion, the more safe and durable it will be. In proportion to the number of hands you intrust the precious blessings of a free government to, in the same proportion do you multiply the chances for their preservation.

The measure providing the means for the purchase of the territory finally became a law, and the United States thereby added to its original domain twelve hundred and sixty thousand (1,260,000) square miles, including Texas, which, in 1819, was relinquished to Spain in exchange for the Floridas, and was re-annexed to the United States in 1845. This vast acquisition was more than one-third greater than the whole area of the United States and their territorial possessions at the time of the purchase.

FEARS OF EASTERN STATESMEN.

The fears entertained by our early statesmen are all forgotten. I have recalled them, not to illustrate any deficiency in the foresight or wisdom of the men of that day, but to show how remarkable has been the progress of improvement, discovery, and invention, by which we have been enabled, during nearly a century of national expansion, to incorporate not only

the Louisiana Purchase, but others of still greater aggregate extent, into the government of the Republic, without endangering its safety, and without any amendment to the Constitution, or any material modification of our form of government, or divergence from the faith or policy of Thomas Jefferson, and others of the Fathers of the Republic.

It is worthy of notice that all of these vast regions were ceded by the nations possessing them, without consulting their subjects, and the cession accepted by the United States without obtaining or even asking the consent of the inhabitants. As was said by Chief Justice Marshall in the opinion already referred to, "the same act which transfers their country, transfers the allegiance of those who remain in it." The power to expand is inherent and limitless. The United States may constitutionally take whatever territory it desires, if it is rightly acquired. The question is one of expediency only, not of power.

It is said that the best and most enlightened thought of New England to-day is opposed to the expansion policy of our Government. We may answer that the most enlightened thought and best statesmanship of New England opposed the purchase of Louisiana, and of the Floridas, and the measures by which we acquired Oregon, and the treaty with Mexico which gave us California. But the enlightening experiences of a century have left their lessons, and there is to-day neither in New England nor elsewhere in the United States, any prominent man in public life who would venture to question the wisdom of the measures by which these acquisitions were made, and which have so benefited and enriched the Republic. And, with distance annihilated by steam and electricity, there is no reason which can be presented why the work of civilization and development which has been so successfully accomplished by the American people in the remote regions of this continent, may not be as effectively done on any soil under the sun.

The doleful predictions of a century ago, like those we are hearing to-day, when our land is teeming with the spirit of acquisition, were born of a fear and timidity which are inimical to great progress; and they represent a mental attitude which is not fitted to grapple with new problems.

This Nation is no longer an infant, but a giant. The sun never sets on the land over which now float the stars and

stripes, and we have need to expand our ideas of our destiny as we have expanded our territory. The present is no time for faint-heartedness in the councils of the Republic.

MODE OF DEFINING WESTERN BOUNDARY.

The western boundary of the vast territory ceded to the United States under the name of Louisiana was a geographical problem, incapable of any other than a forced solution. It was claimed that by the treaty of Utrecht, concluded in 1713, the 49th parallel of latitude had been adopted and definitively settled as the dividing line between the French possessions of Western Canada and Louisiana on the south, and the British territories of Hudson Bay on the north, and that this boundary extended westward to the Pacific. So unreliable was the evidence in support of this claim, that it was finally determined, in the settlement of the western boundary of Louisiana, to adopt such lines as were indicated by nature, namely, the crest of mountains separating the waters of the Mississippi from those flowing into the Pacific. This left in an unsettled condition the respective claims of Spain, Russia, Great Britain and the United States to the vast territory beyond the Rocky Mountains, extending along the 42nd parallel of latitude west to the Pacific on the south, thence north up the coast indefinitely, thence east to the crest of the Rocky Mountains, thence following the crest, south, to the place of beginning. Both our country and Great Britain recognized an indefeasible right in Spain to some portion of this country, but our relations with Spain were such at the time, that this opinion was not openly promulgated. The territory included the mouth of the Columbia, the entire region drained by that river and its tributaries, and an extensive region still further north independent of this great river system. The most valuable portion of it at this early period in our history was that traversed by the Columbia and its tributaries.

DISCOVERY OF THE COLUMBIA BY CAPTAIN GRAY.

Great Britain had no right, by discovery or otherwise, to any portion of this part of the territory. "The opening," says Greenhow, "through which its waters are discharged into the ocean was first seen in August, 1776, by the Spanish navigator

Heceta, and was distinguished on Spanish charts within the thirteen years next following, as the mouth of the River San Roque. It was examined in July, 1788, by Meares, who quitted it with the conviction that no river existed there. This opinion of Meares was subscribed, without qualification, by Vancouver, after he had minutely examined the coast, 'under the most favorable conditions of wind and weather,' and notwithstanding the assurance of Gray to the contrary." The actual discovery of the mouth of the Columbia was made on the 11th of May, 1792, by Captain Robert Gray, a New England navigator, who says in his logbook under that date: "Beheld our desired port, bearing east-south-east, distant six leagues. At eight a. m., being a little to the windward of the entrance of the harbor, bore away, and ran in east-north-east between the breakers, having from five to seven fathoms of water. When we were over the bar, we found this to be a large river of fresh water, up which we steered."

Captain Gray remained in the Columbia from the 11th until the 20th of May, during which time he sailed up the river fifteen miles, gave to it the name it still bears, trafficked with the natives, and named the capes at the entrance and other points above.

ATTITUDE OF JEFFERSON.

The United States had this claim to the mouth of the river and the interior drained by it and its tributaries eleven years before the Louisiana Purchase was made. President Jefferson evidently believed that Gray's discovery fully established our claim to all that region, and that it was not embraced within the limits of the territory ceded by Spain to France in 1800 by the treaty of St. Ildephonso:—for in January, 1803, while negotiations with Napoleon were in progress, and three months before the Louisiana treaty was signed, he sent a confidential message to Congress, which resulted in an appropriation by that body of twenty-five hundred dollars for an exploration of the region. No public documents accessible to me at this time throw much light upon this secret or confidential message, but it is probable that the hidden purpose contained in it was privately brought to the notice of a sufficient number of the members of Congress to insure the small appropriation asked

for it. In a letter to Dr. Barton, dated Feb. 27, 1803, Jefferson refers to these "secret proceedings" as follows:

> You know we have been many years wishing to have the Missouri explored, and whatever river, heading with that, runs into the Western ocean. Congress, *in some secret proceedings*, have yielded to a proposition I made them for permitting me to have it done. * * *

That Jefferson desired to enshroud in secrecy the real purpose of this expedition, and conceal it from the knowledge of Great Britain and the Northwest Company, is evident from his suggestions relative to the title of the bill providing for the appropriation, and from the small number of persons he desired to enlist in the enterprise, as well as from other mysterious and covert suggestions contained in this secret message to Congress, from which I here quote. After outlining a project for the extension of the public commerce among the Indian tribes of the Missouri and the western ocean, he says:

> An intelligent officer, with ten or twelve chosen men, fit for the enterprise and willing to undertake it, taken from our posts where they may be spared without inconvenience, might explore the whole line, even to the Western Ocean, have conference with the natives on the subject of commercial intercourse, * * * and return with the information acquired in the course of two summers. * * * Their pay would be going on while here or there. While other civilized nations have encountered great expense to enlarge the boundaries of knowledge **by** undertaking voyages of discovery *and for other literary purposes*, in **various** parts and directions, our nation seems to owe to the same object, **as well as** to its own interests, to explore this only line of easy communication across the continent, *and so directly traversing our own part of it.* The interests of commerce place the principal object within the constitutional powers and care of Congress, and that it should incidentally advance the geographical knowledge of our own continent, can **not** but be an additional gratification. The nation claiming the territory, *regarding this as a literary pursuit,* which it is in the habit of permitting within its dominions, would not be disposed to view it with **jealousy,** even if the expiring state of its interests there did not render **it** a matter of indifference. The appropriation of $2,500 *"for the purpose of extending the external commerce of the United States,"* while understood **and** considered by the Executive as giving the legislative sanction, *would cover the undertaking from notice,* and prevent the obstructions which interested individuals might otherwise previously prepare in its **way.**

LEWIS AND CLARK EXPEDITION.

The expedition was not organized, however, before the purchase from France was concluded. After that was agreed

upon, Captain Meriwether Lewis, whose grand-uncle married a sister of Washington, and who, at the time of his appointment, was the private secretary of President Jefferson, and Captain William Clark, were, at the instance of Jefferson, appointed to explore the country up the Missouri to its source and to the Pacific. From the moment of their appearance on the Missouri, their movements were watched by the British, and as soon as the object of their expedition was discovered, the Northwest Company, in 1805, sent out its men to establish posts and occupy territories on the Columbia. The British Company proceeded no farther than the Mandan villages on the Missouri. Another party, dispatched on the same errand in 1806, crossed the Rocky Mountains near the passage of the Peace river, and formed a small trading establishment in the 54th degree of north latitude,—the first British post west of the Rocky Mountains. Neither at this nor at any subsequent time until 1811 does it appear that any of the waters of the Columbia were seen by persons in the service of the Northwest Company.

Lewis and Clark arrived at the Kooskooskee river, a tributary of the Columbia, in latitude 46° 34', early in October, 1805, and on the 7th of that month began their descent in five canoes. They entered the great southern tributary, which they called Lewis, and proceeded to its confluence, giving the name of Clark to the northern branch; thence they sailed down the Columbia to its mouth, and wintered there until the middle of March, 1806. They then returned, exploring the streams which emptied into the Columbia and furnishing an accurate geographical description of the entire country through which they passed.

ASTOR EXPEDITION.

Early in 1811 the men sent by John Jacob Astor to the northwest coast in the interest of the Pacific Fur Company, erected buildings and a stockade, with a view to permanent settlement, on a point of land ten miles above the mouth of the Columbia, which they called Astoria. With the exception of one or two trading posts on some of the small streams constituting the head waters of the river, the country had not at this time been visited by the English. Further detail of the history and trials of the Pacific Fur Company is unnecessary in this place, but the reader who desires to acquaint himself

with it is referred to Irving's "Astoria" for one of the most thrilling narratives in American history.

In 1818, after Astoria had been sold by the Americans to the British Fur Company and the stockade occupied by British troops, it was restored to the United States under a provision of the Treaty of Ghent, without prejudice to any of the claims that either the United States, Great Britain, Spain or Russia might have to the ultimate sovereignty of the territory. The claims of the respective nations were afterward considered by the plenipotentiaries of Great Britain and the United States. Messrs. Rush and Gallatin, who represented our Government, proposed that the dividing line between the territories should be drawn from the northwestern extremity of the Lake of the Woods north or south, as the case might require, to the 49th parallel of latitude, thence west to the Pacific. The British commissioners, Messrs. Goldburn and Robinson, agreed to admit the line as far west as the Rocky Mountains. Our representatives on that occasion supported the claim of our Government by citing Gray's discovery, the exploration of the Columbia from source to mouth by Lewis and Clark, and the first settlement and occupancy of the country by the Pacific Fur Company. The British commissioners asserted superior claims by virtue of former voyages, especially those of Captain Cook, and refused to agree to any boundary which did not give them the harbor at the mouth of the river in common with the United States. Finding it impossible to agree upon a boundary, it was at length agreed that all territories and their waters claimed by either power west of the Rocky Mountains should be free and open to the vessels, citizens and subjects of both for the space of ten years; provided, however, that no claim of either or of any other nation to any part of those territories should be prejudiced by the arrangement.

FLORIDA TREATY.

On the 22nd of February, 1819, Spain ceded Florida to the United States, and by the treaty it was agreed that a line drawn on the meridian from the source of the Arkansas northward to the 42nd parallel of latitude, and thence along that parallel westward to the Pacific, should form the northern boundary of the Spanish possessions and the southern boundary of those of the United States in that quarter.

On the 5th of April, 1824, the negotiations between the
United States and Russia were terminated by a convention
signed at St. Petersburg, which, among other provisions, contained one to the effect that "neither the United States nor
their citizens shall, in future, form an establishment on those
coasts or on the adjacent islands north of the latitude of 54°
40', and the Russians shall make none south of that latitude."

These concessions on the part of Spain and Russia left the
United States and Great Britain sole claimants for the entire
territory under consideration, the claim of Great Britain having been fortified by a treaty with Russia in 1825, in which
the Russian Government agreed, as it had done with our Government the previous year, that the line of 54° 40' should be
the boundary between their respective possessions.

The period of ten years' joint occupation by our Government and Great Britain agreed upon in 1818 was now approaching a termination. A new negotiation was opened, and
after submitting and rejecting several propositions for a settlement, it was finally agreed between the two Governments
that they should continue in the joint occupancy of the territory for an indefinite period, either party being at liberty to
demand a new negotiation on giving the other one year's notice of its intention.

The relations thus established between the two Governments continued without interruption until the attention of
Congress was called to the subject by President Tyler in his
message read at the opening of the session of 1842. The subject was referred to the committees on foreign affairs in both
houses of Congress, and a bill was introduced in the Senate
for the occupation and settlement of the territory, and extending the laws of the United States over it. A protracted debate
followed, the bill passed the Senate and was sent to the House
of Representatives, where a report against it was made by
Mr. Adams, chairman of the committee on foreign affairs, and
the session expired without any debate on the subject. When
the report of the debates in Congress reached England, it produced some excitement in the House of Commons, and in
February, 1844, the Honorable Richard Packenham, plenipo-
tentiary from Great Britain, arrived in Washington with full
instructions to treat definitively on all disputed points relative
to the country west of the Rocky Mountains.

In August following the British minister opened the negotiation by a proposition which would have given Great Britain
two-thirds of the entire territory of Oregon, including the free
navigation of the Columbia and the harbors on the Pacific.
This was promptly rejected, and no further attempt at adjustment was made until the following year. An offer was then
made by President Polk, which being rejected, closed the door
to further negotiation. The President recommended to Congress that the agreement for joint occupation be terminated.

FINAL SETTLEMENT OF BOUNDARY.

A very animated debate, which continued until near the
close of the session, sprang up, in which the question of boundary lost most of its national features in the sharp party conflict to which it was subjected. The Democrats, generally
adopting the recommendations of the President, advocated the
extreme northern boundary of 54° 40′, and were ready, if
necessary, to declare that as the ultimatum. A few leaders
among them, of whom Thomas Benton was, perhaps, the most
prominent, united with the Whigs in opposition to this extreme demand, and the line was finally established by treaty
on the 49th parallel.

Hon. James G. Blaine, in a speech delivered at Lewiston,
Maine, on August 25, 1888, said: "The claim of the Democrats
to the whole of what now constitutes British Columbia up to
latitude 54° 40′, was a pretense put forth during the presidential canvass of 1844 as a blind, in order to show that they were
as zealous to secure Northern territory as they were bent on
acquiring Southern territory. President Polk made his campaign on this claim. The next thing the country heard was
that Mr. Polk's administration was compelled to surrender the
whole territory to Great Britain, confessing that it had made
pretenses which it was unable to maintain or defend. Had
his party not forced the question to a settlement, the joint occupation which had come down from Jefferson to that hour
would have peacefully continued, and with our acquisition of
California two years afterwards and the immediate discovery
of gold, the thousands of American citizens who swarmed to
the Pacific coast would have occupied British Columbia, and
the final settlement would doubtless have been in favor of

those who were in actual posssession;—and but for the blundering diplomacy of the Democratic party, which prematurely and without any reason forced the issue, we should to-day see our flag floating over the Pacific front, from the Gulf of California to Behring's Straits."

This mode of settlement probably averted a war between Great Britain and the United States, but after a careful survey of all the facts, including discoveries, explorations and settlements, I cannot but feel that the concessions were all made by the United States, whose title to the whole of the territory was much more strongly fortified than that of Great Britain to any portion of it.

As from our present vantage ground we look back a half century in review of the debates and discussions in Congress upon this boundary question, we marvel at the seeming lack of prescience which the wisest of the public men of that day displayed in estimating the value of these possessions. Even as enlightened and sagacious a statesman as Daniel Webster, in his famous speech delivered on the floor of the United States Senate, on April 6, 1846, while defending his course in advocating the treaty of Washington, in speaking of the value of the privilege granted by England to the citizens of Aroostook County, in the State of Maine, in allowing them free navigation of the River St. John, to the ocean, said:

"We have heard a great deal lately of the immense value and importance of the Columbia river and its navigation;—but I will undertake to say that for all purposes of human use, the St. John is worth a hundred times as much as the Columbia is, or ever will be."

Standing to-day in the valley of the Mississippi and casting our eyes over the Louisiana Purchase and our later acquisitions, upon this continent, we talk of the West,—its cities,—its agriculture,—its progress, with rapture;—a land where but half a century ago, nearly all was bare creation;—whose valleys, now teeming with fruition, had then never cheered the vision of civilized man;—whose rivers, which now afford the means of employment to thousands, and which are bordered by myriads of happy homes, then rolled in solitary grandeur to their union with the Missouri and the Columbia;—to all this we

point with pride as the latest and noblest illustration of our republican system of government. But beyond this West, which we so much admire and eulogize, there has come to us from the islands of the Pacific, another West, where the real work of development is just commencing;—a land whose rugged features, American civilization with all its attendant blessings will soften;—insuring respect for individual rights and the practice of orderly industry, security for life and property, freedom of religion and the equal and just administration of law;—and where man, educated, intellectual man, will plant upon foundations as firm as our mountains, all the institutions of a free, enlightened and happy people;—a land where all the advantages and resources of the West of yesterday will be increased, and varied, and spread out, by educational, industrial and social development, upon a scale of magnificence which has known no parallel, and which will fill the full measure of Berkeley's prophecy:—

"Westward the course of Empire takes its way.
    The first four acts already past,
A fifth shall close the drama with the day.
    Time's noblest offspring is the last."

SOME LEGACIES OF THE ORDINANCE OF 1787.*

BY HON. JAMES OSCAR PIERCE.

It is not the aim of this paper to explain the place of the
Ordinance of 1787 as a constitutional document, or the details
of the movement of which it was the culmination. The general
history of that period has been abundantly written. and the
evolution of the Ordinance has been elaborately traced. While
the present age has recognized this as one of the great constitutional acts in the larger history of our country, the extent of
our indebtedness to it has not been generally observed. We
are now so far removed from that epoch that we can distinguish
some of the legacies which that Ordinance has left for the welfare and prosperity of the present generation, and for which
it and its wise promoters deserve our gratitude.

NATIONALITY.

It is not often possible to mark the precise time when a people became a Nation, or the final step which made it such. All
students recognize historical processes as gradual, including
those by which great governments grow. The historian sees
a people at a certain date unformed, with no institutions definitely or permanently established, and he does not ascribe to
them statehood. At a later period, the same people are recognized as a fully formed nation. In the intervening time, one can
note only a general progress from the earlier status toward the
later, without being able to assign any particular date as that
when the change was consummated. There is a period in
American history which presents difficulties of this character.

On July 4th, 1776, our country ceased to be thirteen British
colonies, and she never reverted to that status. The adoption

* Read at the monthly meeting of the Executive Council, March 13, 1899.

of the Federal Constitution, and the commencement of its operations in 1789, exhibit her as a Nation. It is not easy to define
her exact political status at any time during the interim.
There has been extended discussion upon this subject, developing many and persistent differences of opinion. It is not necessary to attempt to settle these disputes, in order to distinguish
the whole revolutionary and confederate period as one of
progress, from the League of 1774 to the Nation of 1789. There
are some well-meaning and patriotic persons, who argue that
it was not until the results of the Civil War had removed all
doubts, and had cemented the interests of the two previously
discordant sections, that full nationality resulted. The majority of students of our history, however, now agree, as the Supreme Court of the United States has so often held, that the
work was accomplished when the Constitution went into operation in 1789. If we do not concede that the Declaration of Independence initiated nationality, as many constitutionalists
claim, it is easy to conceive of the period of 1776 to 1789 as one
of transition, during which the people were considering the merits of two rival plans of confederation, and were gradually
making their choice between a League and a Nation. The
Ordinance of 1787 furnishes evidence that the choice was made,
and that the people had determined upon the higher and more
vigorous form of political life.

Many of the intervening steps taken by the people indicated
that such was their choice; but it has been argued that these
steps were not necessarily irrevocable or final. The Declaration of Independence itself, professing to be the act of "one people," seemed to imply the creation of a nation composed of thirteen states; and it has often been urged that this was a complete and determinate act, and that we were thus "born United
States." So the Continental Congress, which was the sole
head of the revolutionary government, raised a Continental
Army and placed a general at its head, put afloat a Continental
Navy, created an Appellate Prize Court, sent diplomats abroad,
negotiated and entered into treaties, and discharged other functions properly pertaining only to a nation.

On the other hand, it is urged that these acts do not indicate
the deliberate choice of the people to become a nation, because
they were all compulsory, by reason of the war then existing.
May it not be that these were only temporary expedients, asser-

tions of central sovereignty which was but a simulacrum, and
which the states tolerated only under the pressure of a foreign
war? The scanty grants of power to "the United States in
Congress assembled," under the Articles of Confederation, and
the reservations made therein to the states, have been appealed
to as indicating that the people were not ready to establish
more than a league. It is true, they had adopted one flag,
under which the army drove out or captured the invaders,
under which the navy swept the seas; but may this not have
been the flag of a league, and could it not have been divided
into thirteen flags, with one star in each, if the people so desired? What they chose to do while engaged in resisting
Britain, they might prefer not to do when the pressure of war
was removed, and peace succeeded.

If we concede that these considerations leave it doubtful
whether the people had theretofore chosen to become a nation,
the doubts are resolved when we come to observe the Ordinance of 1787. In that instrument is found evidence of a deliberate choice made in the time of peace, after an extended discussion commencing in the time of war. This debate was protracted for ten years, and was at times exceedingly heated.
The diverse views presented were ardently advocated, and several plans were offered for governing and dividing the Northwestern Territory. When, with all this consideration, after
the pressure of foreign war had been removed, an ordinance of
a distinctly national character was adopted, this may well be
taken as the final determination of the people. By this instrument there was placed upon our government the stamp of Nationality. This was before the Federal Convention at Philadelphia had completed its draft of a constitution. It was fore-
ordained that the work of that body should be the constitution
of a Nation.

The precedent discussion involved the determination of this
precise question, Should America be a Nation or a League?
The matter under dispute had been the proper control of the
unsettled western lands, over which, as a result of the war,
Great Britain relinquished authority. Four of the states laid
claim to some of these lands; and Virginia, whose pretensions
seemed most plausible, claimed all, and proposed to settle for
herself their destiny. Before the war had closed, the smaller
colonies, with Maryland in the lead, were resisting the Virginia

theory, and claiming that the western lands would belong to
the Union of States, because the states had united to wrest
them from Great Britain.   Maryland had declined to ratify the
Articles of Confederation unless her position in regard to the
western lands was adopted, and she yielded her assent to those
articles only when assured that those lands would be ceded to
the general government.   It is true that Virginia and the other
colonies voluntarily ceded their claims to these lands to the
United States.   But it is clear that they did so in response to
that demand, and for the sake of cementing and perfecting the
Union of the States.   The Act of cession by New York recited
that it was designed "to facilitate the completion of the Articles of Confederation."   So the question becomes pertinent,
Upon what legal ground was the claim of Maryland based?   To
what theory did Virginia and New York and Massachusetts
and Connecticut yield, when they chose to cede the lands?

Under the British law, the colonies were crown property.
They belonged to the sovereign.   All the American charters
were based upon this principle.   From the time of James I, this
had been conceded as a canon of the British constitution.   It
was the war jointly conducted, and the victory of the Americans, which secured these western lands by the concession in
the treaty of peace.   The respective colonial charters gave
their holders title only to such lands as they had respectively
occupied with their settlements, which did not reach beyond
the Ohio river.   And as it was by war and conquest, carried
on by a united people, that these lands had been acquired, what
power had thereby succeeded as sovereign to the rights of
King George III?   Manifestly, the people of the United States,
that power which had conquered the territory from him.

The idea that these lands were by right common property
anticipated their actual conquest by many years.   Immediately following the Declaration of Independence, and before
any steps toward a Union had been taken, the Maryland Constitutional Convention, on October 30th, 1776, resolved that "if
the dominion over these lands should be established by the
blood and treasure of the United States, such lands ought to
be considered as a common stock, to be parcelled out at proper
times into convenient, free and independent governments."
The substance of this proposition was offered in Congress in
October, 1777, before the Articles of Confederation were sub

mitted for ratification, but it received the support of Maryland alone. In 1778, Maryland instructed her delegates not to ratify those articles until this question should be settled upon the basis that the lands, "if wrested from the common enemy by the blood and treasure of the thirteen states, should be considered as a common property, subject to be parcelled out by Congress into free, convenient, and independent governments." These instructions, when read in Congress in May, 1779, brought protest and remonstrance from Virginia, based on her claim to individual sovereignty over these lands.

Delaware, New Jersey, and Rhode Island desired to have the unoccupied lands sold for the common benefit, not claiming more than that at first. In connection with a certain contemplated treaty with the Cayuga Indians, it was proposed, in 1779, that the Six Nations should cede a part of their territory "for the benefit of the United States in general."

The controversy of Maryland *versus* Virginia had progressed so far in 1780 as to imperil the success of the contemplated Union under the Articles of Confederation, so that it was proposed that the "landed" states should cede their lands to the Union in order to save the Union. In October, Congress resolved that the western lands, to be ceded by the states, should be formed into distinct republican states, which should become members of the Federal Union on equal terms with the other states. New York had already offered to cede her claims in order "to facilitate the completion of the Articles of Confederation and perpetual Union." In 1781, Virginia offered to cede her claims, on certain conditions, one being the division into new states; and Maryland, having substantially won her controversy, ratified the Articles of Confederation, not relinquishing "any right or interest she hath, with the other United or Confederated states, to the back country." In 1782, Congress, on the motion of Maryland, accepted the offer of New York, and in 1783 that of Virginia. The cession of Virginia was executed in March, 1784; that of Massachusetts, in April, 1785; and that of Connecticut, in September, 1786.

The other branch of the controversy, namely, as to the legal title to the territory, arose, in an acrid form, in 1782. In the discussion over the terms of the proposed treaty of peace with Great Britain, as to the title to the lands to be recovered, the claim of the United States as successor to the British crown

33

was advocated by Rutledge of South Carolina and Witherspoon of New Jersey. A committee of Congress submitted to it two alternative propositions, one that the individual states had succeeded to the rights of the crown, and the other, that these lands "can be deemed to have been the property of his Britannic Majesty, and to be now devolved upon the United States collectively taken." The last named proposition was further expounded by the committee as follows: "The character in which the king was seized was that of king of the thirteen colonies collectively taken. Being stripped of this character, its rights descended to the United States for the following reasons: 1. The United States are to be considered in many respects as an undivided independent nation, inheriting those rights which the King of Great Britain enjoyed as not appertaining to any particular state, while *he* was, what *they* are now, the superintending governor of the whole. 2. The King of Great Britain has been dethroned as king of the United States by the joint efforts of the whole. 3. The very country in question hath been conquered through the means of the common labor of the United States." The Virginia delegates protested against this proposition, asserting the individual sovereignty of their state. Witherspoon argued for the national view, saying: "The several states are known to the powers of Europe only as one nation, under the style and title of the United States; this nation is known to be settled along the coasts to a certain extent." To minimize this controversy, the report was recommitted.

It soon arose more sharply, when the petition of the inhabitants of Kentucky was received, on August 27th, 1782, asking that they be admitted on their own application as a separate and independent state. on the grounds that they were "subjects of the United States, and not of Virginia," and that as a result of the dissolution of the charter of Virginia, "the country had reverted to the crown of Great Britain, and that by virtue of the Revolution the right of the crown devolved on the United States." Lee and Madison of Virginia controverted, while McKean of Delaware, Howell of Rhode Island, and Wither-.spoon of New Jersey, maintained the theory of the succession of the United States to the rights of the crown.

In 1783, in connection with the question of organizing the Northwestern Territory, Carroll of Maryland offered in Con-

gress a resolution claiming the sovereignty of the United States over that territory, "as one undivided and independent nation, with all and every power and right exercised by the king of Great Britain over the said territory." Congress was not ready to adopt the proposition in that form. Then followed the acceptance of Virginia's offer of cession, provided she withdrew certain objectionable conditions, and the appointment of a committee to report a plan for the government of the territory; and, later, the deed of cession by Virginia, Jefferson's ordinance of 1784, and the deeds of cession by Massachusetts and Connecticut, gradually paving the way for the authoritative and comprehensive Ordinance of 1787.

It was, then, the argument of the smaller colonies which prevailed, and to which the larger colonies yielded. The fact of a deed of cession by Virginia does not imply, as Professor Tucker has argued in his Commentaries on the Constitution, that all parties acknowledged the sovereignty of Virginia, because the deeds of cession did not stand alone.   They were given to facilitate the Union of the States, and to enable the general government to exercise her sovereignty over the western territory.   What was in fact done with these lands by the United States, with the assent of the larger colonies, is of greater weight, in ascertaining the ultimate purpose, than the verbal protests of certain dissatisfied statesmen.   That final action was the assertion of full sovereignty by the United States, and the exertion of that sovereignty in establishing government.   "Be it ordained, by the United States in Congress assembled," is the language of self-conscious sovereignty.

It was this legal proposition, advanced by the smaller colonies as their ultimatum in the western land controversy, which the Supreme Court of the United States approved, in the case of Chisholm v. Georgia, as just and sound, saying: "From the crown of Great Britain, the sovereignty of their [this] country passed to the people of it, and it was then not an uncommon opinion that the unappropriated lands, which belonged to that crown, passed not to the people of the colony or state within whose limits they were situated, but to the whole people; on whatever principles this opinion rested, *it did not give way to the other.*"

This proposition of necessity imputed nationality to the people of the United States, and denied the existence of a

league. To this proposition both Virginia and New York assented when they ceded their western lands. By her action in
ceding these lands and participating in the adoption of the
Ordinance of 1787, Virginia, no less than New York, was in
good faith and in honor estopped from ever claiming any other
position than that of a Commonwealth in subordination to the
Nation. That Ordinance, legislating authoritatively for the
government of the territory so acquired, was a national act. It
was the deliberate act of the people of the United States, as-
suming to themselves the power of a nation. Whether America should be a nation or a league, became then a closed question. Thenceforward, it remained only to establish finally the
nationality which the people had assumed, by the framing and
adoption of the Federal Constitution.

THE DUAL SYSTEM OF GOVERNMENT.

The American system of federal government is unique. It
is a happy combination of a strong but limited central government, for all general and external purposes, with state governments which control all local matters and all those affairs
which most concern the body of the citizens in their daily lives.
It was the first experiment of the kind on a large scale, and it
has had a conspicuous success. The novelty consisted in binding together a league of states in such a manner as to give them
a supreme central government which should act directly upon
and command obedience from the individuals of all sections of
the country. Thus every citizen is subordinated at the same
time to two governments, and has a dual citizenship.

The American plan contemplates additions to the group of
states by admission of new ones on equal terms with the first
members. It involves the assertion and exercise, by the people
of the entire nation, of their inherent sovereignty; for no less a
power would be competent to ordain, by authoritative law, the
enlargement of the galaxy of states by the admission of new
ones, possessed of equal rights and privileges, and bound by
equal responsibilities and duties, with the older states. The
sovereign people thus establish the central government which
secures respect and honor for the flag abroad, and authorize
and guarantee the state governments which foster and protect
all the domestic privileges and rights of individuals. The people of all the states finally adopted this plan when they ratified
the Constitution.

The plan was first proposed in connection with the Ordinance for the government of the Northwestern Territory. While the Revolutionary War was still in progress, and before it was settled that America should hold that territory. it was proposed to divide it up, as fast as sufficiently populated, into new states, which were to be admitted to the Union on equal terms with the original thirteen. This provision the people approved, and it was embodied in the Ordinance, and thus became the American plan. Under it, three states were admitted to the Union before the time came for Ohio, a part of the Northwestern Territory, to apply. This form of federalism has succeeded far beyond any possible expectation of its first proposers. To it America owes her great constitutional expansion, the cementing of all her various local interests and feelings, her unusual strength as a large representative republic, and her present proud position among the nations of the earth. The Ordinance in question (including in this term the whole movement for establishing government in the Northwestern Territory) was the first evidence that this had been adopted by the American people as their ideal of government.

FREEDOM.

The war for the preservation of the Union purged the nation from the reproach, and its flag from the stain, of African slavery. This result was not an accident. Its causes were early implanted in our national life. The power that achieved this great work was the strong arms of freemen who were bred in the life of freedom, and devoted as by native instinct to her service. It was largely through the consecration of the Northwestern Territory to freedom by the Ordinance of 1787, that the ultimate nationalizing of liberty became possible. The dedication of that vast domain as the home of a race of freemen furnished the recruiting ground from which to enlist the legions who should sustain the banner of freedom against fierce opposition. If slavery was entrenched by the compromises of the constitution so as to necessitate an internecine struggle for its final overthrow, so was freedom by the Ordinance of 1787 so thoroughly entrenched as to make her banner and her army invincible when the crisis came.

The circumstance that, in the organization of the Southwestern Territory, Congress applied to it all the provisions of the famous Ordinance, except that prohibiting slavery, only

emphasizes the worth of the prohibition as to the Northwestern Territory. No one will now dispute the superior value of the Northwestern over the Southwestern plan of organizing territorial government.

The labored attempt of Chief Justice Taney, in the Dred Scott case, to decry the efficacy of the Ordinance as a charter of freedom, because of a want of expressly granted power, in the Articles of Confederation, for its enactment by Congress, has proved futile. That decision has become null, because it ran counter to the express opinion of the people. The Ordinance did not suffer for want of authority as a charter of freedom, because the people authorized and ratified it; and the well-nigh unanimous opinion of the people, since the close of the Civil War, concurs with and enforces that original opinion, and justifies the far-seeing wisdom of the men who were instrumental in dedicating an empire to freedom by an authoritative law.

RELIGIOUS LIBERTY AND POPULAR EDUCATION

were first adopted, as national ideals, by this Ordinance. They thus became a part of the birthright of the people of the states carved out of the Northwestern Territory. Though these principles were already adopted as fundamental by many of the states, they were by this Ordinance established in advance as parts of the foundations of other states whose ultimate greatness was foreseen. Never before did any great state paper operate to develop these principles on so large a scale.

Most natural was it, that the adjacent portions of the Louisiana Purchase, when organized, should be blessed with the same precious guarantees of education and free thought, by the incorporation of like provisions into the Ordinances enacted for their government. Thus did these peculiarly American institutions, the free church and free school, become a part of our national, no less than of our state, life. Broadened by it from local into continental operation, they are not the least among the priceless legacies left to the citizens of America by the Ordinance of 1787.

THE DUAL ORIGIN OF MINNESOTA.*

BY SAMUEL M. DAVIS.

It is the purpose of this paper to trace the origin and source of the territory now comprised within the boundary of the state of Minnesota. This state occupies the unique position of being the only state in the Union which acquired its territory from the two largest accessions of land to the United States in the early history of this government. I refer to the cession of the Northwest Territory by Great Britain in 1783 and the Louisiana Purchase in 1803. About twenty-nine thousand square miles of territory, including all east of the Mississippi which is now comprised within the boundary of the state, originated in the cession by the treaty with Great Britain in 1783. The remaining part, about fifty-five thousand square miles, was secured from the territory originally purchased from France in 1803. It is my object to sketch the main features connecting these two great treaties of accession of territory, both in relation to the boundary of the territory acquired and also with reference to the government provided for them after the territory was acquired.

CESSION OF THE NORTHWEST TERRITORY.

The Revolutionary War, which began April 19th, 1775, was closed by three separate treaties of peace. The United States and France conducted simultaneous negotiations with different English Commissioners, with the understanding that the preliminaries should be signed the same day. Dr. Franklin wrote to Vergennes on the 29th of November, 1782, that the American articles were already agreed upon and that he hoped to lay a copy of them before his Excellency the following day.

*Read at the monthly meeting of the Executive Council, April 10, 1899.

They were duly communicated, with the exception of a single secret article, but the French diplomat was astonished and mortified to find that they were already signed and therefore binding so far as the commissioners could make them so. The diplomatic game for despoiling the young republic of one half of her territorial heritage was effectually defeated. The French diplomatist reproved Franklin for the course which he and his associates had followed. Franklin replied as best he could, at the same time admitting that nothing more than a slight breach of politeness had been committed. The American people were at first disposed to censure the commissioners, but so anxious were all classes for peace and so much more favorable were the terms obtained than had been expected, that the expressions of dissatisfaction gave way to expressions of gratification and delight. The preamble to the treaty contained the saving clause that it should not go into effect until France and England came to an understanding, which fact Franklin diplomatically pressed upon the attention of the nettled Vergennes. The final treaty of peace between the United States and England was signed September 3rd, 1783. By this treaty Great Britain acknowledged the United States to be free, sovereign, and independent states, and relinquished all claims to the government, proprietary and territorial right of the same and every part thereof. The boundaries assigned proved to be more satisfactory than those which had been proposed in Congress in 1779.

It is not possible to divide among Benjamin Franklin, John Adams, and John Jay, the exact honor due each of saving the West to their country. To the man, however, who goes through the original documents, it would seem that we are not least indebted to John Jay for his distinguished services in this connection.

Great Britain's claim to the Northwest Territory was founded both on conquest and on the charters of the original colonies. Great Britain claimed not only all the land in the western country which was not expressly included in the charters and governments, and all the Mississippi, but also all such lands within them as remained ungranted by the king of Great Britain. England was slow to surrender so much of the Northwest as remained in her hands at the close of the war. Her refusal to surrender this territory was positive proof of the reluctance with which she consented to the north-

western boundaries. The boundaries negotiated by the treaty were much discussed and every proposition with reference to a different boundary had been considered. Mr. Adams tells us that one of these lines was the forty-fifth parallel north of the St. Lawrence river, and the other the line of the middle of the lakes. The British ministers, owing to their desire to give Canada a frontage on the four lakes, preferred the water boundary and chose the line which left the Northwest intact. Their decision was most fortunate for us. If the forty-fifth parallel had become the boundary, nearly half of Lakes Huron and Michigan and of the states of Michigan and Wisconsin, and a part of Minnesota, would have fallen to Great Britain. The boundaries finally decided upon were the middle of the chain of lakes on the north, and the Mississippi river on the west.

There is reason to think that England did not believe the young republic would be successful in maintaining an independent government, and her tardy transfer of the Northwest Territory to the United States was caused by a determination to share in the expected spoil that would result from the failure of our early government. The fact is that neither England nor Spain looked upon the treaty at Paris as finally settling the destiny of the country west of the Alleghany mountains. The war of 1812 no doubt revived England's hopes of again recovering the Northwest; and the efforts of Tecumseh to stay the oncoming tide of white population, and Hull's surrender of the Michigan territory, fanned these hopes into a bright flame. Harrison's success on the Maumee, and Perry's victory on Lake Erie, finally dashed her hopes to the ground. Only three of the thirty-two years between 1783 and 1815 were years of open war, yet for one half of the whole time the British flag was flying on the American side of the boundary line. The final destiny of the Northwest was not assured in its fullest sense until the treaty of Ghent.

The question of boundaries was, by the treaty of Paris, settled upon paper; but the actual boundaries were, for a considerable length of time, undetermined. It was not a foregone conclusion that the West should be delivered to the United States. The retention of the Northwest by Great Britain would have been a serious mischance in case subsequent events had turned out differently. The longer one considers the question, the more will he discover reasons for congratu-

lation that the logic of events gave us our proper boundaries at the close of the War of Independence,* and that we were not left to renew the struggle upon that question in after years with other European nations. The boundaries as determined by the diplomats at Paris, were, no doubt, fixed in good faith; but they had not only to be drawn upon paper, but also traced through vast wildernesses, uninhabited and unexplored. It was natural therefore that some of the lines were found impracticable. Some of the disputes that arose afterward had, however, other sources than ignorance of geography. A serious doubt arose as to the practicability of reaching the Mississippi by a due west line from the northwest point of the Lake of the Woods.† Jay's treaty, in 1794, therefore provided that measures should be taken in concert to survey the upper Mississippi, and, in case the due west line was found impracticable, it was further provided that "the two parties

---

*Article 2 of the Treaty of Paris reads thus: "And that all disputes which might arise in future on the subject of the boundaries of the said United States may be prevented, it is hereby agreed and declared that the following are and shall be their boundaries, namely: From the northwest angle of Nova Scotia, namely, that angle which is formed by a line drawn due north from the source of St. Croix River to the Highlands; along the said Highlands, which divide those rivers that empty themselves into the River St. Lawrence from those which fall into the Atlantic Ocean, to the northwesternmost head of Connecticut River; thence down along the middle of that river to the forty-fifth degree of north latitude; from thence by a line due west on said latitude, until it strikes the River Iroquois or Cataraquy [that is, the St. Lawrence]; thence along the middle of said river into Lake Ontario, through the middle of said lake until it strikes the communication by water between that lake and Lake Erie; thence along the middle of said communication into Lake Erie, through the middle of said lake until it arrives at the water communication between that lake and Lake Huron; thence along the middle of said water communication into the Lake Huron; thence through the middle of said lake to the water communication between that lake and Lake Superior; thence through Lake Superior northward of the Isles Royal and Phelipeaux, to the Long Lake; thence through the middle of said Long Lake, and the water communication between it and the Lake of the Woods, to the said Lake of the Woods; thence through the said lake to the most northwestern point thereof, and from thence on a due west course to the River Mississippi; thence by a line to be drawn along the middle of the said River Mississippi until it shall intersect the northernmost part of the thirty-first degree of north latitude. South, by a line to be drawn due east from the determination of the line last mentioned, in the latitude of thirty-one degrees north of the equator, to the middle of the River Apalachicola or Catahouche; thence along the middle thereof to its junction with the Flint River; thence straight to the head of St. Mary's River; and thence down along the middle of St. Mary's River to the Atlantic Ocean. East, by a line to be drawn along the middle of the River St. Croix, from its mouth in the Bay of Fundy to its source, and from its source directly north to the aforesaid Highlands, which divide the rivers that fall into the Atlantic Ocean from those which fall into the River St. Lawrence; comprehending all islands within twenty leagues of any part of the shores of the United States, and lying between lines to be drawn due east from the points where the aforesaid boundaries between Nova Scotia, on the one part, and East Florida, on the other, shall respectively touch the Bay of Fundy and the Atlantic Ocean; excepting such islands as now are, or heretofore have been, within the limits of the said province of Nova Scotia."

†The maps of the period put down the course of the river above the forty-fifth parallel as "the Mississippi by conjecture."

will thereupon proceed, by amicable negotiation, to regulate the boundary line in that quarter." This boundary was not fixed till more than twenty years later.

A convention was signed in London by the representatives of the two powers on May 12th, 1803, which contained arrangements for determining the boundary from the Lake of the Woods to the Mississippi. At about the same time the treaty for the cession of Louisiana to the United States was signed. When the London treaty came before the Senate the argument was made that the Louisiana Purchase would affect the line from the Lake of the Woods to the Mississippi. Accordingly the Senate struck out the article, and this caused the whole treaty to fall through. By the Louisiana Purchase we succeeded to all rights, as respects Louisiana, that had belonged to Spain or France, and this carried us north to the British possessions and west of the Mississippi river. On October 20th, 1818, the United States and England agreed to a convention which settled the Lake of the Woods controversy and established the boundary between the two countries as far as the Rocky mountains.*

The remaining boundary, from the intersection of the St. Lawrence and the forty-fifth parallel north to the foot of the St. Mary's river, was established in 1823, by a joint commission under the treaty of Ghent; and from the foot of the St. Mary's to the most northwestern point of the Lake of the Wood[S], by the Webster-Ashburton treaty in 1842.

The western boundary of the Northwest Territory was the Mississippi river to its source. All that part of Minnesota east of the Mississippi river was taken from the original Northwest Territory. From the source of the Mississippi river in Lake Itasca the line was drawn due north by 95 degrees and 12 minutes west longitude from Greenwich to a point known as the northwestern point of the Lake of the Woods. This line

---

* "It is agreed that a line drawn from the most northwestern point of the Lake of the Woods, along the forty-ninth parallel of north latitude, or, if the said point shall not be in the forty-ninth parallel of north latitude, then that a line drawn from the said point due north or south, as the case may be, until the said line shall intersect the said parallel of north latitude, and from the point of such intersection due west along and with the said parallel, shall be the line of demarcation between the territories of the United States and those of his Britannic Majesty, and that the said line shall form the northern boundary of the said territories of the United States, and the southern boundary of the territories of his Britannic Majesty, from the Lake of the Woods to the Stony Mountains."

This provision as to the boundary, together with the facts of geography, explains the singular projection of our northern boundary on the west side of the Lake of the Woods.

passes through the western part of the southern half of Red
Lake. The territory now included in Minnesota east of this
line, and east of the Mississippi river, comprises about one
third of the state. The balance of the present state of Minnesota was derived from the Louisiana Purchase.

THE ORDINANCE OF 1787.

In the early days the eastern portion of Minnesota territory
came under the jurisdiction of the Ordinance of 1787. The
vital point in the history of the entire Northwest was the
passage of this ordinance by Congress. The first question
that had to be decided was in regard to the ownership of the
territory ceded by Great Britain. This decision was made in
Congress by an agreement of the representatives of the different states. Seven states, Massachusetts, Connecticut, Virginia,
Georgia, New York, and both the Carolinas, claimed portions
of this territory. The claim of New York was based upon the
ground that she was the heir of the Iroquois Indians. The
other six states based their claims on various charters. None
of these claims were substantial or founded on very tenable
ground.

The first plan for a solution of the problem of sovereignty
over the western lands was brought forward by Maryland on
October 15th, 1777. This was proposed as an article of amendment to the articles of confederation then under discussion.
That amendment read as follows: "That the United States, in
Congress assembled, shall have the sole and exclusive right
and power to ascertain and fix the western boundary of such
states as claim to the Mississippi or South Sea, and lay out
the land beyond the boundary, so ascertained, into separate
and independent states, from time to time, as the numbers and
circumstances of the people thereof may require." The amendment failed, and one of an exactly opposite character was
passed, which put a prohibition on the United States government so that it should not deprive any state of any territory.
The principle contained in the Maryland amendment, however,
was a germinant idea which afterwards came to a fuller realization in the Ordinance of 1787. The Maryland proviso contained two propositions, an end to be reached, and a means of
reaching it. Maryland was one of the states that did not have
any claim to territory outside of her own limits. There were
at that time two classes of states, known as the landed states
and the states without any claim. Maryland was the pioneer

in bringing about a 'solution of the question for nationalizing the western land. She showed great hesitation in joining the confederation as long as the question was unsettled, and insisted that the titles of the claimant states were invalid, that there was no need of asking them to cede what they did not possess, and that the West should be declared outright a part of the Federal domain. The claimant states subsequently ceded their claims, Connecticut being the last, in 1786, to cede all her rights. The non-claimant states thus obtained their object, and the lands included in the Northwest Territory became part of the Federal domain and were nationalized so far as they could be under the Confederation. It was not until the Constitution was adopted that there was a national treasury into which the proceeds from the sale of lands could be turned.

It remained for Congress, under the conditions of the Ordinance of 1787, to determine the terms on which settlers could enter the new lands and on which new states should spring up therein. This ordinance was one of the most important acts ever passed by an American legislative body, for it determined with great wisdom and statesmanship that the new Northwestern states should be free from the taint and curse of negro slavery, and that education should receive just and due attention, asserting thus a principle which later has found expression in its being aided by the grant of a part of the public lands.

The important features of the Ordinance were contained in the six articles of compact between the confederated states and the people and states of the territory, and were to be forever unchanged except by consent of both parties.* It is difficult

---

*Article I declares, "No person demeaning himself in a peaceable and orderly manner shall ever be molested on account of his mode of worship or religious sentiments in the said territory."

Article II guarantees to the inhabitants the writ of *habeas corpus*, trial by jury, proportional representation in the legislature, and the privileges of the common law. The article concludes with the declaration that "no law ought ever to be made, or have force in the said territory, that shall, in any manner whatever, interfere with or affect private contracts or engagements *bona fide* and without fraud, previously formed." A few weeks later this provision was copied into the Constitution of the United States, but this is its first appearance in a charter of government. It was an outgrowth of the troublous commercial condition of the country. Lee, who originally brought it forth, intended it as a stroke at paper money.

Article III contains these words, which should be emblazoned on the escutcheon of every American State: "Religion, morality, and knowledge, being necessary to good government and the happiness of mankind, schools and the means of education shall forever be encouraged." It also says that good faith shall be observed toward the Indians.

Article IV ordained that "the said Territory, and the States which may be formed therein, shall forever remain a part of this Confederacy of the

to determine which of the provisions of the Ordinance were most important, but we cannot doubt that the one providing against the introduction of slavery was the greatest blow struck for freedom and against slavery in all our history, save only Lincoln's Emancipation Proclamation. This provision determined that in the final struggle the mighty and lusty young West should side with the right against the wrong. The fact is that the Ordinance of 1787 was so wide-reaching in its effects, was drawn in accordance with so high and lofty a morality and such far-seeing statesmanship, and was potent with such weal for the nation, that it will ever rank among the foremost of American state papers. "It marked out a definite line of orderly freedom along which the new States were to advance. It laid deep the foundation for that system of widespread public education so characteristic of the Republic and so essential to its healthy growth. It provided that complete religious freedom and equality which we now accept as part of the order of nature, but which were then unknown in any important European nation. It guaranteed the civil liberty of all citizens. It provided for an indissoluble Union, a Union which should grow until it could relentlessly crush nullification and secession; for the States founded under it were the creatures of the Nation, and were by the compact declared forever inseparable from it."*

The Ordinance of 1787 provided that not less than three and not more than five states should be carved out of the territory

---

United States of America, subject to the Articles of Confederation, and to such alterations therein" as might be made, and to the laws enacted by Congress. After some provisions in regard to taxation, it concludes as follows: "The navigable waters leading into the Mississippi and St. Lawrence, and, the carrying-places between the same, shall be common highways and forever free, as well to the inhabitants of the said Territory as to the citizens of the United States, and those of any other States that may be admitted into the Confederacy, without any tax, impost or duty therefor."

Article V provided for the division of the Territory into States, not less than three nor more than five, and drew their boundary lines, subject to changes that Congress might afterwards make. A population of 60,000 free inhabitants should entitle any one of these states to admission, not "into the Union," a phrase that came in with the Constitution, but "by its delegates into the Congress of the United States, on an equal footing with the original states in all respects whatever," and to "form a permanent constitution and State government," with the proviso that "the constitution so to be formed shall be republican, and in conformity to the principles contained in these articles."

Article VI dedicated the Northwest to freedom forever. "There shall be neither slavery nor involuntary servitude in the said Territory, otherwise than in punishment of crimes whereof the party shall have been duly convicted." But this prohibition was coupled with a proviso that stamps the whole article as a compromise: "Provided, always, that any person escaping into the same, from whom labor or service is lawfully claimed in any one of the original States, such fugitive may be lawfully reclaimed and conveyed to the person claiming his or her labor or service as aforesaid."

*Theodore Roosevelt, The Winning of the West, vol. iii, p. 259.

thus acquired. It will be interesting for us to note, in a later part of this paper, the circumstances and conditions which caused a part of this territory to be included in Minnesota after five states had already been admitted.

THE LOUISIANA PURCHASE.

The interest that attaches to the Louisiana Purchase is romantic as well as historic. The vast territory acquired by the United States in its early history laid the foundation for the subsequent greatness of the republic. The soil contained within this area had belonged successively by discovery and conquest to several of the powerful and aggressive nations of Europe. Zealous and pious missionaries traversed its length and breadth in the service of their earthly kings, and for the spiritual welfare of the aboriginal nations inhabiting its wide extended plains. Daring and adventurous explorers and discoverers ploughed its rivers with their canoes and laid open the vastness of its extent, and the magnificent resources and treasures of its wealth, like an open book. At length it was returned to the dominion of France. Napoleon was directing the affairs of the French nation, and was in need of funds to equip her armies for conquest. The United States stood ready to purchase Louisiana. Events were hurrying Napoleon to a conclusion.

On April 10th, 1803, Napoleon called to him two of his counsellors, Marbois and Decres, and addressed them in regard to the cession of Louisiana in that peculiar and vehement manner which he commonly manifested in political affairs. Napoleon's words are given by Marbois, in his History of Louisiana, as follows:

I know the full value of Louisiana, and I have been desirous of repairing the fault of the French negotiator who abandoned it in 1762. A few lines of a treaty have restored it to me, and I have scarcely recovered it when I must expect to lose it. But if it escapes from me, it shall one day cost dearer to those who oblige me to strip myself of it, than to those to whom I wish to deliver it. The English have successively taken from France, Canada, Cape Breton, Newfoundland, Nova Scotia, and the richest portions of Asia. They are engaged in exciting troubles in St. Domingo. They shall not have the Mississippi which they covet. Louisiana is nothing in comparison with their conquests in all parts of the globe, and yet the jealousy they feel at the restoration of this colony to the sovereignty of France acquaints me-

with their wishes to take possession of it, and it is thus that they will begin the war. They have twenty ships of war in the Gulf of Mexico; they sail over those seas as sovereigns, whilst our affairs in St. Domingo have been growing worse every day since the death of Leclerc. The conquest of Louisiana would be easy, if they only took the trouble to make a descent there. I have not a moment to lose in putting it out of their reach. I know not whether they are not already there. It is their usual course, and if I had been in their place, I would not have waited. I wish, if there is still time, to take away from them any idea that they may have of ever possessing that colony. I think of ceding it to the United States. I can scarcely say that I cede it to them, for it is not yet in our possession. If, however, I leave the least time to our enemies, I shall only transmit an empty title to those republicans whose friendship I seek. They only ask of me one town in Louisiana; but I already consider the colony as entirely lost, and it appears to me that in the hands of this growing power it will be more useful to the policy, and even to the commerce, of France, than if I should attempt to keep it.

The ministers thus addressed gave opposite opinions. Marbois declared that France should not hesitate to sacrifice what was about slipping away from her; that war with England was inevitable; that there were no means at hand to send garrisons to protect the province; that the colony was open to the English from the north by the great lakes, and if they should show themselves at the mouth of the Mississippi, New Orleans would immediately fall into their hands; that nothing was more certain than the fate of European colonies in America, and that the French had attempted to form colonies in several parts of the continent of America, but had in every instance failed; and that, in order to make the colony of Louisiana in any degree successful, it would be necessary to have all the labor performed by slaves, although slavery must be regarded as the most detestable scourge of the human race.

Decres, on the other hand, gave an entirely opposite opinion. He pointed out that France was still at peace with England; that the colony had just been ceded to the French, and depended on the First Consul to preserve it; that to retain it would be of inestimable importance to commerce and to the maritime provinces; that France, deprived of her navy and her colonies, would be stripped of half her splendor, and a greater part of her strength; that Louisiana could indemnify France for all her losses; that when an inter-ocean canal should be cut through the Isthmus of Panama, Louisiana, being

on the track of trade thus opened up, would assume an importance of inestimable value to France; and that, if it were necessary to abandon St. Domingo, Louisiana would take its place.

Napoleon terminated the conference without making his intentions known. The discussion had been prolonged far into the night. At daybreak he summoned Marbois, and had him read the dispatches that had just arrived from London. He was informed in them that naval and military preparations of every kind were being made with extraordinary rapidity. Upon hearing of England's preparation for war, Napoleon declared:

Irresolution and deliberation are no longer in season. I renounce Louisiana. It is not only New Orleans that I will cede; it is the whole colony, without any reservation. I know the price of what I abandon, and have sufficiently proved the importance that I attach to this province, since my first diplomatic act with Spain had for its object the recovery of it. I renounce it with the greatest regret. To attempt obstinately to retain it would be folly. I direct you to negotiate this affair with the envoys of the United States. Do not even wait the arrival of Mr. Monroe; have an interview this very day with Mr. Livingston. But I require a great deal of money for this war, and I would not like to commence it with new contributions. For a hundred years France and Spain have been incurring expenses for improvements in Louisiana, for which its trade has never indemnified them. Large sums, which will never be returned to the treasury, have been lent to companies and to agriculturists. The price of all these things is justly due to us. If I should regulate my terms according to the value of these vast regions to the United States, the indemnity would have no limits. I will be moderate, in consideration of the necessity in which I am of making a sale. But keep this to yourself. I want fifty millions [francs], and for less than that sum I will not treat; I would rather make a desperate attempt to keep those fine countries. . . . .

Perhaps it may also be objected to me, that the Americans may be found too powerful for Europe in two or three centuries; but my foresight does not embrace such remote fears. Besides, we may hereafter expect rivalries among the members of the Union. The confederations that are called perpetual only last till one of the contracting parties finds it to his interest to break them, and it is to prevent the danger to which the colossal power of England exposes us, that I would provide a remedy.

Mr. Monroe is on the point of arriving. To this minister, going two thousand leagues from his constituents, the President must have given, after defining the object of his mission, secret instructions, more

34

extensive than the ostensible authorization of Congress, for the stipulation of the payments to be made. Neither this minister nor his col-
league is prepared for a decision which goes infinitely beyond anything
that they are about to ask of us. Begin by making them the overture,
without any subterfuge. You will acquaint me, day by day, hour by
hour, of your progress. The Cabinet of London is informed of the
measures adopted at Washington, but it can have no suspicion of those
which I am now taking. Observe the greatest secrecy, and recommend
it to the American ministers; they have not a less interest than yourself in conforming to this counsel. You will correspond with ⅄. de
Talleyrand, who alone knows my intentions. . . . Keep him informed
of the progress of this affair.*

The import of this declaration was communicated to Talleyrand and soon bore fruit, for on the same day Talleyrand
surprised Livingston with a new offer.   Talleyrand asked Livingston whether the Americans wished to have the whole of
Louisiana.   Livingston replied that we only desired New Orleans and the Floridas.   The French minister said that if they
gave us New Orleans, the rest would be of little value, and
wished to know what we would give for the whole.   Pressed
for an answer, Livingston declared that while it was a proposition he had not thought of, he supposed we should not object
to a price of twenty million francs, if our claims were paid.†
The conversation of Talleyrand at this interview would go to
show that the resolution to sell Louisiana had been taken,
and that now the negotiation was only a matter of price.

The proposition thus suddenly made to Livingston quite
confounded him.   He had been endeavoring for a long time
to bring the First Consul and his Secretary of Foreign Affairs
to some definite proposal with regard to the Louisiana territory, but nothing had been gained, although he had written
and talked much upon the question.   Neither Talleyrand nor
Napoleon could charge that he had been in any sense negligent
in his duties in this regard.   Livingston endeavored, on the
following day, April 12th, to reap the fruits of his labors by
an interview with Talleyrand, without the assistance of Monroe.   Monroe had just come upon the scene, but had not as
yet conferred with Livingston, nor had he been presented
to any of the French officials.   He had that very day reached

*History of Louisiana, Barbé Marbois; American translation, 1830, pp.
274-277.

†Livingston to Madison, April 11, 1803; American State Papers, Foreign
Relations, vol. ii, p. 552.

Paris. Livingston attempted to close the matter up more definitely with Talleyrand, but was unable to do so. The astute Frenchman declared that his proposition was only personal, and that he did not have proper authority to make it binding, and finally excused himself on the ground that, as Louisiana was not yet theirs, he could make no terms for its sale.*

In this same letter Livingston states that Monroe passed April 13th with him in examining documents; that, while Monroe and several other gentlemen were at dinner with him, he observed the Minister of the Treasury, Marbois, walking in the garden; and that, upon invitation, Marbois came in while they were taking coffee. After his being some time there, Livingston and he strolled into the next room, "when," says Livingston, "he told me he heard that I had been at his house two days before, when he was at St. Cloud; that he thought I might have something particular to say to him, and had taken the first opportunity to call on me. I saw that this was meant as an opening to one of those free conversations which I had frequently had with him. . . . . He went away, and, a little after, when Mr. Monroe took leave, I followed him."

The conversation of the leading American and the leading French negotiator of the treaty, as stated in this midnight letter, forms one of the most interesting chapters in diplomatic history. It appears that after a social cup of coffee these two representatives of two great nations practically settled the purchase of half a continent. Both Livingston and Marbois treated each other with perfect frankness and candor, and it is owing to this friendly and informal conversation that the terms of the treaty were settled so easily and amicably. It is certainly true in this instance that the after-dinner coffee and cigars figured as prominently in the negotiations as did the laborious and painstaking diplomacy of Monroe and Talleyrand.

Up to the time of the actual opening of the negotiations for the purchase of Louisiana, Livingston had no direct instructions from Madison, the Secretary of State, to purchase any part of the territory; and on April 17th, 1803, Livingston complained in a letter to him, that the commission contained power only to treat for lands on the east side of the Mississippi. "You will recollect that I have been long pre-

---

*Livingston to Madison, April 13, 1803, midnight.

paring this government to yield us the country above the Arkansas. . . . . I am therefore surprised that our commission should have entirely lost sight of that object."

The following week the ministers passed in attempting to reduce the price asked for Louisiana. They had frequent interviews with Marbois, and pressed upon him to name as early a day as possible for the reception of Mr. Monroe at court. Marbois told Livingston that he would speak to the First Consul at once on the subject of their negotiations, and that he hoped some person would be appointed to treat with the American envoys, even before Mr. Monroe was presented. In consultation, Monroe and Livingston determined to offer fifty million francs, including the debt due to the citizens of the United States from France. "I reminded him of the Consul's promise to pay the debt. I placed in the strongest light his personal obligation on this subject; and desired him to urge it as an additional reason to conclude an agreement which would facilitate the means of doing it. The next morning . . . . I again called to see him. He told me that he had been to St. Cloud; that the Consul received his proposition very coldly; and that I might consider the business as no longer in his hands, since he had given him no further powers; that he had urged the Consul's promise relative to the debt, which he admitted, but said, at the same time, he did not think it had exceeded three millions, though my letter expressly mentioned twenty."*

Livingston had used many and persistent endeavors to consummate the purchase and cession of this territory. He had addressed memorials and notes of great length to the Minister of Foreign Affairs and also to the First Consul, and while they answered these notes politely, the replies were not satisfactory. The vast territory to which France had received title by her treaty with Spain formed the basis of many plans and calculations. Among the most favored projects of the First Consul had been the colonization of Louisiana. He saw in it a new Egypt; he saw in it a colony that was to counterbalance the eastern establishment of Britain; he saw in it a provision for his generals; and, what was more important in the then state of things, he saw in it a pretense for the ostracism of suspected enemies. His advisers generally favored

*Livingston to Madison, April 17, 1803.

the plans of the First Consul, and they would not hear of any disposition of it by sale. A commercial sale of the territory had never been relished by those who controlled the destinies of France. Livingston firmly believed that one of the reasons why a sale was considered at all, was that our debt would be fully and promptly paid. Without ready funds at hand to pay this debt, Napoleon saw that by selling Louisiana not only could he pay the debt, but at the same time raise sufficient funds to wage another war.*

Napoleon drew up a convention which he trusted to Marbois, which outlined certain propositions of the proposed treaty. One of these provided for the disposition of the territory about to be ceded: "In consequence of said cession, Louisiana, its territory and its proper dependencies, shall become part of the American Union, and shall form successively one or more states, on the terms of the Federal constitution." French commerce, at the same time, was to be fostered by the United States, and given all the privileges of American commerce, with a perpetual right of navigation and certain fixed points of entry. In addition, the United States were to assume all debts due to American citizens under the treaty of September 30th, 1800, and to pay in addition thereto one hundred million francs to France.

On April 27th Marbois brought the document proposed by Napoleon to a meeting of the three ambassadors at Mr. Monroe's headquarters. He was forced to admit that Napoleon's plan was unreasonable. He also produced, along with Napoleon's scheme, a substitute of his own, somewhat more reasonable in its terms. Livingston endeavored to give American claims precedence. He desired to have these disposed of in case the cession failed. Monroe thought differently about this matter, and they took Marbois' propositions with a view to considering them. After working over them for a day, the American ministers drew up a series of articles embodying their own ideas. On the 29th they gave Marbois the draft of their articles, proposing to offer fifty million francs to France, and twenty million on account of her debt to the citizens of the United States. Marbois replied that he would proceed only upon the condition that eighty millions were accepted as the price, and to this the American ministers assented; and,

*Livingston to Madison, May 12, 1803.

with this change, Marbois took their proposition for reference to the First Consul. On the 30th of April, Marbois held the final and conclusive consultation with Napoleon, and at this meeting the terms betweeen the parties were agreed upon.

On the following day Monroe was formally presented at court, and dined at the Tuileries with Livingston. At that meeting Napoleon said nothing of the business, except that he agreed it should be settled without further delay, and on the same evening the American ministers had a final discussion of the subject with Marbois. The treaty and convention for the sixty million francs to be paid to France was actually signed on the 2d day of May. The convention respecting American claims took more time and was not signed until about May 9th. All of these documents were dated as of April 30th, the day on which Marbois had his final conference about the business with Napoleon. The treaty of cession was communicated by Livingston and Monroe to Mr. Madison on the 13th of May. In a letter accompanying it they explained some of the difficulties in accomplishing the transaction.

An acquisition of so great an extent was, we well know, not contemplated by our appointment; but we are persuaded that the circumstances and considerations which induced us to make it, will justify us in the measure to our government and country. Before the negotiation commenced, we were surprised that the First Consul had decided to offer to the United States, by sale, the whole of Louisiana, and not a part of it. We found, in the outset, that this information was correct, so that we had to decide, as a previous question, whether we would treat for the whole, or jeopardize, if not abandon, the hope of acquiring any part. On that point we did not long hesitate, but proceeded to treat for the whole. . . . . On mature consideration, therefore, we finally concluded a treaty on the best terms we could obtain for the whole. . . .

The terms on which we have made this acquisition, when compared with the objects obtained by it, will, we flatter ourselves, be deemed advantageous to our country. We have stipulated, as you will see by the treaty and conventions, that the United States shall pay to the French government sixty millions of francs in stock bearing interest of six per cent.; and a sum not exceeding twenty millions more to our citizens, in discharge of the debts due them by France, under the convention of 1800.*

*Livingston and Monroe to Madison, May 13, 1803; American State Papers, Foreign Relations, vol. ii, p. 558.

With the exception of the correspondence of the American ministers, there is no official report to show that the commissioners of the respective governments met in formal conference, nor any record of their proceedings or discussions. No record was left of the date when the agreement was made, although it was one of the most important measures that has ever taken place in American history. There is a cloud of shadow and mystery surrounding it. There is no doubt that the treaty itself, as well as the statements of Livingston, evidences that the consummation of the treaty by all parties was hasty.

The treaty of cession did not attempt to define the boundaries of Louisiana. The words with reference to the boundaries were taken from Berthier's original treaty of retrocession: "Louisiana, with the same extent that it now has in the hands of Spain, and that it had when France possessed it, and such as it should be after the treaties subsequently entered into between Spain and other states." This statement was convenient for France and Spain. All that the United States knew, on the other hand, was that Louisiana, as France possessed it, had included a part of Florida and the whole of the Ohio valley as far as the Allegheny mountains and lake Erie.

The agreed price represented the sum of $11,250,000, and the further sum of $3,750,000 for the payment of debts due to the citizens of America, making a total of $15,000,000 as the price to be paid. The second convention attached to the treaty, relating to the debts of indemnity due from France, was probably not drawn with the greatest degree of skill. This was originally drawn by Livingston and afterwards was modified by Monroe and Marbois, and was not signed until nearly a week after the treaty of purchase. The stipulations in the convention were arbitrary and the document was not accurate. It is probable that neither Livingston nor Monroe gave very careful attention to it. Its most serious defect was in the fact that the estimate of twenty million francs was very much below the amount of the claims which the French admitted in the treaty; besides, there was no rule of apportionment, and the right of final decision was reserved to France in every case. Some of these defects may be accounted for

by the statement of Livingston that the moment was critical and the question of peace or war was in the balance, and that it was important to come to a conclusion before either scale preponderated. As the indemnity provided by this convention was considered to be a mere trifle compared with the great object of the treaty, namely, the purchase of the territory, and as it had already been delayed for a long time, the American ambassadors were ready to take it in almost any form.

This position of Livingston, as viewed in the light of subsequent history, was correct. He was right in securing his main object at any cost. It is true that he might have saved his reputation as a diplomatist if he had given more time to the convention relating to claims. He could, however, have gained no more than he did for the government. The two conventions of 1800 and 1803 gained for the United States two objects of great value. The first released the United States from treaty obligations which, if carried out, would require war with England. The second secured for the Union the whole west bank of the Mississippi and the province of New Orleans, together with all advantages that would subsequently flow therefrom. In return, the United States promised not to press the claims of its citizens against the French government, except to the amount of $3,750,000, which represented one-fourth part of the purchase price of Louisiana. From almost every point of view, the negotiators, as well as their government, were to be congratulated upon the satisfactory terms then consummated.

In the many transfers of this territory, no complete or accurate boundary had ever been drawn. It now became necessary to define accurately the boundaries of the new territory. The treaty of cession had quoted the third article of the treaty of Ildefonso, and Louisiana had been ceded to the United States "with the same extent that it now has in the hands of Spain, and that it had when France possessed it, and such as it should be after the treaties subsequently entered into between Spain and other states." This description is not definite nor certain, and it could only be determined by the rules of international law.

The original province of Louisiana embraced not only the territory west of the Mississippi, but also West Florida to.

the Perdido river. West Florida had already been ceded to France by Spain at the time of the treaty of St. Ildefonso, and by the treaty between Spain and the United States in 1795 the boundary line between the United States and West Florida had been established. This explains the last clause of the third article of the treaty. In the case of Johnson vs. McIntosh, Chief Justice Marshall says that in the discovery of this immense continent, the nations of Europe were eager to appropriate to themselves so much of it as they could respectively acquire; but, as all were in pursuit of the same object, it was necessary, in order to avoid war with each other, to establish a principle which all should acknowledge as the law by which the right of acquisition should be regulated. The principle thus adopted was that discovery gave title to the government by whose subjects or by whose authority it was made, against all other European governments, which title might be consummated by possession. France rested her title on the vast territory she claimed in America on discovery. It was on this ground that she claimed Louisiana, through the discovery of La Salle in 1682.

After the protracted war between England and France, which was terminated by the treaty of Paris in 1763, France ceded to Great Britain all of Louisiana north of the Ohio and east of the Mississippi. This war was really one for supremacy in the western world. When it was over, French power was at an end in America.

The American ministers at first had insisted on defining the boundaries, and Marbois had presented their request to Napoleon. He refused any information upon the matter of boundaries, and intentionally concealed the boundary he himself had defined. A knowledge at this time of the exact boundary claimed by France would have prevented a tedious and humiliating dispute. Being unable to secure any information from Napoleon as to the boundaries, Livingston first went to Marbois.

I called this morning upon M. Marbois for a further explanation on this subject, and to remind him of his having told me that Mobile made a part of the cession. He told me that he had no precise idea on the subject, but that he knew it to be an historical fact, and that on

that only he had formed his opinion. I asked him what orders had been given to the prefect who was to take possession, or what orders had been given by Spain, as to the boundary, in ceding it. He assured me that he did not know, but that he would make inquiry.

Afterward Livingston went to Talleyrand for the same purpose.

I asked the minister what were the east bounds of the territory ceded to us. He said he did not know; we must take it as they had received it. I asked him how Spain meant to give them possession. He said, 'According to the words of the treaty.' 'But what did you mean to take?' 'I do not know.' 'Then you mean that we shall construe it in our own way?' 'I can give you no direction; you have made a noble bargain for yourselves, and I suppose you will make the most of it.'*

The answer of Talleyrand would not have been different, even if Livingston had known that Victor's instructions received from Decres, which began by fixing the very boundaries under discussion, were still in the desk of the astute diplomat.

The western boundaries of the purchase were not more certain. There were joint claims of France and Spain to the territory lying west of the Sabine river. France based her claims upon the occupation of La Salle, and Spain upon the general extent of her Mexican possessions. In acquiring Louisiana, the United States obtained the rights of France to the regions west of the Sabine. At the time of the purchase the western boundary of Louisiana was the Rio Bravo or Rio Grande river, if we concede that La Salle, in taking possession of the Bay of St. Bernard, carried rights to the great river which was midway between his post and the nearest Spanish settlement at Panuco. Jefferson held that this claim was valid.†

It was a question, however, which remained in dispute until 1819, when the United States abandoned all claims west of the Sabine. According to this treaty, the boundary line between the territory of Spain and that of the United States was to run from the mouth of the Sabine river along its west bank to the 32nd degree of latitude; thence due north

---

*Livingston to Madison, May 20, 1803; American State Papers, Foreign Relations, vol. ii, p. 561.

†Letter of Jefferson to John Melish, the geographer.

to the Red river; thence westward along that river to the
100th degree of longitude west from London; thence north
to the Arkansas river; thence along its southern bank to the
42nd degree of latitude; and.thence west along that parallel
of latitude, to the South sea.

The northern boundary of the Louisiana Purchase was, at
the time of the making of the treaty, admitted to be the source
of the Mississippi. It had been assumed by the treaty of 1783
that this source was northwest of the Lake of the Woods and
beyond the 49th degree of north latitude, and Pickering, in a
memoir to Jefferson, intended that the boundary west from
the Lake of the Woods to the Mississippi should be on that
parallel. In 1818 a convention of Great Britain, recognizing
the fact that the "most northwestern point" of the Lake of the
Woods might be distant from the 49th parallel, provided that
the line from that point should be due north or south, as was
required, until it struck that parallel, and thence westward on
that parallel to the crest of the Rocky or Stony mountains.
This line was subsequently agreed upon in the Webster-Ashburton treaty of 1842. There has been considerable controversy as to the northwestern limits of the Louisiana Purchase,
as to whether or not any part of the territory west of the
Rocky mountains was included in the treaty of cession.

Marbois, in his History of Louisiana, published twenty-six
years after the treaty by which the United States acquired
Louisiana, says: "The shores of the western ocean were certainly not included in the cession; but the United States are
already established there." He further states that the boundaries were uncertain, and that in his conference with Napoleon
he spoke to him of the obscurity of that article of the treaty,
and the inconvenience of a stipulation so uncertain, to which
Napoleon replied, "If an obscurity did not already exist, it
would perhaps be good policy to put one there."*

The map which accompanied this work of Marbois, in its
original publication in Paris, showed the territory extending
from the Mississippi to the Pacific ocean, as the "Acquisition
of the United States by the treaty and by its results." This

*Marbois' History of Louisiana, p. 286.

would seem to imply that the whole territory, in the mind of
Marbois, was not acquired by the treaty. General Stoddard,
who took possession of Upper Louisiana in March, 1804, takes
substantially the same view. In giving the boundaries of the
territory, he says that it is bounded "south on the Gulf of
Mexico; west, partly on the Rio Bravo, and partly on the Mexican mountains; north and northwest, partly on the Shining
mountains [Rocky mountains], and partly on Canada [New
France]; east on the Mississippi from its source to the thirty-
first degree; thence extending east on the line of demarkation
to the Rio Perdido; thence down that river to the Gulf of
Mexico."*

The French apparently never actually claimed as far as the
Pacific, but many authorities have held that the right of con-
tiguous territory would give to the United States the entire
country west of the Rocky mountains. Whatever may have
been the boundaries of the territory ceded to us by France,
it was all comprised and included under the name of Louisiana.

The history in brief of the transfers of the territory so
named is as follows: that La Salle, under a royal commission
from Louis XIV, discovered the mouth of the Mississippi in
1682; that in the name of that sovereign he claimed the river
and all its tributaries and all the country watered by those
streams, under the name of Louisiana; that the country was
explored and occupied from the mouth of the Mississippi to
its source; that on the 14th of September, 1712, Louis XIV
granted this territory to Crozat, declaring that the edicts, ordinances, and customs of Paris should be observed; that afterwards, the assignee of Crozat surrendered the country back
to the king; that on the 3d of November, 1762, France ceded
to Spain all of Louisiana west of the Mississippi river, and
all east of that stream and south of the 31st degree of north
latitude, including thus the province of New Orleans; that in
1800 Spain retroceded the same country to France, by the
treaty of St. Ildefonso, except as the territory may have been
changed by the treaties made by Spain; and that on the 30th
day of April, 1803, this same territory was ceded to the United
States, and is known in our history as the Louisiana Purchase.

*Stoddard's Sketches of Louisiana, 1812, p. 148.

TERRITORIAL GOVERNMENTS.

Not only was the area which now comprises the State of Minnesota partially embraced in the Northwest Territory ceded to the United States by Virginia in 1783, but that part was subsequently included successively in the territories of Indiana, Illinois, Michigan, and Wisconsin. The other and larger part of Minnesota, west of the Mississippi, was in like manner successively a part of the territories of Louisiana, Missouri, Michigan, Wisconsin, and Iowa.

On December 20th, 1783, the legislature of Virginia passed an act to authorize the delegates of that state in Congress to convey to the United States all the rights of that commonwealth to the territory northwest of the Ohio river. This act empowered the representatives of that state in Congress, by proper deed or instrument in writing, to convey and make over to the United States for the benefit of said states, all right, title, and claim, as well of soil as jurisdiction, which the State of Virginia had to the territory or tract of country, within the limits of the Virginia charter, which was situated northwest of the Ohio river. The conditions of cession were that the territory so ceded should be laid out and formed into states of suitable extent and territory; that the states so formed should be distinct republican states, and admitted members of the Union, having the same rights of sovereignty, freedom, and independence as the other states; and that the necessary expenses incurred by Virginia in subduing the British possession or in acquiring any part of the territory so ceded should be fully reimbursed by the United States, and that these expenses should be arranged by three commissioners. The deed of cession thus provided for was made on the 1st day of March, 1784, by Thomas Jefferson, Samuel Hardy, Arthur Lee, and James Monroe, the delegates then in Congress from Virginia.

After Congress decided to divide the Northwest Territory into not more than five nor less than three states, as proposed in article five of the Ordinance of 1787, the State of Virginia ratified such action of Congress in 1788 by a special act. This was to avoid any difference of interpretation that might arise from the size of the new states as provided by the original act of cession passed by Virginia in 1784.

Pursuant to an act of Congress approved April 30th, 1802, the people of the eastern division of the territory northwest of the Ohio river, under the name of the State of Ohio, were permitted to form a constitution for state government.

The remaining portion of the Northwest Territory had been constituted a separate territory on May 7th, 1800, and was known as Indiana Territory. On February 3rd, 1809, Indiana Territory was divided into two separate governments, and all of that territory which lay west of the Wabash river and a direct line drawn from the Wabash river and Post Vincennes due north, with all other territory lying between the United States and Canada, constituted a separate territory called Illinois.

By an act of Congress passed January 11th, 1805, all that part of Indiana Territory which lay north of a line drawn east from the southern bend or extremity of lake Michigan until it should intersect lake Erie, and east of a line drawn from the said southerly bend through the middle of lake Michigan to its northwest extremity, and thence due north to the northern boundary of the United States, was, for the purpose of government, constituted a separate territory, called Michigan.*

When the territorial government of Wisconsin was formed by an act of Congress approved April 20th, 1836, it included the whole of the present State of Minnesota.†

*The boundaries of Michigan as established by this act were necessarily changed by the acts of Congress approved April 9th, 1816, June 18th, 1818, June 28th, 1834, and April 20th, 1836. The act of 1818 extended the territory westward to the Mississippi river, and the act of 1834 added the territory between the Mississippi river on the east and the Missouri and White Earth rivers on the west. Michigan territory then extended from Lakes Erie and Huron westward to the Missouri river, and from the States of Ohio, Indiana, Illinois, and Missouri, northward to the British dominions.

†The Territory of Wisconsin was bounded as follows: On the east, by a line drawn from the northeast corner of the State of Illinois, through the middle of lake Michigan, to a point in the middle of said lake and opposite the main channel of Green Bay, and through said channel and Green Bay, to the mouth of the Menomonie river; thence through the middle of the main channel of said river, to that head of said river nearest to the Lake of the Desert; thence in a direct line to the middle of said lake; thence through the middle of the main channel of the Montreal river, to its mouth; thence with a direct line across Lake Superior, to where the territorial line of the United States last touches said lake northwest; thence on the north, with the said territorial line, to the White Earth river; on the west, by a line from the said boundary line following down the middle of the main channel of White Earth river, to the Missouri river, and down the middle of the main channel of the Missouri river to a point due west from the northwest corner of the State of Missouri; and on the south, from said point, due east to the northwest corner of the State of Missouri; and thence with the boundaries of the States of Missouri and Illinois, as already fixed by acts of Congress.

By an act of Congress approved March 26th, 1804, the territory acquired by the Louisiana Purchase was divided into the territories of Louisiana and Orleans. In the original act the former was designated as the "District" of Louisiana; but a supplementary act of Congress approved March 3rd, 1805, names it the Territory of Louisiana. By an act of Congress approved June 4th, 1812, its name was changed to the Territory of Missouri.

In 1834, Congress passed an act relative to certain parts of the Louisiana Purchase, as follows: "Be it enacted, etc., That all that part of the territory of the United States bounded on the east by the Mississippi river, on the south by the State of Missouri, and a line drawn due west from the northwest corner of said state to the Missouri river; on the southwest and west by the Missouri river and the White Earth river, falling into the same; and on the north by the northern boundary of the United States, shall be, and hereby is, for the purpose of temporary government, attached to, and made a part of, the Territory of Michigan, and the inhabitants therein shall be entitled to the same privileges and immunities, and be subject to the same laws, rules, and regulations, in all respects, as the other citizens of Michigan territory." This was the first special provision made for the government of that portion of the Territory of Missouri not included within the boundaries of the State of Missouri, which had been defined by the act of Congress approved March 6th, 1820.

When the territory of Wisconsin was formed, as before noted, in 1836, it included this part of the Louisiana Purchase. Again, after two years more, when the territorial government of Iowa was formed by an act of Congress approved June 12th, 1838, its boundaries included the same part of the present state of Minnesota, west of the Mississippi, which during the preceding four years had been thus successively under the jurisdiction of Michigan and Wisconsin. The act of Congress forming Iowa declares that "all that part of the present territory of Wisconsin which lies west of the Mississippi river, and west of a line drawn due north from the headwaters or source of the Mississippi to the territorial line, shall, for the purposes of temporary government, be and constitute a separate territorial government by the name of Iowa."

Congress, on March 3rd, 1849, passed an act providing for the territorial government of Minnesota. The Territory of Minnesota extended west beyond the boundary of the present State, and included parts of both North and South Dakota. The promoters of the interests of Minnesota also desired and attained the incorporation of a part of the Northwest Territory with that larger tract of the Louisiana Purchase, to form the new territory.

On the west of the St. Croix river and extending to the Mississippi river, there lay a remnant of the Northwest Territory, out of which, by a provision of the Ordinance of 1787, only five states could be formed. After Iowa was admitted as a state, the region north of its northern line and west of the Mississippi, formerly belonging to Iowa as a territory, was known as the Indian country. The Mississippi, from the time of formation of the Territory of Iowa, was the recognized western boundary line of Wisconsin Territory. In the various bills that originated in Congress, and in the two conventions held in Wisconsin to adopt a state constitution, the question of the western boundary of Wisconsin was a leading one. There were many propositions advocated, both in Wisconsin and in Congress. One was to include the entire country east of the Mississippi, and east of a line drawn from its source north to the British possessions, within the new state; another was to make the Rum river the western boundary, thence extending to Lake Superior; another made the St. Croix river the western boundary; and still another, the Chippewa river. It was argued, by those who favored the proposition first noted, that the Ordinance of 1787 made it compulsory to limit the entire Northwest Territory to five states. On the other hand, it was claimed that the fifth and last state to be organized out of the Northwest Territory could be restricted in its boundary, so that a portion of the territory east of the Mississippi could be taken in connection with a portion of the territory west of that river and north of Iowa to make a future state, without in any way violating the provisions of the Ordinance of 1787. In the end this view was carried out, but not before many disputes and contentions arose. A compromise was finally reached between the contending factions, and the boundary line of the St. Croix river was determined upon.

This was approved by the constitutional convention, and was confirmed by a vote of the citizens of Wisconsin. It was finally accepted and approved by Congress in admitting the state to the Union.

When Minnesota was organized as a territory in 1849, its boundaries were fixed in the Enabling Act and extended on the west to the Missouri river.* The territory at that time was little more than a wilderness; and the Indian title to the lands upon the west bank of the Mississippi, from Iowa to lake Itasca, had not been extinguished.

Under successive acts of Congress the Louisiana Purchase had been divided into various territories. By an act of Congress, approved March 26th, 1804, the southern part of the Louisiana Purchase was constituted as the territory of Orleans, its northern boundary on the east side of the Mississippi being at the south line of the Mississippi Territory, and on the west side of the river at the 33rd degree of north latitude. The residue of the Louisiana Purchase was called the District of Louisiana, and was placed under the jurisdiction of Indiana Territory. By a subsequent act of March 3rd, 1805, the District of Louisiana was designated by the name of the Territory of Louisiana. A governor was appointed to serve three years, and a secretary for four years, and the legislative power of the territory was vested in the governor and three judges or a majority of them.

By an act approved June 4th, 1812, Congress changed the name of Louisiana Territory to Missouri, and provided more fully for its territorial government. The executive officers were the governor and secretary, for three and five years respectively. The legislative power was vested in a general assembly consisting of the governor, a legislative council of nine

---

*The boundaries of Minnesota Territory were designated in this act as follows: "Beginning in the Mississippi river, at the point where the line of forty-three degrees and thirty minutes of north latitude crosses the same; thence running due west on said line, which is the northern boundary of the state of Iowa, to the northwest corner of the said state of Iowa; thence southerly along the western boundary of said state to the point where said boundary strikes the Missouri river; thence up the middle of the main channel of the Missouri river to the mouth of the White Earth river; thence up the middle of the main channel of the White Earth river, to the boundary line between the possessions of the United States and Great Britain; thence east and south of east, along the boundary line between the possessions of the United States and Great Britain, to Lake Superior; thence in a straight line to the northernmost point of the state of Wisconsin in Lake Superior; thence along the western boundary line of said state of Wisconsin, to the Mississippi river; thence down the main channel of said river to the place of beginning."

35

members appointed by the president, for five years, five of whom were to constitute a quorum, and a house of represent-atives elected by the people to serve for two years. The judicial power was vested in a superior court and such inferior courts as would be found necessary. Among the provisions of this act we find two that seem worthy of mention. One of these shows that the principle of the government holding public lands was fully understood and approved at this time. It reads as follows: "The general assembly shall never inter-fere with the primary disposal of the soil by the United States." The other enactment referred to taxation, and pro-vided that "the lands of non-resident proprietors shall never be taxed higher than those of residents."

ADMISSION OF MINNESOTA TO THE UNION.

On December 24th, 1856, there was a bill introduced into Congress by Henry M. Rice, delegate from the Territory of Min-nesota, authorizing the people of that territory to form a con-stitution. The bill was referred to the Committee on Terri-tories, of which Galusha A. Grow of Pennsylvania was chair-man. A substitute bill, which afterwards became the En-abling Act, defined the boundaries of the proposed state as they now exist.* This act changed the boundaries some-what from those provided by the bill of Mr. Rice. John S. Phelps, of Missouri, in commenting upon the boundaries of the proposed state, declared that, since five states had already been formed from the Northwest Territory, it would be a vio-lation of the Ordinance of 1787 to incorporate a part of that territory into a new state. Advocates of the measure, how-ever, did not look upon it in that light. The bill was brought

---

*"Beginning at the point in the center of the main channel of the Red river of the North. where the boundary line between the United States and the British possessions crosses the same; thence up the main channel of said river to that of the Bois des Sioux river; thence up the main channel of said river to Lake Travers; thence up the center of said lake to the southern extremity thereof; thence in a direct line to the head of Big Stone lake; thence through its center to its outlet; thence by a due south line to the north line of the State of Iowa; thence east along the northern boundary of said state to the main channel of the Mississippi river; thence up the main channel of said river, and following the boundary line of the State of Wis-consin, until the same intersects the Saint Louis river; thence down said river to and through Lake Superior, on the boundary line of Wisconsin and Michigan, until it intersects the dividing line between the United States and the British possessions; thence up Pigeon river, and following said dividing line, to the place of beginning." Congressional Globe, vol. 43, Appendix, p. 402.

to vote with very little debate, and was passed by 97 in favor
to 75 against it.

In the Senate the debate was more prolonged and somewhat acrimonious. Senator Thompson, of Kentucky, made a
speech of strenuous opposition, in which the fact that he was
a partisan upon the question of slavery distinctly appeared.
When Minnesota asked for admission to the Union two opposing forces were contending for supremacy in the territory secured by the Louisiana Purchase. The party in favor of slavery were zealous to maintain their rights, and to reserve as
much as possible of the new territory for the propagation of
their peculiar institution. Previous to the admission of California, in 1850, which was the last state received into the Union
before Minnesota, there were fifteen states in which the institution of slavery was permitted, and the same number in which
it was prohibited by law. This great contest was renewed
with increased vigor by the Kansas-Nebraska bill of 1854; and
when, two years afterward, Minnesota applied for admission
to the Union, the pro-slavery and the anti-slavery forces were
striving in every way to gain the mastery in Kansas. Senator
Thompson said:

> These Minnesota men, when they get here and see my friend
> from Michigan [Cass] and my friend from Iowa [Jones] struck down,
> will grapple up their bones from the sand, and make handles out of
> them for knife blades to cut the throats of their Southern brethren. I
> want no Minnesota senators. . . . . I know some men talk about an-
> nexing Canada and all New France; but I hope that, when they come
> in, we shall go out. I do not wish to have any more of Mexico annexed,
> unless you annex it by a treaty so controlling its regulations and mu-
> nicipal institutions as to erect it into a slave State. The equilibrium
> in the Senate is destroyed already. There is now an odd number of
> States, and the majority is against the slave-holding States. I want
> no hybrid, speckled mongrels from Mexico, who are free-state people.
> It is bad enough to have them from New England, Christianized and
> civilized as they are. . . . . My notion of governing the territories
> is, that they ought to be governed by a proconsul, and pay tribute to
> Caesar. I would not puff them up with Treasury pap or plunder in
> the way of public lands, like an Austrian horse that is sleek and
> bloated with puff, instead of real fat and strength, by putting arsenic
> in his food. Are you to stall-feed the people in these Territories? No,
> sir. I would treat them differently. Like boys that get too big for
> their breeches, they ought to have rigid discipline administered to

them; they ought to be made to know their place, and constrained to
keep it. We are told of there being two hundred thousand people in
Minnesota. I do not care if there are five hundred thousand. . . . .
Minnesota is undoubtedly a portion of the Louisiana Purchase. . . . .
This, it seems to me, under the treaty of Louisiana, is incontestably
slave territory.*

It is worthy of notice that the principles laid down in the
Ordinance of 1787 dominated all of the state papers relating to
the admission of Minnesota to the Union. The provisions of
that ordinance are clearly to be found in the organic act for
the establishment of the territorial government, passed March
3rd, 1849, as also in the act authorizing the state government,
passed February 26th, 1857; and finally they were embodied
in the constitution of the state itself. We find, of the main
articles of the Ordinance of 1787 which have been thus preserved, article one, referring to religious belief; article two,
forming the bill of rights of the people; and article three,
relating to education and good government.

It is also noteworthy that these same provisions, which related to all the Northwest Territory under the Ordinance of
1787, have passed over to, and have been dominant in, the
constitutions and governments of almost all the states that
have been carved out of the Louisiana Purchase. This fact
alone would seem to show the great importance and enduring
character of the principles laid down in the ordinance itself.
The territory which accrued to the United States by the cession
of Great Britain in 1783 was not nearly as extensive as that
obtained from France in 1803, yet the principles early laid
down for the government of the smaller acquisition have prevailed in the commonwealths formed from either. Thus the
Ordinance of 1787 became a protecting ægis which extended
its authority and power far beyond the limits to which it originally applied. This is clearly seen in the state of Minnesota,
which formed a connecting link binding parts of the two great
cessions into a single commonwealth; but, if further proof
were required, it would be discovered in the constitutions of
nearly every state between the Mississippi and the Pacific.

*Congressional Globe, vol. 43, p. 850.

549-550

CELEBRATION OF THE FIFTIETH ANNIVERSARY
OF THE ORGANIZATION OF THE MINNESOTA
HISTORICAL SOCIETY, IN THE HALL OF THE
HOUSE OF REPRESENTATIVES, ST. PAUL,
MINN., WEDNESDAY, NOVEMBER 15, 1899.

FIFTIETH ANNIVERSARY COMMITTEE OF THE
EXECUTIVE COUNCIL:

HENRY L. MOSS,   WILLIAM P. CLOUGH,
RUSSELL BLAKELEY,   GEORGE H. DAGGETT,
GREENLEAF CLARK,   WILLIAM G. LE DUC,

WARREN UPHAM, Secretary.

FIFTIETH ANNIVERSARY ADDRESSES.
AFTERNOON SESSION.

The meeting in the afternoon, at half past two o'clock, was opened by Hon. Henry L. Moss, chairman of the Anniversary Committee, who said:

Ladies and Gentlemen: Fifty years ago, on November 15th, 1849, the Minnesota Historical Society was organized under an act of the legislature of the Territory at its first session, which received the approval of Governor Ramsey on October 20th, 1849. To-day we have with us, as the present president of the society, that first Governor of the Territory of Minnesota, and I have the pleasure of now asking him to take his seat and preside on this occasion.

As Governor Ramsey stepped forward, he was greeted with great and prolonged applause. The order of the program was then taken up, including the following invocation and addresses.

INVOCATION.

BY REV. ROBERT FORBES, D. D.

Almighty God, our Father, we bow reverently in Thy presence. We draw nigh unto Thee. We come with reverence that Thou art the great and mighty God. We approach with filial confidence because Thou art our Father. We render thanks unto Thee that in the order of Thy providence we are permitted to assemble in this place. We remember that every good and perfect gift cometh from Thine hand, and we thank Thee for all that life is and all that it means to us. We give thanks unto God for all the beautiful sights that please the

eye, for this beautiful world in which we live, for the forest
and the field, for the mountain and the valley, for the land and
for the sea, for the sun that shines by day and the moon and
the stars by night.   Glory be to God the Father, the Son,
and the Holy Spirit.   We thank Thee for the pleasant sounds
that fall upon the ear, for the words of wisdom that Thou
revealest to babes, and for the life of childhood.   We thank
Thee for the world within, the world of reason and memory
and hope and imagination.   We give thanks for our country,
this great land we so proudly call our own, the land of our
birth and of our fathers' graves; and we pray, O Lord God,
that Thy blessing may still rest upon this nation, so that the
world shall continue to rejoice in the light of America's civilization and her pure form of Christianity.

We pray for the blessing of heaven to come upon this
great State, this State of Minnesota.   O, we thank Thee for
what it is, for the prairie and the forest and the mine, for
all the treasures that are here; not only for material blessings, but we thank Thee for home and school and college and
church, and for all the benevolent institutions that exist.   God
grant His blessing upon this great State.   Let Thy mercy come
to the men and the women who are here to-day and are particularly interested in the work of this Historical Society.   We
thank Thee for the brave, manly men, and the womanly women, who came here in the early days and laid the foundations
of this State.   The wise man said, long ago, "The hoary head
is a crown of glory if it be found in the way of righteousness"; and we have ourselves observed that nearly all the
hoary heads are found in the way of righteousness.   "The
wicked shall not live out half their days."   God grant His
blessing upon the men and women here assembled, and upon
all the interests they represent.   We thank Thee for our civilization, for the hope given unto us in the Gospel, for the idea of
our immortality.   O, Lord God, bless the churches of every
name, Catholic and Protestant, Jew and Gentile, orthodox and
heterodox.   This poor old world is not so rich in goodness,
truth, and devotion and loyalty, and love and self-sacrifice,
that we can afford to slight any agency that promises to do
even a little good.   God bless the churches and the schools, and
the teachers in the schools, and the professors in our colleges

and universities, all the people who in any way mold and direct public sentiment, and guide us all by Thy counsels.

And we thank Thee for the pleasant, the beautiful dream of the hereafter,—that land where every winter turns to spring, that land that is fairer than day, the land of which the poets have sung, the land of which our mothers have told us, and the land in whose existence we most certainly believe in our own highest and best moments. We thank Thee for the idea that we shall never die, that we shall simply lay this throbbing dust aside and step out into the unending life.

O God of our fathers, help us to be good and true, to walk in the way of righteousness. Bless us and our children, and our children's children, and all the people everywhere, and bring us at last to the glory of that better land. In Jesus' name. Amen.

GREETING.

BY HON. JOHN LIND, GOVERNOR OF MINNESOTA.

Human development and culture, in their inception at least, are probably the outgrowth of the unconscious activity of the race to adjust itself to the varying phases of physical nature,— of its environment. Every new condition to which man has been subjected has developed and called into play new faculties, and has added new powers to the individual, and new forces to society. It is for this reason that every migration has resulted in advancement, both of the individual and of the social body of which he became a member.

This principle is nowhere more forcibly illustrated than in our own land, and, I might say, than in our own state. The character of all of our people has been shaped by the influence of one or more successive migrations. That the original settlers on the Atlantic coast, within a few generations, differentiated from the populations from which they had descended, and developed new traits and characteristics in response to the new environment and new conditions to which they were subjected and which they had to meet, is a matter of history. That every subsequent migration to the westward contributed to this accumulation of human experience new elements of the most

varied and comprehensive character, cannot be questioned. As a result, I believe it safe to say that we have in the West, and particularly in the Northwest, a population which for energy, versatility, physical and mental power, and genius, is not excelled in the world. This, if I am right in the proposition suggested, is in part due to their manifold experiences inherited and acquired. The wonderful pluck and energy of the pioneers of this state; the ease and facility with which they adjusted themselves to frontier conditions; the phenomenally short time in which they transformed these conditions into those of culture and civilization, and the forethought and acumen with which they shaped our institutions and established agencies for the future development of a high degree of culture and civilization among our people, as evidenced by this society and by our magnificent common school system, seem to me confirmatory of the view advanced.

That our incomparable growth and progress as a nation and as a state have been in a large measure due to the opportunities which a rich and new country have afforded, and to the dormant faculties in the human mind which new conditions and the new environment have tended to stimulate and develop, is probably conceded by all; and, if conceded, it also admonishes us of the fact that these factors will not be so actively operative in the future as they have been in the past, and one might conclude from this premise that our continued advancement will not be as rapid as heretofore. I think, however, that it is safe to assume that society, at least in this country and in our own state, has arrived at a stage of development and culture whence it will consciously and knowingly continue to guide the development of a higher civilization and better social conditions, notwithstanding that the factors which have unconsciously contributed to that end are not so active as they have been in the past. And to this conscious, positive work for the betterment of society, it seems to me that no single factor, except our common schools, will contribute more than the work of this society and the material which it has accumulated. History has been defined as the biography of society. We know that the individual profits by the conscientious study of the life of other great individuals. As suggested, I believe that civilization has now reached a point where society can profit by the study of its own biography.

Your society has written and is writing a biography, not only of pioneers, but of a young commonwealth. No greater work, nor one fraught with more promise for the future, could be undertaken. The people are beginning to appreciate its value, as is shown by more liberal contributions, both from individuals and from the state, from time to time.

On this memorable occasion it does not become me, belonging as I do to a later generation, to occupy much of your time. I congratulate those of you who were present and co-operated in the establishment of this society, fifty years ago, on the work that you then did, and on the wisdom and public spirit that prompted you to such action, and I trust that the present and future generations may profit by your example. Especially does it afford me pleasure to see present with us to-day the Hon. Alexander Ramsey, who occupied the position which I now hold at the time this society was organized, and who has contributed so much to the growth, development, and honor of our state. I know that I voice the feelings of all present when I express the hope that he may long continue with us, enjoying the same physical and mental vigor which have always been his portion. No higher tribute can be paid to the memory of the patriotic men who founded this society, nor any greater compliment to the early members thereof who are still with us, than is implied in the very fact that a commonwealth so young as ours is enabled to celebrate the fiftieth anniversary of its Historical Society.

To this celebration the honor has been conferred upon me to formally extend you the State's welcome, which I do most heartily, both as a citizen and as the Chief Executive of our great State.

RESPONSE.

BY THE PRESIDENT, HON. ALEXANDER RAMSEY.

The members of the Historical Society of Minnesota, after fifty years of effort to bring it to its highest degree of usefulness, which have immeasurably succeeded, felt that upon this occasion, fifty years having transpired and still a number of those who came here at that early day being amongst us, it

was a proper thing to have a celebration of the organization of this society. We all feel proud at the response which you have given to the suggestion from us, and hope that you all and others will also be present here to-night.

My friends, if you had been here with us at the earliest days when the light began to shine upon this province of ours, you would scarcely have expected to find in fifty years so large, bright and intelligent an audience as I see before me, now collected here. It is not an ordinary thing to raise upon the plains of a new and primitive country, yet inhabited by its oldest possessors, a population and measures of progress such as we see instituted in this country, such as we have now here. When I came here in 1849 and looked out upon the new State or Commonwealth (which we anticipated it would be in a short time) of Minnesota, you can scarcely imagine what it was like. It was one vast, unoccupied, unpossessed, unimproved country, spreading far and wide, with beautiful plains green with herbage, large and small rivers running to the sea, and in every way a beautiful and hopeful prospect. I am glad we have advanced as far as we have. I have been in the whole history of this northwest country, and I might say in the whole history of the United States during the same period of fifty years. There is scarcely an instance in which a population as large and as progressive and intelligent as ours has been brought together in so short a time. Then there was scarcely anything that could be dignified with the name of town or village. I landed here in St. Paul, and, looking around, I saw here and there, and at another distant place, a small cabin, half a house, or something of that kind. When I revisited my old home in Pennsylvania, it was after Mr. Neill had built the first brick house in St. Paul, up near where the Metropolitan Hotel stands. Some of my old neighbors, with the intent, I suppose, of triumphing over a little pride I was exhibiting, asked me, "Have you a brick house in town?" "We have a brick house," said I; and it was the only one we had. It saved me the mortification of saying we had none.

This country, as you know, the territory of the State of Minnesota, is quite large. It is, indeed, within a small fraction of figures, as large as the States of Pennsylvania and New York, which are in the first rank, as to area, among the states

of the Union. Nearly all of Minnesota, about as large as both those states, was owned at that time by the Indians. Two great tribes that figure conspicuously in Indian history, the Dakotas and the Ojibways, were here, the Dakotas occupying nearly half the area, and the Ojibways the other half in the north. We happened to be located with our towns and earlier settlements in the southern part of this region, in the Dakota country. And from that early beginning, in fifty years, with the country occupied in wars and troubles of one sort and another, we have been growing to an extent that no one probably at the time anticipated. By even the most farsighted, it could scarcely have been anticipated. We have large towns, quite large towns. Here is one close west of us, probably with a population of two hundred thousand, or more; we in the capital city count somewhat less, but we are very willing to be equal with our neighbor, and may some day attain it. We have other towns of sixty, and twenty, and twelve thousand inhabitants. We have a university which would be the pride of any state, surpassed in its number of students by only one or two others in the Union. We have every kind of institution which usually shows the growth of civilization and increased population, and all this has been achieved in fifty years of time. I doubt whether in the whole history of our country any instance of so great progress of a new state can be pointed out.

So late as 1851, after the treaties with the Dakota Indians at Traverse des Sioux and Mendota, I was instructed by the government to take a party and proceed to the Red river valley, near the British line, to make a treaty with the Ojibways of Red river, and with those on the west side of the river, for the extinguishment of their title, that the government might distribute lands for homes among the settlers who had come down in great numbers from the Red river country, as it was then called, comprising the Selkirk settlements. This was probably in the month of August or September of 1851. We had a military escort, not a very large one, for our protection in the Indian country; and a great number accompanied the expedition, for one purpose and another. We proceeded to Sauk Rapids. The roads of course were very indifferent, the settlements had just commenced, and there with considerable difficulty we were assisted in crossing the Mississippi river,

and thence passed out to the Bois des Sioux river, which is one of the headwaters of the Red river of the North. We passed down the far side of the Red river, and at a point which I suppose to have been about ten miles west of where the city of Fargo now is, we came across a monstrous herd of buffalo. I think there must have been five thousand in it. We traveled with them, and they with us. We were indifferent to each other. We occasionally killed one. And so we went down to near the crossing of the river, near the present town of Pembina. There we camped for three or four weeks and negotiated a treaty with those Indians. In all that distance, I was going to say, in all that long line of four hundred miles, we did not see, excepting those who belonged to our own party, a white man or a white woman, an Indian, or a mixed-blood,— not one in over four hundred miles. We saw no other human beings than those who were with us. Since that time progress has taken place in that formerly uninhabited and unimproved country. Now all that country is occupied by farms, villages, and towns; it is cut up into counties; and the organizations which characterize a prosperous and cultured people have followed. Schools have been erected, colleges established, and every kind of benevolent and charitable institution. You have them everywhere, just as perfect as in any state in this Union.

But I need not further recall the past, nor contrast it with the present time, tracing the steps of our advance. These themes will be well considered by those gentlemen who have been specially appointed to address you. They will review the work accomplished by this Historical Society, and the progress of Minnesota and of the United States, during the fifty years since the organization of our society and of Minnesota Territory.

Wm. G. Le Due
Hastings, Minnesota

ORGANIZATION AND GROWTH OF THE MINNESOTA HISTORICAL SOCIETY.

BY GEN. WILLIAM G. LE DUC.

Because I am one of the few surviving members of the Minnesota Historical Society whose record of membership dates back to the year 1850, the year in which the active life of the society began, I have been assigned the task of reciting such of the incidents of organization and growth as may be recapitulated in the brief period of ten to fifteen minutes. The limitation of time will therefore permit me only to outline the beginning and somewhat of the progress of a beneficent literary institution, which in the most unpretentious manner began its existence in a frontier log tavern on Bench street in the then village of St. Paul, fifty years ago. This subject has heretofore been treated by other members of the society, and I can add but little, if anything, beyond a repetition or verification of statements made at previous meetings.

The society had its origin in the suggestion and action of one whose unpopularity at that time and afterward tended to hinder, rather than to promote, any scheme he might have proposed or been associated with. Seeking the real genesis of the Minnesota Historical Society, the reason why the Secretary of the Territory, Charles K. Smith, took active interest in this matter, I found in the printed records of the society, in an address made by our venerable President Ramsey, that he surmised that Mr. Smith had been connected with a historical society in his native state, Ohio, and saw the importance of collecting the past and current history of the new country to which he had been sent as secretary of the territorial government. This suggestion is very close to the truth.

Mr. Smith and other young men of his age, living in the interior and western part of Ohio, were enthused by the writings and lectures of the learned antiquarian and historian of that state, Hon. Caleb Atwater, a prominent lawyer, member of the legislature, author, lecturer, and United States official, a graduate of Williams College, who emigrated from Massachusetts in 1811 and settled in Ohio at Circleville. This town was located on the banks of the Scioto river, upon the site of what had evidently been a very large and important town of the mound builders, whose circular earthwork gave name to the modern American town of Circleville. The valley of the Scioto had been occupied by a numerous population well enough advanced in the arts and sciences of construction to measure accurately, lay out geometric forms, and construct earthworks that were in a remarkable state of preservation hundreds of years after their abandonment by the builders. No historic record of that people could be found, other than the mounds and fortifications upon which oak trees had grown and fallen and decayed, giving place to others that had grown to the maturity of hundreds of years. Mr. Atwater devoted much time to a patient examination of these earthworks at Circleville and other places in Ohio, making surveys, maps and records of the contents of mounds, and preserving whatever he found of pottery, stone or metal implements, and other remnants of a vanished and forgotten race, whose monuments proved them to have been a numerous and agricultural people. He published, among other books, a volume entitled "Western Antiquities," which attracted much attention to historic matters. I was a school boy in Ohio at that time, and I speak from personal knowledge of the influence of Mr. Atwater's books and lectures on the youth of that period. We were all antiquarians, collectors, and historical society boys.

Charles K. Smith, who lived at Hamilton, not far from Circleville, was thus indoctrinated with the historical fervor which manifested itself later in the southeast corner room of Robert Kennedy's log tavern on Bench street, St. Paul. This room was Mr. Smith's office as the territorial secretary. Here he drew up an act, in two sections, to incorporate the Historical Society of Minnesota, and included as incorporators, with

himself, the names of eighteen others, embracing the members of the territorial government (excepting the governor, Alexander Ramsey), and the principal other persons then in Minnesota Territory who would probably feel any interest in the subject. None of the incorporators were consulted; it was assumed that they would not object to be included in an act of incorporation which contained only two sections, and by which no apparent responsibilities were incurred. This act was approved the 20th day of October, 1849, by Governor Ramsey. A certified copy was made November 10th, 1849, by Mr. Smith; and the society was formally organized on November 15th, 1849, in the office of Secretary Smith.

This meeting consisted of the chairman, William Henry Forbes, a Canadian born, then in the service of the American Fur Company, the secretary, Charles Kilgore Smith, and others of the corporate members. L. A. Babcock, David Olmsted, J. C. Ramsey, and Henry L. Moss are shown to have been present by the record of motions which they proposed. The organization of the Society was completed by the election of officers. Alexander Ramsey was elected as president; David Olmsted and Martin McLeod, vice presidents; William H. Forbes, treasurer; and C. K. Smith, secretary. A committee, consisting of L. A. Babcock, Franklin Steele, Judges Goodrich and Cooper, H . L. Moss, Dr. T. R. Potts, and D. B. Loomis, was appointed to draft a constitution and by-laws and report at a meeting to be held on the second Monday in January, 1850, the date of the first annual meeting fixed by the charter.

Secretary Smith now enlisted the willing services of the Rev. Edward Duffield Neill to attract attention to the society. At a meeting held January 1st, 1850, in the Methodist church, on Market street, an address was delivered by Mr. Neill, the subject of which was, "The French Voyageurs to Minnesota during the Seventeenth Century." This address, which was the first of a series of most interesting and instructive historical contributions made by Rev. Dr. Neill to the Historical Society, attracted the attention of the people of Minnesota Territory; and, as it was published and widely distributed, it received praise from many scholars and historians, and put the Minnesota Historical Society upon a plane of respectability.

36

With this lecture the rude methods of tradition passed for Minnesota, and the pen of our historian and beloved comrade Neill began the record.

The annual meeting, having been advertised in the Chronicle and Register (an administration paper published in St. Paul), was held on Monday, January 14th, 1850, at the office of C. K. Smith. It secured an attendance of eight, four of whom were of the incorporators; but none of the officers who had been elected was present, excepting the secretary. Six of those recorded as present were young lawyers, whose time was not so much occupied with the duties of their profession at that time as it was subsequently, for they all became active and influential citizens. These were L. A. Babcock, who was attorney general for the Territory, appointed by the governor; Henry L. Moss, who was the first United States attorney for the district of Minnesota; A. Van Vorhes, afterwards a land officer for the United States at Stillwater; James B. Wakefield, who was lieutenant governor of Minnesota for the years 1876 to 1880; Michael E. Ames, an astute lawyer, whose services were in demand in the more important cases in court while he lived, but who died early; and Morton S. Wilkinson, known to most of this audience, who represented the state in the National Congress, first in the Senate, and later in the House of Representatives. Only one of the eight present in that meeting survives, the Hon. Henry L. Moss, whom we are happy to hear answer to the call of his name at each monthly council meeting of the Society, and who is the chairman of the committee in charge of the organization and conduct of this semi-centennial celebration.

Judge David Cooper, who had been named as one of the incorporators, presided over the meeting. A report of the committee on a constitution and by-laws was called for, and was made nominally by Mr. Babcock as chairman, and was read by the secretary. This required discussion and amendment; and, on motion of Mr. Wilkinson, the constitution and by-laws were taken up article by article, amended, and adopted.

To this constitution and the by-laws were appended the names of one hundred and twenty-two persons as resident

members, embracing nearly every white man in the Territory, who by article tenth of the by-laws were expected to pay the initiation fee of one dollar and sign the constitution before participating in the business of the society. The list contains the names of a few who came somewhat later than January, 1850, my own name being one of these.

The next meeting of the Minnesota Historical Society was its second annual meeting, held in the Methodist Episcopal church, on January 13th, 1851. It was presided over by the president of the society, Governor Ramsey, assisted by the vice presidents, Hon. David Olmsted and Martin McLeod. On this occasion the president delivered an address; and Hon. Martin McLeod read an interesting letter from the Rev. S. R. Riggs, the subject of which was "The Destiny of the Indian Tribes." This letter included a brief and modest notice of the work of the author in compiling a dictionary of the Dakota language. Mr. George L. Becker also read a paper, contributed by Henry R. Schoolcraft, LL. D., on the "History and Physical Geography of Minnesota."

Subsequently, at an adjourned meeting held on January 29th, with Governor Ramsey presiding, the society adopted a resolution pledging its aid for the publication of a "Dakota Lexicon," compiled by Rev. Mr. Riggs and his associates of the Dakota Mission. A committee of twenty-one members was appointed to procure subscriptions for this purpose. In June, 1852, this work, comprising a grammar and dictionary of the Dakota (or Sioux) language, was published by the Smithsonian Institution, under the patronage of the Historical Society of Minnesota. It forms a quarto volume of 338 pages, being the fourth volume in the series of Smithsonian Contributions to Knowledge.

This unique publication, and its distribution among colleges, libraries, and historical societies, gave rise to much favorable comment and expressions of admiration for a state in embryo whose people had taken such timely action in the preservation of the unwritten language of a nation of aborigines, who must necessarily disappear or be absorbed by the English-speaking white race. It was also the means of securing many and valuable exchanges and donations of books for our library.

From that second annual meeting may be dated the active virile existence of the Minnesota Historical Society, whose birth and nursing care up to this time had been the one notable, commendable public work of Charles Kilgore Smith. He became very unpopular and objectionable to the people of Minnesota; and complaints sent to Washington, demanding his removal, became so frequent and earnest that his sponsor, Secretary Thomas Corwin, a relative by marriage, advised his resignation. He left the Territory some time during the season of navigation in 1851.

The Executive Council of the Historical Society filled the vacancy in the office of secretary resulting from Mr. Smith's departure by the election of the Rev. Edward D. Neill, November 18th, 1851. No better appointment than this could have been made. The business of the society was now entrusted to a man who graduated from Amherst College before he was nineteen years old, was the next year a student in Andover Theological Seminary, and then completed his studies in theology with that eminent master and scholar, the Rev. Albert Barnes. Mr. Neill was an enthusiastic, tireless student of history, who mined to the bottom for facts; and facts only, as he understood them, would satisfy his truth-loving nature. He entered upon his duties as secretary, and prosecuted his work for the society during twelve years as a labor of love and not of profit. His contributions to the publications of the society commenced with the first address in the Methodist church on New Year's day, 1850, and continued with more or less frequency throughout his service as secretary; and even to the very day of his sudden and lamented death, in 1893, he constantly had in contemplation some interesting topic for the Historical Society records.

To the Rev. Dr. Neill this society is chiefly indebted for the high position it attained in the favorable estimate of scholars during his secretaryship, for the great increase of its library and museum, and for its growing popularity with the intelligent reading members of our legislatures and with scholars everywhere. Amid all the varied duties of his life, as organizer of churches, schools, and colleges, superintendent of education for the Territory and State, chaplain of the immor-

tal heroes of the First Minnesota Regiment in the Virginia campaign, secretary to Presidents Lincoln and Johnson, consul in Ireland, and professor in Macalester College, whatever time was not occupied in the faithful discharge of the duties of his position, he gave to historical studies and publications, which, continuing through more than forty years, contributed greatly to the honor of the Minnesota Historical Society.

Among the early and zealous friends of our society, to whom much praise is due, was another immigrant from Ohio, Daniel A. Robertson, who was the editor of a Democratic paper in Territorial days. He deplored the impecunious condition of our society, whose meetings were held at the offices or rooms of the members, and whose freight bills and postage expenses were matters of personal solicitation. Resolutely he set about the task of collecting money to purchase lots and erect thereon a suitable fireproof building, in which to preserve our valuable accumulations that were then stored, on sufferance, wherever rents were not demanded. Mr. Robertson joined with him other prominent citizens, and made earnest and persistent application for a room in the capitol, which was finally granted for temporary use. November 27th, 1855, the society met for the first time therein. We were extremely gratified to see our books arranged on shelves, and the donations of various kinds properly displayed, even though it was but a temporary shelter enjoyed at the will of state officials.

Mr. Robertson vigorously pushed his scheme for raising money from the sale of life memberships. At the annual meeting on January 15th, 1856, he reported the sale of sixty-two life memberships at twenty-five dollars each, and was authorized to close a conditional purchase he had made of two lots on Wabasha street. Here it was determined to excavate and lay the foundation for the proposed building.

By means of a grand parade and ceremony in laying the corner stone, it was expected that favorable attention would be drawn to the building proposition, that life memberships would sell freely, that citizens would make liberal subscriptions, and that the legislature would contribute what might be lacking. The laying of the corner stone June 24th, 1856, was the occasion of the most notable procession and public

display that had ever occurred in Minnesota. The military authorities at Fort Snelling sent their full band. Major Sherman and his battery (not W. T. Sherman, afterward General, but Thomas W. Sherman, who had won fame in Mexico with his "Flying Artillery") headed the procession, which marched through the streets and to the foundation, where the corner stone was to be laid.

Hon. George L. Becker, who was mayor of St. Paul at that time, being then as now an honored citizen of Minnesota, delivered an address. Lieut. M. F. Maury, of the United States Navy, who had already distinguished himself and honored his country by his original scientific work in charting ocean currents and making routes for the safer and more speedy navigation of the Atlantic Ocean, also gave an address. The corner stone was laid with Masonic ceremonies; and there, I trust, it remains safe, with its contents undisturbed, up to this day.

The financial storm of 1857 was approaching, and life memberships were unsalable; conditional subscriptions stopped at $15,000, some were withdrawn, and others were expected to be withdrawn; and the legislature declined to make any appropriation for the building. Col. Robertson, discouraged and beaten, went to Europe for a year's rest and recreation.

The room at the capitol occupied by our society was demanded for the use of the state auditor, and the Executive Council rented a small room adjoining the St. Paul Library room in the Ingersoll Block, at the southeast corner of Third and Wabasha streets. This was the humble home of the society during the incumbency of Mr. Charles E. Mayo as secretary, from 1864 to 1867, a period in which the unsettled condition of public affairs prevented any considerable growth.

On the 21st of January, 1867, John Fletcher Williams was elected secretary. He served in that capacity faithfully and efficiently until his resignation in 1893, a period of twenty-six years, during which time there was a constant and increasing interest exhibited by the people of the state and by the successive state legislatures. The society was recognized as a state institution by appropriations of money that enabled its officers to largely extend its usefulness, and to increase ma-

terially its valuable library of books and newspapers. Notwithstanding the impairment of its property by the fire that on March 1st, 1881, destroyed the old capitol, in which were its library and museum, the society has experienced a constant and healthy growth, under different secretaries, up to the present day. Now, under the present careful and efficient management, it is in the front rank with any similar institution of the same age in any state or country.

I have passed lightly over the more recent growth of the society, for it would require an extension of the time allotted to me for the presentation of this subject. To realize that our growth has been phenomenal for the half century, it is only necessary to enumerate the number and consider the value of the publications of the society, and the catalogue of its library, which now contains a grand total of 63,500 volumes, bound and unbound; and to note that our unique and most valuable collection of Minnesota newspapers commences with the first number of the first paper published in Minnesota Territory in the year 1849, and continues down to the present day. The library is now receiving regularly four hundred and twenty-one daily, weekly and monthly newspapers of Minnesota, which are bound when volumes are completed, and are carefully preserved in a fireproof room.

These daily and weekly newspapers and periodicals afford the truest, the fullest, the most impartial image of the age we live in, that can be derived from any single source; and this collection is recognized as invaluable for reference by students of history and of politics, by lawyers and searchers for titles of real estate in all parts of Minnesota, and for many other matters of record nowhere else obtainable. Constant use is made of these files, by personal inspection, by all classes of citizens, who often come to the library for this purpose from distant parts of the state.

The young men who met just fifty years ago, on November 15th, 1849, for the organization of the Minnesota Historical Society, and on January 14th, 1850, to discuss and adopt its constitution and by-laws, in the little room of the log tavern, were there at the solicitation of Secretary Smith, who was pushing a fad, for which presumably none of his associate in-

corporators of the society had much if any sympathy. They, like others, were absorbed in the strife for the human necessities of food and clothing, and in the endeavor to acquire a competency, if not wealth, through the opportunities offering in a newly settled country. It is safe to say that no one of them, not even our worthy chairman of the committee having this celebration in charge, ever imagined he might live to see that society an honored institution of the state, with a library of between sixty and seventy thousand volumes, referred to by persons from every county in the state, while the work of the society in gathering and publishing the history of Minnesota and of the Northwest is known and highly esteemed throughout the civilized world.

As those of us pioneers who survive to celebrate this half century of existence and growth of our society contemplate the result of our seemingly fortuitous action, we now see the fact that, while we were mostly absorbed in the development of our heritage, in the conquest of this portion of our peerless continent, by the plowing, the planting, the harvesting, trading, and building towns and cities, we did not recognize, as we might have done, the invincible spirit of human progress which was then as now the directing power that suggested action. In our forecast of the possibilities of the next fifty years, it is well to remember that this is the electric age, and that our society is a component part of the model state of the world, the State of Minnesota. All things attainable by any people are also possible to the people of Minnesota and to this Historical Society.

THE LIBRARY, MUSEUM, AND PORTRAIT COLLECTION OF THE MINNESOTA HISTORICAL SOCIETY.

BY NATHANIEL PITT LANGFORD.

In the legislative act incorporating this society, approved by Governor Ramsey October 20th, 1849, nearly four weeks before the first meeting and organization of this society, its object was stated to be "the collection and preservation of a library, mineralogical and geological specimens, Indian curiosities, and other matters and things connected with, and calculated to illustrate and perpetuate the history and settlement of said Territory."

Wider scope of the society's duties to the Territory was declared in an additional act passed somewhat more than six years later, as approved March 1st, 1856, of which the third section says: "The objects of said society, with the enlarged powers and duties herein provided, shall be, in addition to the collection and preservation of publications, manuscripts, antiquities, curiosities, and all other things pertaining to the social, political and natural history of Minnesota, to cultivate among the citizens thereof a knowledge of the useful and liberal arts, science, and literature." In view of this exceedingly generous definition of its fields of labor, this society may well affirm, as did the Apostle Paul, "All things are lawful unto me, but all things are not expedient."

The work of the society in accumulating material possessions has been limited, first, to its large and very valuable library, open from half-past eight o'clock in the forenoon until five o'clock in the afternoon as a public and free reference library; second, the collection of a museum of historical relics, illustrative of the conditions of the pioneer settlement of

Minnesota, of the Sioux war, and the civil war, of the aboriginal people who built the thousands of prehistoric mounds in this state, and of the Sioux (or Dakotas) and the Ojibways who were living here when the first white men reached this region; and, third, its collection of portraits of pioneers and other prominent citizens of this state, with other portraits, pictures and framed documents, illustrating the history of Minnesota, of the whole Northwest, and indeed of the whole United States.

THE LIBRARY.

In the few minutes allotted to me for these remarks I wi ll speak first and chiefly of the historical treasury which the society has gradually provided for itself and for all the people of Minnesota, in its carefully selected library, now numbering about 63,500 titles of books and pamphlets. While the aim of the society has constantly been to gather and preserve all publications issued in Minnesota, and all relating to Minnesota, wherever they may be published, we have also given great attention to the collection of everything published concerning local history, as of townships, in all the older states, as also in the new states of the West and of the Pacific coast.

What immigrant from any eastern part of our country, or son or daughter of such immigrant, does not still feel an interest in the old home and hearthstone, the old township of their nativity, or the homes where lived fifty years ago the fathers and mothers of the present generation?- Many who came here in the early times, and have endured hardships and won success in building up this great Commonwealth, now, in the well-earned leisure of declining years, go back in memory to the old township of their childhood in the Granite State, it may be, or the Bay State, or the Keystone State, which, with all the other states east of us contributed largely to the building up of Minnesota.

This society's library contains many volumes, mostly nowhere else to be found in this state, concerning the detailed local history of all those older parent states. To particularize and give more definite expression of the richness of the library in this department of American township histories,

it may be noted that, according to the librarian's inventory made two months ago, our number of bound volumes of township and strictly local histories was 90 for Maine, 100 for New Hampshire, 35 for Vermont, 469 for Massachusetts, which is richer in these histories than any other state, 40 for Rhode Island, and 100 for Connecticut; besides many for New York and all the states reaching thence southward and westward.

Our collection strictly relating to Minnesota, however, far exceeds that here gathered for any other state, if we include the narrations of explorers, visitors, and the many observant travelers who have written about us, and the books issued from our territorial and state government, as the journals and laws of the legislature, reports and proceedings of the departments of state executive affairs, and similar publications of our universities, colleges, commercial, charitable, and religious institutions. All these books describing Minnesota, her people, their work and their history, number about 1,075 volumes, besides about 1,500 pamphlets in this department. To every one who wishes to know with accuracy any part of our state history, its resources, what it promises to any contemplated new industry or investment, we would say, Come to this society's library, ask for its information on the subject, and you will understand the utility of this storehouse of knowledge.

These Minnesota books and pamphlets, although of inestimable value, are yet very far surpassed, in respect to numbers, magnitude and historical importance, by this society's great department of Minnesota newspapers. Our earliest newspaper issue for this state was the first number of the Minnesota Pioneer (which has now become the Pioneer Press of St. Paul), published by James M. Goodhue on the 28th of April, 1849, a few weeks previous to the establishment of the government of Minnesota as a Territory. A complete series of that newspaper, and of nearly all others published in Minnesota during the past fifty years, has been collected and preserved by our society. We are now receiving, by donation from the editors and publishers, 421 newspapers of this state, daily, weekly and monthly. They are preserved with the greatest care and are bound in ponderous volumes, the yearly increase of this depart-

ment being about 300 bound volumes. Their number on September 1st of this year was 4,250 volumes. They are a priceless treasury of materials for future historians, being in fact a detailed history of the development of the state, of all its counties and of its separate townships, from their beginning to the present time. This newspaper collection is kept in an extensive fireproof vault, which is a part of the society's rooms in this building. It is accessible to all who wish to consult it, and it is so arranged that any paper of any date can be readily found.

There are also other departments of the library which are of great interest to our people, and which are daily consulted by many readers. The growth of our patriotic societies has brought increased attention to histories of the Colonial and Revolutionary times preceding and beginning our national existence, with inquiries for records of ancestry, in the hope of tracing descent from soldiers of the Colonial wars and of the American Revolution. To all desiring to make any research of this kind, the very comprehensive department of American Genealogy, represented in this library by more than 1,100 bound volumes, and about 450 pamphlets, affords very ample resources of information, equalled only by three or four other libraries in the whole United States.

Another and much larger part of the library consists of the publications of the general government, such as the Congressional Record, and the reports of the many departments and bureaus of the Federal service, among which those of the United States Patent Office are perhaps the most frequently consulted. All the books, pamphlets, and maps issued by our national government are received gratuitously, this being a designated depository library.

THE MUSEUM.

One of the parts of the society's proper work which has received little consideration, is its museum. The needs of the library forbid the use of space in the present rooms to display a great portion of our museum collection, that which presents the work of the aboriginal people of Minnesota, the builders of the mounds, and the Indians of more recent times who have been displaced during this half century. The society is in-

debted to one of its life members, Hon. J. V. Brower, whose
report upon the sources of the Mississippi river forms the sev-
enth volume of the society's publications, for gifts of many
thousand stone and copper implements and other products of
aboriginal handiwork, which will form a most instructive exhibit of our museum when the society shall remove to the
ampler rooms assigned for it in the new Capitol. We are assured by the most learned archæologists of America, who have
examined some of these relics, that they were buried in the
mounds where they were found long before the Christian era.

PORTRAITS.

But I must hasten to add a few words concerning the society's collection of portraits. A hundred and twenty portraits are now displayed in the rooms of the society, besides
twenty group pictures which comprise 788 portraits. Nearly
all these are of pioneers and founders of Minnesota, or of citizens who in more recent years have had a prominent part in
the history and development of the state. There are also
many other pictures, as of ancient buildings, monuments,
paintings of historic scenes, etc., and many framed documents,
including a letter of George Washington, written in 1754,
which is in the case holding the Washington chair. This collection is the most interesting and attractive part of the society's possessions for visitors who have only a short time to
spend in our rooms.

Sitting in the monthly meetings of the Executive Council
of this society, I have often thought of the great work done
by the founders and leaders of Minnesota, whose portraits
look forth from the walls of our assembly room. Observing
the earnest, resolute expression of those faces, I recall what
Horatio Seymour said to me in our native state of New York,
nearly fifty years ago: "It is work, with its reward or failure,—the experience of life,—which is expressed by faces and
portraits, rather than the deep inherent character received
from ancestry."

INCREASE OF THESE COLLECTIONS.

The present space occupied by the library, portrait collection, and museum, is quite inadequate. Each of these fruits
of the society's work tends to grow, and they have outgrown

the limits which seemed very liberal when the present rooms began to be occupied sixteen years ago. The growth of a man continues only fifteen or twenty years, and that of a tree perhaps half a century; but of a living and useful library or museum or state portrait collection, there is no natural bound of growth. The duty and destiny of the society here founded and active, to-day completing its first fifty years, imply for it a continuance in the accumulation and preservation of these possessions for the educational and the moral advancement of the people.

The poet Milton gave expression to the duty of preserving valuable books, when he wrote:

"As good almost kill a man, as kill a good book. Who kills a man, kills a reasonable creature, God's image; but he who destroys a good book, kills reason itself, kills the image of God, as it were, in the eye. Many a man lives a burden to the earth; but a good book is the precious life-blood of a master spirit embalmed and treasured up on purpose to a life beyond life. It is true, no age can restore a life, whereof perhaps there is no great loss. . . . We should be wary, therefore, what persecutions we raise against the living labors of public men,—how we spill that seasoned life of man preserved and stored up in books;—since we see a kind of homicide may thus be committed, sometimes a martyrdom; and, if it extend to the whole impression, a kind of massacre, whereof the execution ends not in the slaying of an elemental life, but strikes at that ethereal and sift essense, the breath of reason itself,—slays an immortality, rather than a life."

The volumes on our library shelves have been characterized by some writer as our truest friends, who are never applied to in vain, who are never out when we knock at the door, of whom the announcement "not at home" is never made when we call. They are friends who in the highest as well as in the deepest moods may be applied to, and will never be found wanting.

RETROSPECTION.

It is time to bring these considerations to a close.

The men and women of the half century which we review to-day, have built this great Commonwealth. They and we

shall vanish, but our work as citizens of this state, and as members of the Minnesota Historical Society, will endure, and will be carried forward by others. Let them rightly value their heritage, and transmit it, increased, to their successors.

Few of those who placed themselves in the van of the movement for the organization of this society have lived to witness this day of her grandeur and triumph. It is said that, when two armies have joined battle, the report of musketry and cannon shot does not fall on the listening ear with regularity, but at intervals, now perhaps with a steady roar, and now in groups of sharp explosions, and then again in single scattered shots along the field, and then, after a long interval, and when there seemed a flag of truce hung out, startling us with a succession of quick reports, and strewing the ground with the slain. This is the way our own ranks have been thinned, sometimes in single scattered strokes; but we can see that the fight with the Great Conqueror has lately grown warm on this part of the field, when we number those of our members who within the last half of this decade have gone from us. But a time should never come, in the history of Minnesota, when the memory of those who, in the beginning, as in the later years, laid deep and broad the foundations of this society, should cease to be venerated. And as we crown the graves of the dead with flowers, let the pathway of the living be brightened by the rewards of a grateful people.

RECOLLECTIONS OF PERSONS AND EVENTS IN THE HISTORY OF MINNESOTA.

BY BISHOP HENRY B. WHIPPLE.

Mr. President, Members of the Historical Society, Ladies and Gentlemen: I preface my address by saying that I have an abiding faith in the Providence of God. Since the day when Bishop Stephen Langton, at the head of the nobles of England, wrung from King John the Magna Charta, the English-speaking race has stood for constitutional government. And this race, made up of the best blood of the northern races of Europe, represents loyalty to government and the rights of the individual. One hundred and fifty millions of men speak the English language, and one-third of the population of the world are under English-speaking governments. This loyalty is the characteristic of the people of the North Star State.

The development of the West in the last sixty years is a marvel. In my boyhood, after the journey by stage-coach from Syracuse to Cleveland, I remember standing on the wharf in Cleveland and watching the vessels as they were loaded with flour and pork for the border settlers on lake Michigan. In 1844 I travelled from Cincinnati to Cumberland, Maryland, by stage-coach. The people of the East were prejudiced against the West, as the home of chills and fever and other kindred diseases. Minnesota was a *terra incognita*, and the school maps showed the Falls of St. Anthony as the outpost of civilization.

My friend, Mr. Trowbridge of Detroit, who came in 1820 as a clerk to Governor Cass of the same city, copied the first United States census of the west, which included all trading posts as far as the Rocky mountains. There were nine thou-

sand eight hundred and seventy souls. There were three white citizens in Chicago, Dr. Westcott, physician to the Indians, Beaubien, a fiddler, and John Kinzie, an Indian trader. General Sibley, when a boy, was clerk for the Northwest Fur Company, and it was his duty to go for the mail which was brought to Detroit once a week on horseback.

When Minnesota was admitted to the Union, Congress generously gave two sections of land in each township for school purposes, the reason being that Minnesota was so remote from civilization that it would be generations before it was settled.

I visited Minnesota in 1853, and well remember the shout of laughter from my fellow travellers on the steamboat, as they saw among some scattered houses at Winona, a shanty bearing the sign, "Bank." St. Paul and St. Anthony were then flourishing villages. A friend who had come to Minnesota in 1844, and who had a small interest in the townsite of Minneapolis, said afterward to me, "I was sure that it could never be a town. I had received for my share the lots on which the Nicollet Block stands. I traded them for a pair of horses which I sold for one hundred and fifty dollars, and, feeling sure of the location of the future city of the Northwest, I invested it at Point Douglas." He added, with a smile, "I have it today."

As we were coming up the Mississippi on one occasion, a passenger, who spoke disparagingly of the West, was asked by a borderman, where he was from. "From Vermont," was the answer. "I am from Vermont," said the first speaker. "I know Vermont and I know Minnesota. My father had three sons, and two of us came to Minnesota. Last year I went home to the old farm, and in the morning I went out to look at the fields. When I came in, I said to my brother, 'How are you getting on, John?' 'O,' he answered, 'we manage to get a living, and that is about all.' 'Why, John,' I said, 'I don't wonder that you are poor. If I had a man in my employ who would reap a field of oats and leave as much standing as there is in that field yonder, I would discharge him at once.' 'Why, Bill,' exclaimed my brother, '*that's* the crop!'"

In 1859 I was elected the first Bishop of the Diocese of Minnesota. The State was then beginning to feel the tide of its incoming population, and the east had begun to give ear to the rumor of a western state free from malaria, with fertile soil,

37

good water, and abundant forests. It brought to us an intelligent population, many having been drawn hither in quest of health.

I doubt if any state in the Union has had a better class of pioneers to lay its foundations. They were honest, industrious, courageous, and hospitable. I have no memories dearer than those of the warm-hearted welcomes of those early settlers.

When I was in England in 1864, where there was much prejudice against the North, on account of the Civil War, one of the Fellows of Oxford, at a dinner given in my honor, spoke warmly of the South, and said: "I have been told that there is very little culture in the North, and that gentlemen are to be found only in the South. I have heard that it is not an uncommon thing in the West for two men to occupy the same bed." Then turning to me, he asked if it were true. I answered, with a smile, "It is quite true. I have thirty clergy in my diocese, and I have slept with eighteen of them." The guests looked incredulous, and I continued: "Gentlemen, my diocese is as large as England, Scotland, and Wales. I drive three thousand miles a year over the prairies. On a winter night, with the thermometer below zero, I come to a log house containing one room. I receive a hospitable welcome. When bedtime comes, a sheet is fastened across one end of the room, an impromptu resting place is made on the floor for the family and the only bed is given to me. Since having been lost on the prairie in a blizzard, I have often taken one of my clergy with me on my journeys. Will you tell me what I shall do? Shall I share my bed with my brother, or shall I turn him out in the howling storm to freeze to death? Even English hospitality cannot exceed that of the frontier settler." The look of surprise gave way to hearty cheers.

The spirit of pioneer kindliness was everywhere, and to none am I more indebted than to the drivers of the Merriam, Blakeley and Burbank Stage Company. Whenever I drove up to an inn, some one of the cheery voices would cry out, "Bishop, I know just what old Bashaw wants. Go right in, and I will give him the best of care!" I would as quickly have offered a gratuity to my dearest friend as to one of those generous souls.

Time would fail me to tell the story of the brave lives of some of those frontier men who gave me their love,—men like Peter Robert, the Indian trader, who, when asked if he knew

Bishop Whipple, answered, "Yes, he's a sky pilot, and always straight!"

The early history of the State was marked by very great trials. The attempt to build our first railways and its failure led to repudiation of the state bonds. It gave us a dishonored name in financial circles in the East, and deprived us of that sympathy and help which is so needed in the founding of a new state. I have often blushed when eastern friends have asked, "Why has Minnesota repudiated her bonded debt?" But all honor to the brave hearts who unfalteringly labored to re move the stain!

Then came the massacre of 1862, which desolated our entire border, and swept eight hundred of our citizens into nameless graves. In this brief review of events and men that have helped to form the history of the state, I must not omit a tribute of love to the heroic red men who have been a part of the flock entrusted to my care. You all know the sad condition of our Indian affairs forty years ago. In my acquaintance with sin and suffering, I had found nothing more terrible than the degradation and misery in the Indian country, much of which was the result of the wrong and robbery which we had inflicted on this hapless race. During that holocaust of murder in August, 1862, the only light which came was in the bravery of the Christian and friendly Indians, who, surrounded by thousands of their hostile brethren, did all that it was possible for them to do to ameliorate the condition of the suffering captives, and who rescued two hundred white women and children whom they delivered to General Sibley. The names of these brave heroes cannot be too often repeated. Among them were Other Day, Simon Anagmani, Paul Mazakuta, Lorenzo Lawrence, Taopi, Iron Shields, Good Thunder, Wakinyantawa, and others. After the failure of the special agent to report facts, the Secretary of the Interior asked me to send him a list of the Indians who had shown their fidelity to the whites throughout the massacre. I spent three weeks in careful investigation, and submitted my report to General Sibley and Dr. Williamson, who endorsed it. To make assurance doubly sure, I asked the Government to employ Dr. J. W. Daniels to distribute the funds appropriated, and to make further investigations. He found my report in every respect true.

General Sibley made Good Thunder one of his chiefs of scouts, and I have several letters from General Sibley testifying to the absolute fidelity of Good Thunder throughout the entire massacre. I knew him then, as I have known him all through these forty years, as a hero.

Some years later, General Custer asked me to send him thirty of these friendly Indians as scouts, when he made the reconnoissance of the Black Hills. On their return, he wrote me: "I cannot permit these Indians to return to their homes without testifying to their uniform good character. I do not simply say that they have been obedient, but I doubt whether any village could turn out more exemplary men."

The Government confiscated all the annuities and lands of the Sioux, making no discrimination in behalf of those who had imperilled their lives for us. And to this hour this great wrong has not been redressed.

A few years after the outbreak, came the plague of locusts, which lasted for several years. One day the Governor of the State met me and said: "There is a scare in the southwest about the locusts, and as you are travelling over that part of the country, will you send me the facts about the matter?" When I reached Fairmont, I saw near the inn a field of wheat four or five inches in height, and a few hours later every sign of vegetation had disappeared. I swept my hand through the cloud of locusts and placed the result in a wide-mouthed bottle —a hundred and twenty in number—and sent it to the Governor. When experiments were being tried in vain to destroy the plague, I stopped one day at a house where I saw a distressed farmer gazing upon his half-ruined fields, and asked if he had read in the Pioneer of a way in which the crops could be saved. "What is it?" he asked. "Put a windrow of moistened hay," I replied, "on the windward side of your field and set fire to it, and the smoke will drive the locusts away." The farmer gave a low whistle, and answered, "Bishop, I tried it, and the little pests came down to warm their legs by my fire."

The settlements at that time were scattered, and very few of them numbered a thousand inhabitants. The farming communities were isolated, and I often drove twenty miles without seeing a house. My first service in Minneapolis was in a rude wooden chapel, while in other parts of the state I held service in wayside inns, stores, log-houses, and in the forest.

Nothing added more to the promise of the new state than the high character of its professional men. Wherever the men of the legal profession are men of high character, there will be found in the community a nice sense of commercial honor; and wherever there is the reverse, trickery and fraud will follow. I could call over a long roll of the legal profession of our state, the peers of their brethren of the most favored cities of the East.

Let me mention one name, that of Edward O. Hamlin of St. Cloud, the honored judge of that circuit. A murder had been committed, and the exasperated citizens judged the criminal by mob law, and hanged him. Some of the most prominent citizens of the county notified Judge Hamlin that he must not charge the grand jury with reference to this deed, and that if he did, he could never again be elected. Judge Hamlin paid no attention to the threat, but charged the jury in one of the most manly appeals which ever came from a judicial bench. When I read it, I said to my friend, "Hamlin, I would rather have made that charge of yours than to be President of the United States."

Minnesota has a long list of jurists like Nelson, Mitchell, Ripley, Williston, Gilfillan, Severance, and others, whose judicial ermine is without a stain. There are, however, some exceptions among the lawyers. I remember one of my Indians who employed a lawyer to prepare some legal papers. On paying him his fee, the Indian asked for a receipt. "You do not need a receipt," said the lawyer, "why are you so anxious about it?" .The Indian answered, "Since becoming a Christian I have tried to keep my accounts square, and when the Day of Judgment comes I can't take time to go to the bad place to look you up to get my receipt."

The medical profession has been nobly represented. When I visited Dr. Willey on his death bed, I remember with what loving interest he called over the names of his professional brethren, who, he said, would be an honor to any state.

Many of those early settlers are now occupying positions of trust and eminence in commercial circles, reached by integrity and industry. While our state has been represented by men of different religious creeds, there has been unusual freedom from the rancor and bitterness of sectarian strife.

The character of our people has been exhibited in its citizen soldiery. I can never forget a Sunday in 1861, at the beginning of our Civil War, when I stood on the field at Fort Snelling in the midst of a thousand men and preached to them on love and loyalty to country. That night they enlisted as the First Regiment of Minnesota Volunteers. I met them again at the battle of Antietam, when the ground was covered with the dead and dying, and received scores of last messages from brave hearts to the loved ones at home. That night, when at General McClellan's request I held a thanksgiving service at his headquarters, he said to me, with tears in his eyes, "Bishop, it would wrong other brave men to say that your Minnesota boys are the bravest men in the army, but I will say that no general ever commanded braver men than the Minnesota First."

Some months after the battle of Gettysburg, I celebrated the Holy Communion at the headquarters of General Meade, when he paid a like tribute to the bravery of Minnesota soldiers.

One looks back with amazement at the ignorance manifested as to the resources of Minnesota. I was in London when our esteemed friends, Edmund Rice and Colonel Crooks, sought to interest English capitalists in our railways. I was asked by some bankers as to the character of the country along the line of the proposed St. Paul and Pacific railway. I said that there was no better land in the world, and that if the country west of St. Paul and tributary to the Red River Valley were cultivated as in England, it would feed the entire population of England. My remarks were received with incredulity.

In 1870 some Holland bankers, whom I met in Italy, asked my opinion of the same St. Paul and Pacific railway, and stated that they held a large amount of its bonds. I said, "The railway has been built in advance of the population. It may be years before it becomes a paying investment, but the day will come when it will be one of the foremost railways in the world." They, too, doubted my statement. I advised them to care for this property, and suggested the names of General H. H. Sibley, John L. Merriam, and J. E. Thompson, as men upon whose advice they could rely. They did not seek the

advice, and some years later disposed of their property to Mr. Hill and his associates at a great sacrifice.

Time will not permit me to call over the names inwrought in the history of our goodly state. There was Henry T. Welles, the most generous of men, a clear thinker and scholar, who stood through his entire life for the best interests of the state.

General H. H. Sibley, who came here as the chief factor of the Northwest Fur Company, when the only settlement in Minnesota was the trading post at Mendota, was one of the most genial, clear-headed and warm-hearted men I have known, the friend of the Indians and an honored and loyal citizen.

Col. D. A. Robertson, an encyclopædia of learning, was one of those rare men whose friendship is a lifelong blessing. Henry and Edmund Rice were the most generous of friends, whose names will be remembered as faithful public servants. I have not spoken of the living members of this society, Ramsey, McKusick, Le Duc, Pillsbury, Blakeley, Moss, and others, whose lives are inwrought in the history of the state.

In its early history, our state had a goodly number of devoted clergy, as the Rev. Dr. Mattocks, beloved of all; the Rev. Dr. Neill, the painstaking historian; the Rev. Dr. Gear, the scholar and Christian priest; the devoted Father Ravoux; and many other sainted men who lived and worked for others.

I have spoken of the absence of strife among Christians. In 1863, President Lincoln appointed Bishop Grace of the Roman Catholic Church, the Rev. Dr. Williamson, Presbyterian, and myself, to visit the Ojibways and make a report upon their condition. At the outset I suggested that, as we were to sleep in the same tent, eat together, and live together for some weeks, we should avoid all questions upon which we differed. I said, "I have the only interpreter. As there are Indians who have been baptized by Father Pierre, I will have my interpreter bring them to Bishop Grace for counsel. There are a few scattered Indians who were baptized by the Rev. Frederick Ayer, and they shall be brought to Dr. Williamson for instruction. As Christian men, we shall certainly ask a blessing before meals, and I propose that Bishop Grace shall ask God's blessing at breakfast, and Dr. Williamson at dinner, and I at supper." We were together three weeks; we encountered many hardships, and one night nearly perished from cold; but the

Christian courtesy and gentleness of my companions is a pleasant memory.

I mentioned this incident at a breakfast given me in London by Sir Henry Holland, at which Lord Houghton, Ranke,
the historian, Lord Salisbury, and George Lewes were present.
They exclaimed, "Do you say that you were together three
weeks without a ripple of discord? Minnesota must be the
beginning of the millennium. It could not have happened on
English soil."

In my first visits to the Indian country I found a few of
the voyageurs and employees of the Northwest Fur Company.
They were devoted to the Indians, and at all times gave me
their hearty sympathy. Allan Morrison and Mr. Fairbanks
of Crow Wing, Philander Prescott, Alexander Faribault,
Borup, Oakes, N. W. Kittson, Alexis Bailly, Mr. Shubway of
Red Lake, and others of this class of early traders, were men
of integrity and generous of their substance. Before the Indians came into the treaty relations with the Government, the
relation between the trader and Indian was one of mutual good
will.

One of the most remarkable men of the State was Joseph
R. Brown, known to the older members of the Historical Society. He possessed great executive ability, and a rare knowledge of Indian character. The gains which he received from
Indian contracts he expended with lavish hand for his retain-
ers among the Indians.

Another who had a deep love for the Indians was George
Bonga, an interesting mixed-blood negro, living at Leech Lake,
who was my voyageur and interpreter.

I think that I may say without question that the state has
been fortunate in the character of its newspaper press, although sometimes, in the heat of partisanship, unjust to opponents, yet for the most part taking a firm stand for education, morality, and religion.

As I was the only citizen of Minnesota who could not move
out of the state (for a diocesan bishop of our church must die in
his see), I have always taken a keen interest in all political
questions which affected its welfare. Our first representative
in Congress, H. H. Sibley, delegate for the Territory of Minnesota, of whom my friend Robert C. Winthrop said, "He is
one of the noblest and purest members of Congress," is but one

of the many representatives of incorruptible integrity, who were devoted to the interests of the commonwealth.

It is difficult to realize the marvelous changes which have taken place in the material developments of the state within my memory. Duluth, which at the time of my first visit had but five families, is now one of the greatest grain markets in the world. I remember the first shipment of wheat from Minnesota. Wonderful strides have been made in all lines of manufacture, mining, and commercial life.

When I came to Minnesota our trade with the Northwest British possessions was carried on by Red River carts, rude structures without a particle of iron, the parts held together by pegs and withes and drawn by a single ox in thills. As the cart wheels were never oiled, their screeching could be heard miles before the caravan came in sight. They were laden with furs, and returned with merchandise.

Our intercourse with the outside world was, in the summer, by the Mississippi steamers, commanded by Captain Orren Smith, Russell Blakeley, and Commodore Davidson. Many here present will remember with delight the days spent on the beautiful Mississippi before its navigation was interrupted by sandbars. In the winter, the journeys to Dubuque were made in Walker's rude stages, before the day of the luxurious coaches of Burbank and Company.

The inns on the frontier were of the rudest character, and well deserved the name which one bore, "Hyperborean Hotel." Every summer I travelled on foot hundreds of miles in our northern forests, visiting the scattered bands of Indians.

I have never looked upon scenery more beautiful than that surrounding the lakes of northern Minnesota. Every variety of tree was to be seen, while the earth was spread with a brilliant carpet of wild flowers of every hue. The lakes and rivers were filled with fish, and game was found in great abundance. I have seen buffalo west of Yellow Medicine, elk on the prairies south of Sauk Center, and moose, bear, and foxes in our northern forests. If the National Park, which would include some of our most beautiful lakes, is established and properly cared for, it will be a rich inheritance for future generations.

I have alluded to the rude homes of the frontier population, forty years ago, a majority of whom were of foreign birth.

There are no foreigners in the brotherhood of the nation. In no one direction has the state made more wonderful advances than in its agricultural population. Our State University and primary schools have proved an inestimable blessing. These country homes are surrounded by comforts, and no state in the Union has a more intelligent rural population, keenly alive to the state's interests. It is a fact full of promise, for this new blood from the country homes reinforces the life of the cities, and adds to the civil welfare. Nothing in our history, to my mind, gives greater hope for the future; for the strength and safety of the nation is in its Christian homes. In the past they have always been the best resource of the nation in the hours of her trials.

When I think of our beautiful halls of education, our thronged university, our hospitals and homes of mercy, our churches with heavenward-pointing spires, our teeming warehouses, our busy manufactories, our world-famed flour mills with their vast exportations, and that tremendous tide of living souls that comes to us year by year from other shores to become incorporated into our citizenship and to form the new race which God is raising up here to be in the forefront of great achievement, I can only say with a grateful heart: "What nation is there so great who hath God so nigh unto them as the Lord our God in all things that we call upon Him for?"

In conclusion, to speak last of the missionary work for the Christianization of the Indians of this state and of all the country westward, there are those present, members of your society, and representatives of the press, who have always given me their sympathy in my efforts for these brown children of our Heavenly Father. And I am sure that they will rejoice with me that there are now over twenty-five thousand Indian communicants of Christian churches; over twenty-two thousand Indian children in schools; and thirty-eight thousand who speak English. As a people, they are fast learning the civilization which will make them our fellow-citizens.

PROGRESS OF MINNESOTA DURING THE HALF CENTURY.

BY HON. CHARLES E. FLANDRAU.

Mr. President, Ladies and Gentlemen: I have been chosen to present to you, on this unusually interesting occasion, a subject which, if treated in the usual way, would be a dismal array of heavy statistics. Whether the selection was made with reference to my peculiar talent for dullness, I am unable to say; but, fortunately for you, I am limited to half an hour, in which to tell you all about the growth of Minnesota in the last fifty years. Think of it! I am expected to compress that vast subject into the space of thirty minutes. It looks to me a good deal like holding up a man and saying to him, "Write me the history of the world while I wait."

If I desired to let you down easily and shield you from dreary figures and calculations, I could say, go out into the state anywhere and look about you and whatever you see, or hear of, which represents the handiwork of man, may be taken as part of the growth of the state in the last half century. Fifty years ago it was almost in the exact condition in which it was left by its generous and bountiful Creator, and now it is one of the great and prosperous states of the American Union. Great cities have arisen where, at the beginning of the period, were empty and nameless spaces, only inhabited by the primitive savage. Distances have been annihilated; localities that were then thirty days apart are now within reach in a few hours' journey. The luxurious Pullman car has superseded the Red River cart and the Indian pony; the frontier camp has given way to the comfortably appointed hotel. The varicolored dress of the picturesque half-savage voyageur has

yielded to the somber costume of the civilized citizen. The farmer has usurped the place of the hunter; the old frontier guide, whose unerring instinct would pilot you safely across the continent, is now lost in the bewildering intricacies of artificial civilization; and the original proprietor of the land is a miserable prisoner, corralled, dismounted, and disarmed.

It is not for me to decide upon the justice of all these vital changes. It is accepted by the nations in the progress of the world. The stronger despoils the weaker, on the plea of the necessities of the advance of civilization, to which has recently been added the elusive generality of manifest destiny. The Boer must yield to the Briton, the Spaniard and Filipino to the American; and no doubt, should the autocratic Russian outstrip them all in the race for power, which is by no means impossible, and, according to the recognized authorities, quite probable, they may all have to succumb to his brutal dictation under the very adaptable name of benevolent assimilation. To what ends the selfish passions of man may ultimately lead, and to what judgment his unrighteous deeds may subject him, the Great Spirit can be the only arbiter.

There has been more justice, and less arbitrary exertion of force, in the absorption of the country of the North American Indian, than in similar cases in other lands. We have made a show of purchasing his domains; but had he declined to part with them, he would have fallen under the wheels of the juggernaut of advancing civilization, as have all the weaker nations.

With these reflections, I will take up the subject that I have been asked to consider.

When what is now Minnesota came from the hands of its Creator, I can say, without exaggeration, it was about the best equipped country, of equal size, to be found in North America. It is located on the summit of the continent, where the waters flow in three directions, the Mississippi due south to the Gulf of Mexico, the Red river of the North due north to mingle with the waters of the Arctic sea, the St. Louis river east to the waters of lake Superior and thence to the St. Lawrence and the Atlantic. On its fair bosom were ten thousand beautiful lakes, great and small, filled with delicious fish. A large portion of its surface was covered with a mighty forest of pine

and hardwood trees, giving a home to myriads of wild animals, moose, deer, cariboo, elk, bear, wolf, and others. Its streams were the home of the beaver and the otter; and its vast prairies swarmed with the buffalo and the antelope. Sugar maple groves and wild rice fields abounded. Nothing that contributes to the well-being of man seemed wanting.

Its climate was salubrious beyond comparison with any other portion of the earth's surface. There were no indigenous diseases, and in fact no excuse for sickness or death. So thoroughly was this idea impressed upon the mind and belief of the old settler that there was a universally accepted saying, that no one had ever died in Minnesota but two men, one of whom was hanged for killing the other. I can well remember that the first natural death that I heard of, after my settlement in the Territory, caused me a greater shock than the thousands that have since occurred.

The soil was phenomenally rich and fertile. It was especially adapted to the production of the greatest of all staple grains, wheat; and it was unexcelled in the growth of all other cereals.

The first inhabitants were the Indians, and the commerce which arose from their hunting of fur animals soon attracted the white men. The first white occupants were the fur companies and the missionaries, the first for gain, and the missionaries to introduce among the savages the teachings of Christianity. The fur trade may be said to have been the first business transacted in Minnesota. The men controlling it were of a higher type than generally appear on the border in the first instance, Henry H. Sibley, Henry M. Rice, Norman W. Kittson, William H. Forbes, and others. The business expanded to great proportions and made St. Paul one of the largest fur markets in America.

Very little was known of Minnesota outside of its fur trade, until its organization as a Territory in 1849; although the attractions presented by its pine forests had drawn within its borders a few lumbermen before that event, who were settled about the Falls of St. Anthony, and in the valley of the St. Croix. They soon increased in number, built sawmills, and in these fifty years have pushed the lumber business from a very small beginning to such immense proportions that there were cut in the last season 1,629,110,000 feet. Preparatory to the

census of 1880, the United States government had an estimate made of all the standing pine in the state, and called it 10,000,-000,000 feet, which was far below the truth, as the amount cut annually since proves. But the encroachments made on the pine forests have been sufficient to create fear that they will soon become exhausted if measures of preservation are not speedily taken, and earnest work is being done to preserve them through government reserves and parks. This effort may succeed, but it is so complicated by private ownership that it looks improbable. Many large fortunes have been made in lumber in Minnesota.

The first Territorial Legislature convened in St. Paul, in the dining room of the old Central House, on the third day of September, 1849. The councillors numbered nine; and the members of the house, eighteen. The governor,—now the honored president of this society,—delivered a message that was admirably adapted to the situation, and was intended to attract attention to the Territory and invite immigration. It succeeded to the fullest extent, and the Territory began to grow in population rapidly.

The census that had been taken in 1849, under the organic act, gave the whole Territory, which then extended to the Missouri river and included the greater part of what is now North and South Dakota, four thousand seven hundred and eighty inhabitants, of which St. Paul had eight hundred and forty. The immigration was moderate until the year 1855, when it began to develop enormously. It came from all directions, by wagon trains from Iowa, Wisconsin, Illinois, Indiana, and other states, and by steamboats from everywhere. Its magnitude can best be understood, when I tell you that the packet company running boats on the Mississippi brought into St. Paul that year thirty thousand immigrants. These people generally sought farms, and spread themselves over the country; but no agriculture worth mentioning, except such as was necessary for home consumption, was developed until after 1857. The census of 1895, taken by the state, gives us a population of 1,574,619. The growth since will undoubtedly swell the present total to nearly 2,000,000.

The newcomers naturally located along the Mississippi and Minnesota rivers, and gradually extended into the interior; but so many of them remained in the cities and engaged

in speculation that a financial panic ensued in 1857, which drove the idlers to work. In a very few years we had large areas of our agricultural lands in southern Minnesota under cultivation and many millions of bushels of wheat for export. This was our second step in material progress, and it continued until the lands so cultivated began to show symptoms of exhaustion, when the farmers in our southern counties partially abandoned wheat culture, and adopted butter and cheese making, with great success. About this time the wonderful possibilities of the valley plain of the Red river of the North appeared in evidence, and the principal theater of wheat-raising was transferred to that area. This change in no way diminished the culture of wheat in the state, but simply removed it from its old grounds. Last year the state produced seventy-eight million bushels.

As soon as the production of wheat began to exceed the domestic wants of the state, the water powers at St. Anthony Falls and elsewhere were utilized for its manufacture into flour; and to such an extent did the industry progress that the output at Minneapolis for the year 1898-9 was 15,164,881 barrels, and at Duluth-Superior for the same period (the only other places where records are kept) 2,637,035 barrels, while the estimate for the whole state is twenty-five million barrels.

In the years 1871 to 1874, the Hungarian process of milling our spring wheat was introduced into Minnesota, with the advantage of producing a grade of flour superior to that of the winter wheat of more southern latitudes, while at the same time it reduced the quantity of wheat necessary to make a barrel of flour, of 196 pounds, from five bushels to four bushels and seven pounds, thus increasing the value of our wheat fully twenty per cent.

One of the most remarkable features regarding the general growth of our state was connected with the first session of our legislature in 1849, and I never think of it without being impressed profoundly with the sagacity of our early settlers. Where was there ever a body of men assembled for the first time to administer to the welfare of an extreme frontier territory, that rose much above the realm of townsites, sawlogs, and peltries? But in our case we find that small collection of men comprehending the intellectual wants of future generations, and providing for them by the establishment of a his-

torical society for the record of events yet unborn. Esthetic conceptions of this nature are usually the result of necessity, arising from neglect of the former generations to supply such records, but here we have the whole thing anticipated at the initial step in our history. This fact stamps our first legislature with a remarkable degree of wisdom, and goes a great way to account for the intelligent administration of our subsequent affairs, and for our phenomenal growth.

While dealing with the growth of our state, I must admit that the legislative department has expanded immensely in numbers. The legislature is now composed of sixty-three senators and one hundred and nineteen representatives. Does it give us laws of value equal to its progression in numbers? If I may be allowed an opinion, I would say, no. If I should be asked whether it would be improved by being diminished two-thirds, I would say, yes.

About the third step in the progression of the state's growth was the dairy industry. It had a small beginning, and was in imitation of the farmers of Iowa, who had undergone the same experience in over-taxing their lands with wheat. It soon, however, assumed great proportions, and made the southern counties of the state the most prosperous region within its boundaries. There are now about seven hundred creameries, using the milk of 410,000 cows, and, in 1898, producing 63,000,-000 pounds of butter, of which 50,000,000 pounds were exported. The gross receipts amounted to $10,400,000, and the sum paid to the patrons of the creameries amounted to $8,600,000. Minnesota butter has carried off the prizes at all the expositions where it has been exhibited.

While these various industries were growing and expanding, manufactures of almost every nature were being established throughout the state, as boots and shoes, agricultural implements, clothes, fur garments, pottery, bricks and building material of all kinds, breweries, distilleries, packing houses, and in fact almost everything pertaining to a young western state. I shall have to except distilleries from my industries, as they have ceased. Whether this result was on account of our people preferring Kentucky whisky to the domestic article, or the work of the trusts, I can't say, but I don't believe the amount consumed has to any great extent decreased. It is impossible to estimate the aggregate of these manufacturing

industries, as no branch of them is fully reported, but on the whole they probably exceed all others in magnitude.

Transportation, of course, kept pace with the general growth of the state; and, by reason of a wisely selected distribution of Congressional land grants in the beginning for our railroads, Minnesota has become a great center of an immense railroad system extending over the whole continent. In 1849 there were no railroads west of Chicago. Now we have connection with all existing roads, and two trans-continental roads are especially our own, the Great Northern and the Northern Pacific, which will, at no distant date, encircle the earth with their locomotives and steamships. In Minnesota alone there are twenty-six distinct railroad corporations, operating six thousand and sixty-two miles of main track, with quite a substantial addition in course of construction.

Another immense source of wealth to the state is its iron ore. Mining operations commenced about the year 1884, and in that year 62,124 tons were mined on the Vermilion range in St. Louis county, north of Duluth. The production rapidly increased, and in 1898 there were mined, on the Vermilion and Mesabi ranges, the enormous amount of 5,878,908 tons of ore, and for the period since the opening of the mines in 1884, the grand total of twenty-eight and a half million tons. The most of this industry is in private hands, but the state owns a large amount of mineral lands from which it receives royalties on the ore produced by its tenants at the rate of twenty-five cents per ton of 2,240 pounds, which carries its income to the present time up into the hundreds of thousands of dollars, with the promise of continual increase.

The banking facilities of the state have grown from Borup and Oakes, Truman M. Smith, Bidwell's Exchange Bank, Charles H. Parker, and A. Vance Brown, all of whom, except Borup and Oakes, went under in the panic of 1857, to one hundred and seventy-two state banks with a paid in capital of $6,736,800, and sixty-seven national banks with a capital of $11,220,000, besides numerous private banks, of which the authorities do not take cognizance, with an estimated capital of $2,000,000.

The growth of the state is not to be computed solely upon the basis of its material and physical prosperity. One of the most important elements in the consideration, is its intellectual

38

and esthetic advancement. Minnesota had a more generous endowment, in an educational point of view, than any other state in the Union. When it was organized as a Territory fifty years ago, it was granted by the United States government one eighteenth of its whole lands for school purposes. It also had a generous donation of lands for its university and agricultural college, and it has carefully and faithfully cared for these splendid gifts, until its schools have reached a plane of excellence unsurpassed in any other state, and its university takes rank with the highest educational institutions in the country. The last published catalogue of the State University gives it 2,925 pupils, and I am glad to be able to say that it has never been disgraced by any of the scandalous student demonstrations so common at other colleges.

It is unnecessary to say much about the religion or politics of the state. We don't profess to be superior to our neighbors in either of these respects. We have in great abundance nearly all known denominations of Christianity. The Catholics have deemed our growth and standing sufficient to entitle us to an archbishopric, and have given us John Ireland to fill the exalted ecclesiastical office of that jurisdiction, a priest who has no superior in the world as a statesman, a churchman, and a diplomat. The Protestants have supplied us with representatives of many varieties of creeds and forms of church government, from the stately Episcopalian, with its world-renowned Bishop Henry B. Whipple, to the Christian Scientist, if the latter may be catalogued among Protestant religions. In this connection I am tempted to relate an anecdote of a Frenchman, who returned to his country from a tour of America, and was asked what he thought of the Americans. His reply was, "They are a most extraordinary people; they have invented three hundred religions, and only one sauce."

While on the point of intellectual growth, I must mention the progress made in the publication of newspapers, which, say what you like, have greater influence on the education of the public than any other instrumentality. In 1849, James M. Goodhue established the first newspaper in the Territory and called it the "Minnesota Pioneer," the first issue of which appeared on the 28th day of April of that year. It was a stunner, and Goodhue was the man of all men to edit it. He was energetic, enterprising, brilliant, bold and belligerent. He

naturally got into fights and scrapes, and died from a wound received in an encounter with a brother of Judge Cooper, growing out of an article he had published concerning the judge. It is only fair to say that his assailant died from a wound inflicted by Goodhue in the same affair.

From this beginning the growth of newspapers in the state has been marvelous. We now publish five hundred and seventy-four in the state; some daily, some weekly, and some monthly. They appear in many different languages, for immigrants from as many lands, English, French, German, Swedish, Norwegian, Danish, Bohemian, and one in Icelandic, which last is published in Lyon county. Files of nearly all these papers, donated by their editors and publishers, are carefully preserved in the archives of this society, where will be found 4,250 bound newspaper volumes, which include nearly every paper that has ever been published in the state.

It is sometimes a good method, in presenting the growth of a state or country, to make comparisons between it and other well known countries. I will take California as an illustrative instance. It had in 1849 a wonderful introduction to the country and the world by the discovery of gold within its limits, and people flocked thither in numbers unprecedented in the history of American immigration. The gold was there in fabulous amounts, and much of it was mined for many years. It has the finest harbor and seaport on the Pacific coast. It is nearly twice as large as Minnesota, having 158,360 square miles, while we have but 84,287. Its climate is delightful, and its soil is productive of almost everything that grows outside of the tropics. It has the great ocean for its commerce with the world. It was admitted into the Union eight years before Minnesota. Notwithstanding all these apparent advantages, California has been outstripped by Minnesota in population and general growth. The census of 1890 gave California 1,208,130 people, while Minnesota had at the same time 1,301,826; and no doubt the last ten years have widened the disparity. There is no other way to account for this superiority on the part of Minnesota than upon the basis that our resources are more stable and permanent in their nature, presenting attractions to the immigrant to come to us, and advantages sufficient to hold him afterward.

Having said all I can in the brief time allotted me to present the half century's growth of Minnesota, I cannot round out my conclusions better than by slightly paraphrasing the panegyric of Daniel Webster on Massachusetts, pronounced in the Senate of the United States, in 1830.

Mr. President, I shall enter on no encomium of Minnesota. She needs none. There she is. Behold her, and judge for yourselves. There are her history, her resources, her enterprise, her intelligence, her growth, as I have related them. Her past is at least secure; her future depends upon the fidelity of her people. I commit her to your keeping, with hope undiminished and confidence unimpaired.

Preceding Judge Flandrau's address, Mrs. Jane Huntington Yale, of St. Paul, sang "The Song of the Flag" (by De Koven), with piano accompaniment by Mr. Charles G. Titcomb. Following this address, the afternoon exercises were completed with the singing of "Auld Lang Syne" by the audience, led by Mrs. Yale.

AULD LANG SYNE.

    Should auld acquaintance be forgot,
        And never brought to mind?
    Should auld acquaintance be forgot.
        And days of auld lang syne?

        For auld lang syne, my dear,
            For auld lang syne,
        We'll take a cup of kindness yet
            For auld lang syne.

    We two have paddled o'er the wave
        From morn till sun's decline;
    We'll have a thought of kindness yet
        For auld lang syne.

        For auld lang syne, etc.

EVENING SESSION.

Captain Russell Blakeley, the senior vice president of the society, presided in the evening session, which began shortly after eight o'clock. In taking the chair, Captain Blakeley said:

Ladies and Gentlemen: It is unpleasant to me to announce that it is very doubtful whether Governor Ramsey will be here this evening. He left word that he wishes me to preside if he does not come, and we have waited now somewhat longer than was expected. It will not be my purpose to consume a moment of the time of the audience this evening, except to render my unfeigned thanks on behalf of the Historical Society for the interest that you all have manifested in attending these meetings.

An audience of about five hundred people was present in the afternoon, and fully seven hundred in the evening. The several addresses in this session were as follows.

OPENING ADDRESS.

BY HON. JOHN S. PILLSBURY.

It is certainly very pleasant to meet so many pioneer settlers of this state who are members of this Historical Society, and who have always taken so much interest in the work which this institution has accomplished. The members and officers are entitled to the thanks of the people of this state, for the preservation of the records of the early events of Minnesota as a Territory and as a State. These historic records will be of great value to the future generations, who will consult this society's library for matters of importance which cannot be found elsewhere, and which in after years will be invaluable.

It is said that fifty years is but a small period in the life of a state. There are several members, however, of this society here tonight, who were here before the state or even the territory was organized. The character of these early settlers, many of them members of this institution, gave shape largely to the affairs and reputation which the state now enjoys. Had it not been for the sterling character of these early pioneers, I am sure that this great commonwealth would not have reached the high standing which she now occupies among the other states of the Union.

The early settlement of Minnesota was slow. It had to contend with many drawbacks, because the state was on the extreme frontier of the country and was considered almost worthless for agricultural purposes. General Hazen, while stationed at Fort Buford, in his report to the United States government, represented this country to be a portion of the great American desert, ill adapted for settlement. The geographies used in the common schools also represented this section to be a part of the great American desert. Horace Greeley and other editors advised settlers to go to Kansas and Nebraska, saying that Minnesota was too far north. During the contest which raged at this time as to whether Kansas and Nebraska should be made free or slave states, they advised settlers to go to these territories instead of Minnesota, which was reputed to be a cold and barren country.

Consequently settlement for many years was slow; but there was a class of settlers who believed in Minnesota. Some of those men are members of this Society, and are here tonight. They were frontier settlers of Wisconsin Territory, while that included a part of what is now Minnesota, and were also residents of the Territory of Minnesota before it was organized into a state. What is more wonderful, these men have lived to see that territory developed into the states of Minnesota and North and South Dakota, with increase of population from less than five thousand in 1849 to over two millions today. What is more remarkable still, they have lived to witness the growth, in Minnesota, of two great cities of about 200,000 population each. So much cannot be said of Kansas or Nebraska, or of any other state at the end of the first fifty years from its admission to the Union, or, I should say, from the beginning of its existence as a territory.

General Sibley told me, before his death, that he held jurisdiction, as a Justice of the Peace, over more territory than
any other living man. While a resident of Mendota, in 1838,
he held jurisdiction over a portion of the present states of Wisconsin, Minnesota, Iowa, and North and South Dakota.

In 1854 there were only five or six school districts in our territory, and not more than a half dozen log schoolhouses, of
very little value, with no organized public school system. Then
we had no public school fund. Today there are upwards of
seven thousand school districts, with over ten thousand school
teachers, to whom we pay more than $3,500,000 in salaries an-
nually. Our school buildings at this day are valued at more
than fifteen million dollars. Our public schools have an en-
rollment of more than four hundred thousand pupils; and our
school system is among the very best in the country, with a
permanent school fund which now reaches the magnificent sum
of thirteen million dollars. We have in addition a State University at the head of our public school system, ranking second
only among the state universities in the country, with an en-
rollment at the present time of upwards of thirty-two hundred
students.

Today Minnesota is one of the best agricultural and stock-
raising states in the Union. It produces more and better wheat
than any other state; and, what is more remarkable, it manufactures more flour than is manufactured in any other state or
province on the globe, the product for the year ending September 1st, 1899, being twenty-five million barrels, of which fifteen
million were made in Minneapolis. These facts give the state a
wide reputation throughout the world; and this all has been attained within the memory of those here tonight. All this we
have from a country which was pronounced by eastern editors
worthless for settlers.

The development of our resources has been rapid, not only
in the production of wheat and the manufacturing of flour,
but in our mineral products. In 1884 we produced 62,124 tons
of iron ore. We shall supply the markets this year with more
than 12,000,000 tons of the very best of iron ore. To show how
rapidly the iron industry has developed, I have only to relate
an instance of what I witnessed a few years since at West Superior, in Wisconsin, adjoining our city of Duluth. Two whaleback steamers were to be launched, and a large number of our

citizens were to witness the launching of these great steamers. A special train of cars took us to West Superior, a place which but a few years before was the roving ground for the Indians. We found there fine public buildings, elegant schoolhouses, nice churches, paved streets, good hotels, and some 10,000 enterprising people. A large rolling-mill had been erected and was manufacturing 125 tons of steel daily, used for the plating of these large whaleback vessels. To our great astonishment, we were informed that the ore from which the steel was manufactured was lying in its native soil, in the part of Minnesota north of lake Superior, some six months before.

Not until 1864 did we have a mile of railroad within the limits of this state; today we have thirteen trunk lines of railroad reaching St. Paul and Minneapolis, over which two hundred and fifty-five trains of cars arrive and depart every twenty-four hours. A person can now take a seat in the cars on the Atlantic coast and cross the continent by the way of Minnesota to the Pacific coast with but one change of cars, and with but two changes can reach China or Japan.

Consider also the growth of the mail service. In 1850 the government asked for proposals to carry the mails leaving St. Paul once a week, on Sunday, to reach Prairie du Chien, 270 miles distant, the Sunday following, and to come back by the next Sunday. The notice contained the significant statement, that "more frequent supply will be considered." Compare that service with the service of today and how wonderful is the change!

The number of vessels that passed through the Sault Ste. Marie canal in 1855 was less than 100, with a tonnage of 106,-296, the valuation of which was less than one million dollars. The number of vessels that passed through the canal in 1898 was 17,761, with a tonnage of 21,234,661, of the value of $233,-069,739. The volume of business through the Sault Ste. Marie canal in 1899 will be four times that of the business through the Suez canal.

Minnesota as a producer of wealth during the half century past has forged ahead so rapidly that today she outranks those states which came into the Union about the time she was admitted. Her valuation of property did not exceed fifteen millions in 1850; today her valuation is upwards of $600,000,000, and as a wealth-producing state she ranks well up with the

leading states in the Union. For the proof of this statement, I shall only have to cite the fact that the annual value of our wheat product is nearly as great as one-half of all the gold annually mined in the United States.

Our state has been highly honored by the appointment of two of her distinguished citizens to cabinet positions under the presidents of the United States. Under President Hayes our distinguished citizen and president of this society, Governor Ramsey, served as Secretary of War. Senator Windom served as Secretary of the Treasury, with signal success, in President Garfield's cabinet, and also in the cabinet of President Harrison. In one of the greatest international complications of this half century, Minnesota is again honored by the President of the United States in the appointment of our distinguished senator, C. K. Davis, as one of a commission to adjust our difficulties with Spain and to effect a treaty with that government.

The people of Minnesota, when taking a retrospective view of the past half century, have great reason to be thankful for the progress that has been made in every direction during that period; thankful that our State has always been ready to render loyal service to the general government in defense of our common country; thankful, also, that our people are living under the laws of the most liberal and beneficent government ever devised, and at the same time sufficiently powerful to guarantee to the most humble citizen ample protection of life, liberty, and the possession of property.

It has been truly said that, next to the love for one's home, is the love for one's state and country. We who have lived in the state of Minnesota have rejoiced to see the development of the resources of our state, and her growth in everything relating to the interests of her people. We have watched the pioneer fell the tree, plough the furrow, and build the schoolhouse and the church. In all this, through seasons of prosperity and seasons of adversity and discouragement, our attachment to our state and our pride in our state have never failed. The state of Minnesota has steadily advanced in prosperity; she is rich in the bounties which nature has bestowed upon her, rich in lakes, in forests, in mines, and in her broad prairies. Progress and hopefulness in the development of her many resources are on every side; everywhere order, thrift, and contentment prevail.

EDUCATION IN THE UNITED STATES AND IN MINNESOTA DURING THE PAST FIFTY YEARS.

BY CYRUS NORTHROP, PRESIDENT OF THE STATE UNIVERSITY.

The great work of the present generation is to prepare the coming generation to take our places. The progress of civilization is assured when it is certain that the men and the women of the future will be in all respects superior to their predecessors. The reliance of the present age for the accomplishment of this work is largely on schools and colleges. It is therefore an interesting task to look back on the educational situation fifty years ago and to compare it with the situation now.

THE COMMON SCHOOLS.

Fifty years ago the chief institutions of education were the common school, the academy, and the college. The common school was not free to all without payment of school rates. The studies pursued in the common schools were reading, spelling, writing, arithmetic, geography, and grammar. Webster's spelling book was an essential work. First the alphabet must be learned, letter by letter, a process long and laborious for some scholars, and very trying to the teacher. Then came "a b, ab," then "cat" and "dog." and after a while a notable advance was made to "baker;" and from that to the triumphant spelling in class of "incomprehensibility" was a long educational journey. It did not matter very much when there was so little to be learned beyond. But the process did make better spellers than the average of college students today.

Now the little child first learns to read, and afterward learns his letters. In two months he can learn to read with a

knowledge of the sound of the letters, without any knowledge of their names. Now he is to a large extent put into graded schools, and each grade has its own specific work in preparation for the next.

The old common school (and for that matter the common school of today is like it) was not graded. It had one teacher for all work, from the alphabet up to grammar,—in summer, a more or less intelligent young lady who wanted to earn a little money before getting married, and in winter a man who had been working on a farm or at something else during the summer, and who, having no regular employment in winter, was glad to find occupation in teaching. I do not mean to say that these were poor teachers—they were not such always,— but they were not trained teachers. By the light of their experience they did as well as they could with the knowledge they had, sometimes succeeding and sometimes not. Very few of their scholars expected to go to the academy or the college. Their work therefore was circumscribed within definite limits, and only the brightest of the scholars ever advanced so far as to be masters of grammar and arithmetic. Practically, then, the common education of fifty years ago included little more than reading, writing, spelling, geography, and the simpler parts of arithmetic.

ACADEMIES.

But there were academies for students desiring to go further in their learning than the common school could carry them. These were sometimes endowed institutions, like Phillips Academy at Andover, Mass., another Phillips Academy at Exeter, N. H., and the Hopkins Grammar Schools at New Haven and at Hartford, Conn. Sometimes they were private institutions without endowment. Their aim in all cases was to fit students for college if any of their students desired to go to college, and to prepare the larger number of their pupils who would finish their education in the academy for somewhat higher and better work than they could otherwise do. The range of studies included Latin, Greek, and mathematics, as a preparation for college, and a review of grammar and arithmetic, with higher work in the same than could be found in the common schools. Sometimes book-keeping and surveying

were added, if the principal happened to be able to teach these. Practically no science was taught. Possibly a little of natural philosophy and of astronomy might find a place in the curriculum of some academies; but most of them were destitute alike of laboratories, apparatus, and scientific teachers.

Many of these academies were taught by more or less broken down clergymen, who were not wanting in earnestness and fidelity, and who made a lasting impression on their pupils, but all of whose work was limited by the character of the training they themselves had received. I am bound to speak with respect and admiration both of the work done by these teachers in the academies and of the results as shown in the lives of their pupils. What they did they did thoroughly and well. Education for them was not a process of cramming, but of training. They were not trying to see how many things and how much of many subjects they could make their pupils understand and remember. On the contrary, they dealt with few studies, and they made thorough work of those according to the idea of the time. They built up character. They awakened enthusiasm. They taught boys to think,—and there resulted a more virile, independent, self-reliant class of scholars and men than are usually produced by the educational processes of the present day. They faithfully served their purpose in filling the gap between the common school and the college, and they made life to thousands who could never go to college a sweeter and nobler thing than it would have been but for their training.

COLLEGES.

The same in substance might be said of the college fifty years ago. It did good work and produced good results, but its range of studies was narrow. During the first two years it carried on exclusively Latin, Greek, and mathematics. During the last two years it gave instruction in political economy, psychology, logic, history to a very small extent, astronomy, natural philosophy, geology, and chemistry, but without any practice in laboratories. It had practically no instruction in literature, in biology, or in modern languages. Its library was accessible only at stated times, and then not for research but to draw out a book. Its curriculum of the junior and senior

years was enriched with more Latin and Greek if desired. It had no sociology, no psychology except the results of introspection. It was a bare, rugged skeleton, without flesh, skin, or beauty; and the wonder is that it could contain life as it did. Such as it was, it drew to itself a few hundreds of young men, ambitious to enter what were called the learned professions, and very few others. Schools of science were few and all of them young; and business men rarely thought of the college as a preparation for their work.

Apparatus for teaching was insignificant. A student in astronomy might possibly get a chance to look at the moon through an inferior telescope; the class in chemistry could look on, while the professor performed various more or less successful experiments with his chemicals; the class in natural philosophy could see how an old air-pump, Atwood's machine, and a few other things, worked; and the class in geology could see the various kinds of stones and minerals, and handle them if so disposed. But it was all lecture and text-book work; nothing was learned by personal experiment, and by doing for one's self the things which were exhibited by the professors in their experiments. As a result, the men were rare who had any knowledge of science that was worth much. In short, most men came out of college about as it was intended that they should, not knowing much, but trained to study and fully capable of mastering other subjects in future if they got a chance.

DEVELOPMENT OF OUR EDUCATIONAL SYSTEM.

The Hon. W. T. Harris, United States Commissioner of Education, has said that "by common consent the teachers of the United States would choose Massachussetts as the state possessing the most interesting educational history." How numerous and important are the educational problems which Massachusetts has solved for her own good, and incidentally for the good of other states, will clearly appear from an enumeration of some of the most important, as given by Mr. Harris. "The adoption of a course of study and the fixing of the amount of instruction to be given in each branch, and the time when it is best to begin it; the relative position of the disciplinary and the information studies; the use and disuse of

corporal punishment; the education of girls; written examinations; the grading of schools; the relation of principal and assistant teachers; professional instruction in normal schools; religious instruction; unsectarian moral instruction, and secular instruction; the separation of church and state; government by centralized power, and then by distribution of power to districts, realizing the extreme of local self government, and then the recovery of central authority; public high schools, and private academies; coeducation and separate education of the sexes; educational support by tuition fees, rate bills, general taxation and local taxation; general and local supervision by committees and by experts; educational associations and teachers' institutes; large and small school buildings and their division into rooms, their heating, ventilation, and lighting; evening schools, kindergartens, industrial art instruction, free text books,—all these problems have been agitated in Massachusetts."

Many of these problems had been solved fifty years ago, but some of the most important did not find a solution till some time within the last half century. How persistent the conservative element has been in resisting changes may be seen in "the long battle against the district system, lasting over fifty years," with six victories won alternately by the opposing factions, until at last the opponents of the district system won a final victory in 1882 and the district system was abolished, only forty-five towns out of three hundred and fifty having retained it up to that time. From the experience of Massachusetts the other New England states and many western states largely settled by New England people learned wisdom, and were able to settle their educational policy wisely without passing through the contention and experiments by which Massachusetts had felt out her course.

Fifty years ago the district school was still in its glory in a large part of New England. "Each school district," as a writer has said, "became a center of semi-political activity. Here was exhibited, in all its force, what Guizot so aptly terms 'the energy of local liberty.' The violence of ebullition is inversely as the size of the pot. Questions involving the fate of nations have been decided with less expenditure of time, less stirring of

passions, less vociferation of declamation and denunciation, than the location of a fifteen by twenty district schoolhouse. I have known such a question to call for ten district meetings, scattered over two years, bringing down from mountain farms three miles away men who had no children to be schooled, and who had not taken the trouble to vote in a presidential election during the period."

These were not the only contests. The district committee was an important matter. This committee could usually hire the teacher, and either because some family was angry at the teacher, or because some other family had a relative whom they desired for teacher, there was constant and sometimes acrimonious contention over the election of the school committee.

But on one point there was entire harmony. This I know both by my own observation and the testimony of others. This point was as to what was essential for the site of a schoolhouse. "The land must be valueless, or as nearly so as possible, for frugality was ever a New England virtue. A barren ledge by the roadside, a gravelly knoll, the steeply sloping side of a bosky ravine, the apex of the angle of intersecting roads, such as these were choice spots." The schoolhouse where I first went to school, in Connecticut, stood in such an angle where four roads converged or diverged, the inclosed space being in the highest degree rocky; and the schoolhouse stands there to-day, the building somewhat better than its predecessor, but the environment substantially as it was, the site of the schoolhouse not having cost the district a penny for a hundred and fifty years.

Of the rude equipment of the schoolhouse, the absence of desks and chairs, the absence of every thing conducive to comfort except the chance to learn such elementary subjects as the untrained teacher was able to teach, I need not speak. It is a wonder that so much was accomplished, where so little was expended to make learning either attractive or possible.

Time will not permit me to speak at length of the teachers of the district schools, whether men or women, whether ugly or sweet, whether experienced or fresh. I have already indicated the range of study in these schools. It is customary, I believe, to regard these district schools as mighty factors in

the production of a noble generation of clear-thinking and intelligent men. Undoubtedly there were many such men fifty
years ago, and undoubtedly the district school had something
to do with making them what they were. That is, the district
school started them towards their career. As some one has
said: "The power and majesty with which the Mississippi
sweeps by New Orleans to the Gulf were not brought by it out
of lake Itasca. But let us give the lake credit for what it did
do,—it set the rill a flowing. So did the district school. It
gave the key to the world's literature. What that key was
worth, depended on the use made of it."

If there had been nothing more invigorating fifty years
ago than the district school, the children could not have known
much, for little was taught; and they could not have had very
lofty ideals, for none were to be found in the district schools.
As the intellectual life of a majority of the people was bounded
by these schools, the vigor of the age must have been small
indeed but for forces outside, forces to which I can only allude,
—the pulpit, religion, religious thought, argument on high
themes of state and of future destiny, being a few of the most
potent.

Happily for the boy with a bright mind, a taste for knowledge, and an ambition to be and to do something more than
his sluggish school-mates, there opened that gate to all possibilities, the old-fashioned country academy. There he could begin studies that would lead to the college, studies of which the
district school never dreamed. And these New England academies, narrow in their scope, compared with our high schools,
but intense and thorough, transformed tens of thousands of
men who could not go to college into able and influential public
men, and gave a breadth to culture in the community that the
colleges alone could never have produced.

Dummer Academy, the first of the noble company, founded
in 1761, educated under its first master fifteen members of Congress, two chief justices of the Supreme Court, one president
of Harvard College, and four college professors. The record of
Leicester, Munson, Williston, Andover, and a multitude of
other schools of the same type, would show results quite as interesting and creditable.

Of course, every boy who went to an academy had to pay tuition. There was no free education of so high a type as that furnished by the academy. Of course, also, as a consequence it was only the sons of the wealthier class, at least it was very rarely the sons of the very poor, who went to the academy.

If that state of things had continued to the present time, the sharply defined distinction of classes at the present day would be very much more evident than it is. For nothing has done so much to rub out the lines of separation among our people as free public education from primary school to university.

This magnificent system of public education, free to all, is wholly the development of the last half century; and nowhere does it exist in nobler form or with more beneficent influence than here in the Northwest. By a well arranged order of schools of different grades, the children of the state are enabled to advance from the lowest to the highest grade without interruption and without hindrance because of charges for tuition. The high schools, coming into existence about thirty years ago, and multiplying everywhere until they cover the country far better than the academies ever covered even New England, not only furnish to all their students an education quite equal to that of the colleges not so very many years ago, but they fit them in an admirable manner for the larger work of the modern university.

NORMAL SCHOOLS.

It is only sixty years since the first normal school was established in this country for the systematic training of teachers. Up to that time teaching had not been regarded as an art for acquiring which special training was needed. Knowledge was imparted in various ways according to the taste and temperament of the teacher. Such things as method and science to be used in ordinary teaching were unknown. While the object of teaching was to enlighten, fructify, and stimulate the mind of the pupil, no one thought of making the mind of the pupil a study in order to know how best to affect it.

Systematically trained teachers would have been an incalculable blessing in the olden time, when the things to be taught and the pupils to be instructed were alike comparatively few. In the present age, with the multitude of subjects, and with

39

pupils as the sand upon the seashore in numbers, such trained teachers are indispensable. Normal schools have multiplied in the last thirty years; and trained teachers, of whom fifty years ago there were but a few hundred, are now to be found by the tens of thousands. Those of them who have a knowledge of the subjects to be taught, as well as of the right methods of teaching, are doing a work which fully justifies all that has been done for normal schools.

INSTRUCTION IN SCIENCES.

Perhaps in no more striking way can I illustrate the progress in education, particularly in the teaching of sciences, than by a comparison of the apparatus and methods in use in some particular sciences fifty years ago and now. I select for this purpose Natural Philosophy, a science well developed a half century ago, and Botany, a science of later development. I have asked the professors in charge of these subjects in the University of Minnesota to prepare statements, and what immediately follows is their report upon their respective departments.

PHYSICS.

Professor Frederick S. Jones, of the Chair of Physics, says:

The science of modern Physics may be said to have grown from infancy to maturity during the first sixty years of the present century. During this period more important discoveries in physical science were made than in any other equal period of its history, and they justified the differentiation of the old science of Natural Philosophy into its constituent parts, of which Physics is one of the most important.

Without attempting to give a detailed account of all that was accomplished, it will be of interest to note some of the most remarkable points. In 1800, Volta closed his acrimonious debate with Galvani, and gave to the world the electric battery. This marks a turning point in the history of electrical science. Davy immediately proceeded to obtain sodium, potassium, and many other metals, by electrical methods; he discovered the voltaic arc, and the electric light was the result. Oersted announced the action of electric currents on magnets; Ohm and Ampère formulated and proved the laws which form the basis of the mathematical theory of electricity; Young and Fresnel established the undulatory theory of light; Carnot, Helmholtz, Joule, and Mayer, gave exact form to the laws of the conservation of energy and the principles of thermodynamics; Kirchhoff invented the spectroscope and analyzed the sun's light; and Faraday, the scientific Nestor of them

all, discovered electrical induction and made possible the modern applications of the dynamo, the motor, the telephone, and the electric light. All this accumulation of knowledge had to be formulated, put into tangible and teachable form, and given to the student of science; and it necessitated a radical change in methods of instruction, and an enormous increase in apparatus, books, and accessories. It made the modern physical laboratory a necessity in every educational institution.

Fifty years ago the ordinary lecture on Natural Philosophy was almost entirely devoid of practical illustration and therefore apt to be unintelligible. Great scientific truths had to be taken on faith, for the student had no chance to verify by personal experiment. A meager supply of the most primitive instruments constituted the "cabinet" of the ordinary academy or college. Some idea of the utter poverty of American colleges in instrumental appliances may be had from the report of the President of Harvard College, made in 1865, in which he said: "A new hall should be erected, suitable for the accommodating of the Hollis Professor of Natural Philosophy and the Rumford Professor of Applied Science. At the same time there is urgent need that both these professorships have additional endowments, neither having any income whatever for the supply of illustrative apparatus or machinery. The professors have even been compelled to borrow articles from the factories and shops and return them at the close of the lecture; and five courses have been given without any illustrative apparatus whatever. The special departments of Literature, the Greek and Latin classics, English belles lettres, and pure mathematics, have moderate endowments; but the modern physical sciences exist in vain for the Harvard student or professor, unless he chance to have private means of large amount."

At that time the Lawrence Scientific School offered no instruction whatever in Physics; although it did give its students the privilege of attending these experimental lectures. A physical laboratory was unknown at Harvard for the next ten years, and at Yale for the next twenty years. But such conditions could not long exist. The subject to be taught was too rich and complex, and its application to the needs of civilized life too important; the physical laboratory and the properly equipped lecture-room became necessities in every college, and even in the high schools and academies.

During the past twenty years the erection of appropriate buildings for physical investigation has gone steadily on, and elaborate instrumental equipments have replaced the old philosophical cabinets. One of the most recent creations, the McGill laboratory, built and equipped at a cost of $350,000, represents more than the entire value of philosophical apparatus in all the American colleges of fifty years ago. The total valuation of scientific apparatus in American colleges now exceeds $16,000,000, and is constantly increasing. Faraday's experiments were not repeated to any extent in teaching physics even twenty years after their publication; but Roentgen's famous X-ray work in 1896 was

reproduced before every college audience in the country within two months of the date of its announcement, the tendency of modern laboratories being to keep their equipment fully abreast of scientific discovery.

Such has been the progress in the science of physics during the past half century. The instrumental and library facilities of the early fifties bear about the same relation to those of the present time, as did Galvani's twitching frog to the exquisite electrical mechanism of modern times. The causes for the advance are, first, the general improvement in teaching all branches of knowledge; second, the impetus given by practical applications of electricity; and, third, the achievements of the preceding half century, which required experimental illustration and elucidation.

BOTANY.

Professor Conway MacMillan, of the Chair of Botany, says:

The science of Botany is of modern development. Fifty years ago it did not exist; nor was it possible for it to be born until the epoch-marking discovery of a primal living substance common to plants and animals. Up to that time plants were of interest almost solely for their various medicinal or other economic relations. Suddenly they were discovered to be relatives of man and became interesting for their own sake. The studies of Hoffmeister and Darwin, looking toward a unification of plant and animal development, served to strengthen the position that plants had acquired upon the discovery of protoplasm.

From that time, about fifty years ago, it became a matter of altogether secondary importance to decide what specific names should be applied to plants. The botany of Tournefort, Linnæus, Bentham, and Gray, concerning itself principally with petal-counting, with systematic arrangement, with species description, and with bibliographic research into questions of nomenclature, was recognized to be a merely mechanical process, useful in botanical institutions just as a card catalogue is useful in a library, but having little or no relation to a real scientific inquiry into plant-life. As a matter of fact, the identification of species, the collection of herbaria, and the revision of nomenclature, which were to Linnæus almost the whole of botany, are not now considered by the best informed to be botanical science at all. Yet so persistent are the notions of the past that even today in many institutions herbalism still passes for botany. Hence it is common to hear that Linnæus was the father of botany. This is not true. Linnæus was the father of plant nomenclature; but Von Mohl and Hoffmeister, Knight and Senebier, were the fathers of botany.

Modern botany, in its pure form, bases itself upon the dictum, *"Plants are alive; they are worthy of study";* and, in its economic form, takes its stand upon the proposition, *"Plants are human food-supply, the human shelter, and the human environment; they should be understood and*

fully utilized." As a preliminary to all this, they may properly enough be named and classified, and even preserved in herbaria and museums as objects of interest. But taxonomy, as the old botany is now termed, has after all only a subsidiary interest.

The divisions of pure botanical science are these: the study of structure, or morphology; the study of function, or physiology; the study of development, or embryology; the study of environmental relations, or ecology; the study of positions on the earth's crust, or distribution.

Of economic botany some principal divisions are horticulture, agriculture, pharmacognosy, forestry, arboriculture, fiber culture, landscape gardening, bacteriology, plant pathology, and plant breeding.

There are, moreover, many special fields that lend themselves to ready definition: thus algology is the science of algae; mycology, the science of fungi; bryology, the science of mosses; pteridology, the science of ferns; cytology, the science of the cell; anatomy, the science of tissues; plant paleontology, the science of past vegetation; seminology, the science of seeds; and a hundred other "ologies," limited in their relation to the general subject, but fast becoming unlimited in their literature, their technique, their application, and their contents.

So broad is the field of modern botany that a student may work throughout his college course, through his years of graduate study to his doctorate, and during all his life as a professional investigator and teacher, without ever needing to refer to the works of Linnæus, and without ever "analyzing a flower or collecting a herbarium specimen."

Under the modern conditions the maintenance of a botanical institute becomes a complex matter. There must be museums, herbaria, libraries, publications, expeditions, gardens, lectures, laboratory exercises, seminars, and journal clubs. The machinery of the chemist and the physicist, of the engineer, the architect, the artist, and the electrician, may be drawn upon. Thousands of chemical reagents must be kept in stock. Hundreds of machines and utensils, such as microscopes, clinostats, thermostats, recording apparatus, microtomes, thermometers, barometers, spectroscopes, ovens, paraffine baths, freezing chambers, incubators, air pumps, filter pumps, auxanometers, dynamometers, projection apparatus, photographic appliances, card catalogues, bibliographic conveniences, dialyzers, glassware, and tubing, must be constantly on hand. A systematic collection of paraphernalia is absolutely necessary before the plant can be questioned and its secrets of structure, of function, and development, can be unveiled.

The director of a botanical institution must keep everything swinging in union to accomplish his best work. Illustrative material for dissection, for comparison, for experiment, and for demonstration, must be accessible at the "psychological moment" in his lecture or in his laboratory instruction. The periodical literature in his specialty, numbering now some hundreds of regular journals, must be at hand.

It is the function of the modern botanical institute not to analyze flowers, not to stimulate a *dilettante* interest in the field and meadows, not to accumulate innumerable desiccated curios of plant life, not to affix Latin names to defenceless vegetation; but to be ready to push forward the scientific investigation of those microcosms, the plants, and to help others to probe nearer the secret of their existence. All this looks toward the advancement of human knowledge and the uplifting and broadening of human life.

After having been begun as an amusement, continued as a purveyor of drugs to the medical profession, developed for a time as a systematic classification of natural objects, Botany fifty years ago took its place as a branch of the science of life. In its field are being solved some of the questions of deepest moment to the human race. In the modern study of plants lies the hope of the future, as to the advancement of agricultural methods, the limitation of disease, the lengthening and the comprehension of life. Botany is not merely a division of the natural sciences; it is one phase of the world problem.

SUMMARY AND STATISTICS OF EDUCATIONAL PROGRESS.

Time will not permit me to enter into further details. The progress of the last fifty years may be briefly summarized. Its most striking features have been: 1. The establishment of grades in schools, and special provision for the youngest children in kindergartens; 2. The establishment of training schools for teachers; 3. The establishment of scientific and technical schools; 4. A wonderful increase in appliances and aids, as libraries, laboratories, and apparatus; 5. Great endowments of colleges and schools, by the national government, state governments, and individuals; 6. Increased attention to literature in the study of language; 7. A marvelous extension of all kinds of scientific study, including agriculture, the most important of all; and 8. The establishment of graduate courses, enabling students to carry their studies much further than formerly.

Fifty years ago every college in the country was poor; and no college had an equipment, excepting its library, equal to that of the best high schools today. Now, the annual income of Harvard University is more than one and a half millions of dollars. Its productive funds exceed nine millions of dollars. Its library has 545,000 volumes. Yale has 285,000 volumes; and the University of Minnesota has 60,000 volumes. I need not mention in detail the great gifts which have founded and

built up Johns Hopkins, Chicago, and Leland Stanford Universities, gifts amounting to $25,000,000. The University of California has recently received from a lady a gift of six millions of dollars for buildings, twenty-five thousand dollars being given just for architectural plans.

Fifty years ago, Connecticut had a school fund of $2,000,000, and it was deemed magnificent. Today such a fund is small in comparison with the larger funds of many states, our own state already having a fund more than five times as large and likely to become ten times as large.

There are today in the United States 472 Universities and Colleges of Liberal Arts, at which more than 150,000 students are in attendance. The total annual income of these institutions is nineteen millions of dollars. The bound volumes in their libraries number 6,700,000. The value of their scientific apparatus is more than $16,000,000. The value of their grounds, buildings, and productive funds, is $240,000,000. And the benefactions they receive, while varying from year to year, amount to several millions yearly. The United States, in its magnificent proportions of today, is not grander, in comparison with the infant republic of 1776, than are the educational forces of the country today as compared with those of fifty years ago.

DONATIONS THIS YEAR FOR PUBLIC EDUCATION.

In conclusion, I may say that the donations to educational institutions of the United States have not been as large in any previous year as in 1899. Already there have been received by these institutions, during the present year, nearly $30,000,-000. The wealthy people of the country are beginning to understand that it is better to be their own administrators, and to give their wealth while they are alive, rather than to bequeath it at their death; and that there is no nobler use to which they can put their money than in endowing and making powerful universities for the education of the people. How general this disposition to promote education is becoming, will appear, I think, from the following list of the principal benefactions during this year 1899. It will be noticed that in this splendid list the University of Minnesota does not appear, as the recipient of any large private benefaction.

Mrs. Leland Stanford, to Leland Stanford University	$15,000.000
Estate of John Simmons, for the Female College, Boston..	2,000,000
Henry O. Warren, to Harvard College	1,000,000
G. W. Clayton, for a university at Denver	1,000,000
P. D. Armour, to Armour Institute	750,000
Maxwell Somerville, to the University of Pennsylvania....	600,000
Edward Austin, to Harvard College	500,000
Lydia Bradley, to Bradley Polytechnic Institute	500,000
Samuel Cupples, to Washington University	400,000
Jacob Schift, to Harvard College	300,000
Marshall Field and J. D. Rockefeller, to the University of Chicago	300,000
Edward Tuck, to Dartmouth College	300,000
J. D. Rockefeller, to Brown University	200,000
Caroline L. May, to New York Teachers' College	200,000
Edwin Austin, to the Massachusetts Institute of Technology	200,000
R. C. Billings, to the Massachusetts Institute of Technology	100,000
O. C. Marsh, to Yale College	100,000
Andrew Carnegie, to the University of Pennsylvania	100,000
Unknown donor, to Wesleyan University	100,000
George R. Berry, to Baltimore Female College	100,000
J. D. Rockefeller, to Denison University	100,000
W. K. Vanderbilt, to Vanderbilt University	100,000
Unknown donor, to Princeton College	100,000
R. C. Billings, to Harvard College	100,000

Besides these, there is a multitude of smaller gifts, the total of which rises to the millions. May the liberality thus manifested toward the highest institutions of learning continue to promote education in the years to come, and thus nobly supplement the grand work of the states in their provision for public and universal education.

PROGRESS OF THE UNITED STATES DURING THE HALF CENTURY.

BY HON. CUSHMAN K. DAVIS, UNITED STATES SENATOR.

The progress of the United States, during the half century now about to end, is a trite subject for discussion. I do not believe that the present generation can adequately estimate it. To us it is commonplace. The things that we ourselves have done always so appear. We become so familiar with them, so used and wonted to them by daily contact and elaboration, so versed in the small and myriad details in which any great achievement is necessarily involved, that the entire perform- ance is, to us, like a stage play to its actors, the mere routine of daily life, however gorgeous and spectacular it may seem to the audience. It would be easy enough to treat this progress with sounding and general declamation; to say in elaborate phrase what everyone knows, and to gratify ourselves with self-praise. I am not sure that it would not be entirely proper to do so; for surely the men and women of any eventful epoch about to close have a right to look back proudly over its great results, and to say "all of this have we seen, and of it we have been a great part." But we need not fear that this will not be abundantly done on other occasions.

It has therefore seemed to me that I shall perform a very pleasant duty most usefully by indicating some of the general lines along which this progress has been made.

All National progress is valuable only so far as it benefits humanity. Any other progress is illusory, and does not de- serve the name, although it has often received it. The develop- ment of the United States during the last fifty years has, in my opinion, this for its distinguishing trait, that it has bene- fited man more as an individual, given him more liberties, func-

tions, opportunities, comforts, enjoyments, luxuries even, than he has received in any other half century since time began. The social has been greater than the political progress, and one great excellence of this evolution will consist of the reaction of man as an individual upon political questions, which will be subjected to a higher intelligence than has ever before operated upon them.

The principal progress of humanity had, for many generations, been toward the acquirement of political rights. The struggle was to emancipate man from political restrictions of many kinds, imperial, social, and commercial. Our fathers rebelled to secure political rights. They fought for the right to govern themselves, and they secured it. That the American people, as individuals, should be raised to a higher enjoyment of personal dignity, privilege, and comfort, was not the immediate object of our fathers. Their task was the proximate one to secure that political independence which is the condition precedent to every ultimate social and personal benefit. Thus, up to about fifty years ago, political debates, speculations, and divisions, were largely of a general character, and, to a certain extent, abstract, even in their connection with the most practical questions.

But about the year 1850 a force, then recent, and which had been merely a weak and derided protest, became all at once a controlling power. It was generated by a great conception of the rights of man as an individual. This force manifested itself by an attack made by the intelligence and conscience of the Nation upon the institution of African slavery. The slave was liberated. It was a great achievement in itself, but it went far beyond its own consummation.

Pause for a moment and look back. You cannot help seeing how many vast, perilous, and intricate questions, involving asserted personal rights, have most forcibly presented themselves since 1850, and how rarely they appeared in any form before that year. These have not usually been political. They have been social, industrial, and economic agitations of popular intelligence and sentiment, which have more often enforced themselves by usage and custom than by legislation.

Perhaps the most universal and beneficent of these improvements in social conditions by which the individual has been benefited has been in regard to the status of woman. Her emancipation from an almost complete merger of her personality has been nearly accomplished. Fifty years ago her power in literature, art, and affairs, was small indeed. Today she owns and manages her own property; she is arrayed in nearly every rank of endeavor; she has become a function in all the concerns of life, beyond what was conceivable or dreamed of in former times. New fields of employment have been occupied by her. The doors of universities have been unbarred, and she walks, queenly and triumphant, in the cloistered halls of learning. She has ceased to be merely the satellite of man, shining with a reflected light, and, too often, eclipsed by his shadow, and has become another sphere of humanity shedding a milder and purer radiance upon all human concerns; and to her attractive power and beauty the tide of human welfare has risen to a greater height.

The last fifty years have not been an imaginative period. They have been intensely practical. More useful inventions have been made since 1850 than for two hundred years before. They have lightened labor and utilized waste substances. They have doubled time and shortened the duration of the act of production. They have thus given rest and leisure for intellectual improvement. They have cheapened products and they have not reduced wages. They have not barred any of the opportunities for employment, but have, on the contrary, created and increased them. For it is a truth that every invention which has produced a machine which can do the work of many hands has wronged no toiler, but has, on the contrary, improved his condition. The benefits have been universal. An inventory of the utensils of any household will disclose many devices to lighten toil, to shorten hours of work, and to produce a better result, which were unknown fifty years ago.

Education has become universal and its scope immensely greater. The school of whatever grade of that time was not the school of today. The difference is that the school now connects itself immediately with the practical life of after years, whereas it formerly did this in scarcely any degree.

People are better fed, better housed, and better clothed, than they were fifty years ago. The number of books in lowly houses has increased tenfold, and I think that the family life is better and closer now than it was then.

This is a self-governing people, and we look to see what effect this great progress towards individualism has had upon political affairs. It is to be noted, in the first place, that this individualism is simply the result of mental independence. Mental independence is the product of the resources of knowledge and thought. These resources have been partly the result, and partly the cause, of the personal advancement which I have indicated so imperfectly.

That this independence should assert itself in political affairs was inevitable. Accordingly, this half century has been signalized by great manifestations of free political action. Formerly political inconsistency was an unpardonable apostasy; it is now merely venial. Formerly the masses followed; now they lead. Their leading is not always wise,—but that is not the question. The fact is what we are seeking.

This independence of thought and action has been asserted and sustained by an unprecedented intellectual activity. The crowd often now debates ably, whereas formerly it merely hurrahed or dogmatized.

The political contest of 1896 was upon abstract and most difficult questions of finance and economics. I say nothing here as to the merits of that most remarkable controversy, but I will say that no political subject was ever debated so thoroughly and well by the masses of the people. There was, of course, much unfounded assertion and a deal of delirious prophecy; but, allowing for all these, there was a stock of information, and a vigor of argument employed by men talking with each other, never before equalled..

This is as it should be in a nation whose people settle everything. A people so endowed as ours will settle a disputed issue wisely, and much more speedily than was done in the earlier times, when irreflection, ignorance, and passion, were too often the prey of the demagogue or the victim of the wise man gone wrong. No more potent guaranty of our power and perpetuity has been produced, in our one hundred and twenty-

five years of development, than this subjection of political questions to individual independent opinion.

Of course, individual independence of action upon political subjects is sometimes ruinously destructive. Free thought is always in rebellion. If resisted too obdurately by ancient and evil institutions, it crushes and wrecks, by force irresistible, the entire social fabric of which they are a part. The French Revolution was such an event. It was the product of individual thought which for fifty years protested, remonstrated, suffered, and was often crushed only to rise again, until it possessed itself of the physical force of thirty millions of people, and swept into one chaos of destruction the good and the bad of a state which had stood for nearly a thousand years. The most salutary changes, both in the social and in the material world, are gradual; and the more imperceptible in their progress, the better they are. Had France been plastic a hundred years ago, the lava of the Revolution would not have buried so many institutions under its tide of fire, and Napoleon would never have appeared as conqueror, emperor, and reformer.

It is not to be doubted that the people of the United States will assimilate, and will concentrate into unitary action, the many and diverse forces of individual thought and action. They have always done so. If we look back over our history, we see many great events and emergencies of the most dangerous character which our fathers never foresaw, which were encountered, controlled, and settled, in every instance, to the increase of our power and stability. What other nation could have suffered and triumphed as did the United States in our civil war? Unprecedented as the mere military result was, it was slight compared with the fact that, during the generation which suffered and prevailed in it, the people of the North and South speedily reunited in a great National identity of patriotism and power.

The Louisiana purchase was an event of unexampled magnitude of its kind. To many of our greatest and purest statesmen, it seemed sinister, and manifestly destructive of our institutions and polity. But with the cession from Mexico it has become the very essence of our invincible strength as a Nation.

Present conditions of a similar character, which at once create anticipations of benefit, or apprehensions of evil, that

have no limits in the compass of the imaginations which conceive them, will, by the wisdom of a great people whose thought, speech, and action 'are free, be settled and wisely adjusted to the conditions and destinies of a civilization which has moved from its European and American seats across the great oceans, and which is touching with its creative hands the dark and inert masses of Oriental and African humanity.

Considering the evolution of the last fifty years, its mass, its spirit, its momentum and direction, we are warranted in believing that our country is now, as it has been heretofore, an agency of that Providence which guides and moves nations to the realization of every aspiration of humanity for better conditions, moral, intellectual, spiritual, and physical.

NOTE BY THE SECRETARY.

An address on the first of the two following subjects was expected to be given by Senator Knute Nelson, and on the second, completing the series of this Anniversary Celebration, by Gen. James H. Baker.

Senator Nelson, however, having recently returned from a long visit in Norway, his native land, found many and important duties requiring his attention before the opening of Congress, so that he felt obliged to decline the invitation of the Anniversary Committee. At the monthly meeting of the Historical Society, November 13th, the Committee secured the promise of Gen. John B. Sanborn to speak on the same subject that had been assigned for Senator Nelson, the address being thus without time for studied preparation.

Still later, a telegram was received from Gen. Baker, detained by business which had called him to New York City, saying that he could not be present at the Anniversary. In his place and on the subject announced for him, when only a part of one day remained, Col. William P. Clough consented to speak, that each theme in the series planned by the committee might be presented.

MINNESOTA IN THE NATIONAL CONGRESS DURING THESE FIFTY YEARS.

BY GEN. JOHN B. SANBORN.

Mr. President, and Ladies and Gentlemen: It was only at the close of the Historical Society meeting, on Monday evening, that I was notified by the committee and asked to fill this place. Hence I appear before you with no preparation whatever, except what any man has who has been identified with the affairs of Minnesota for forty-five years. In the celebration of this anniversary, a day of so much importance in the history of our Society and our State, all papers should be prepared with a great deal of care, every idea being thoroughly considered and fairly expressed. It seems scarcely proper, therefore, for me to proceed with any remarks upon this subject, which had been assigned to Senator Nelson.

It can be treated of course in a great many ways, but it cannot be treated by me in any adequate manner this evening. The addresses that have already been given, and the papers that have been prepared and read, have made frequent reference to the grand achievements of the people of this State. One of the most distinguished parts of this history of fifty years consists in the patriotic and honorable public services of her senators and representatives in Congress.

Minnesota had no life, corporate or otherwise, until Congress passed the act providing for the organization of the territory, on the third day of March, 1849. The land had been a wilderness, as it then was, from the dawn of creation. Of course, Adam was the original owner of this territory, and I think (although this may differ a little from the ideas of our distinguished Bishop Whipple) that the people whom we found

here when this was organized as a territory had descended from Cain and not from Abel. Under the marked influence that he has brought to bear upon them, however, it would be difficult now to substantiate the idea that they were descendants of Cain.

The organization of Minnesota as a territory brought her into immediate contact with the great powers of Congress and of the United States. No such powers of government exist anywhere else on the earth, nor have they ever existed, I think, in any period of the history of the race. When we speak of the authority of Congress, that does not fully come to our mind. It comprises the power of negotiating treaties with foreign nations, of regulating commerce with foreign nations, with the several states of the Union, and the Indian tribes; the power to raise and support armies, all expressed in five words, from which at times spring armies of a million men to protect and maintain these powers and enforce them; to provide and maintain a navy, from which navies sometimes spring, under the operations of Congress, that are capable of sweeping all other navies from the seas; and then that last, grand, transcendent power, to make laws to carry into effect all the foregoing powers and all other powers vested in the government of the United States or in any department or office thereof.

When Minnesota sent her first territorial delegate to Congress, and more definitely when statehood entitled her to send senators and representatives to Congress, she became a participant in the administration of those powers. She shared in the deliberations of Congress by her successive territorial delegates; and since her admission to statehood she votes on all questions, as when war shall be declared, or peace made, and what action shall be taken in regard to commerce and all those great relations which make states and make nations. This commenced, as I stated, on the third day of March, 1849. The white inhabitants of this territory were then few. My friend Moss was here at that time, and there were three or four thousand others.

But what was done then? From the provisions that are included in that act have flowed all the great results which have been referred to by the previous speakers. Among these are

the thirteen million dollars of our permanent school fund, and the State University. The simple enactment by Congress that sections 16 and 36 in each township of all the public domain in the territory and future states growing out of this region should be set apart for school purposes has brought about this result. Now to whom is that due in the main, to the greatest extent? Unquestionably to the first delegate from Minnesota who was there present, giving direction to legislation for our territory at that time, General H. H. Sibley. Thence followed the marvelous educational growth which has since appeared. It was the touch of the wand of the magician to the whole territory. Hitherto it had continued as it was in the beginning. Its only inhabitants had been untutored savages. Six thousand years had passed away without making any material changes, excepting here and there a mound to mark the burial places of a departed race.

There is little that I can say in regard to the part performed by Minnesota in the administration of the powers vested in Congress, except what was said by my predecessor, Governor Pillsbury, that she has always been thoroughly true and loyal to the federal government. Minnesota has always voted for the patriotic use of every power vested in the Congress of the United States, when it has been exerted for the preservation and development of our national life, and for the upbuilding and advancement of the whole country. At the same time there has been constant watchfulness for all the interests of the Northwest and of this State. There have been fifteen United States senators from Minnesota, and about three times as many representatives, forty-three, in the House of Representatives; but in no instance has the vote of the State been adverse to the loyal and patriotic exercise of any power granted by the Constitution to Congress or to any department of the federal government.

When the civil war commenced, the Minnesota senators were Morton S. Wilkinson, a republican, and Henry M. Rice, a democrat. Both were most ardent supporters of the government. To my astonishment, I heard Senator Wilson, of Massachusetts, chairman of the committee of military affairs, say to Mr. Rice, long years after the war, "I don't know how we could ever have

mobilized our armies, if you had not been on the military committee of the United States Senate;" and he went on to state
that they got more information and knowledge from Mr. Rice,
as to what was required to move a regiment or any organized
force of the army, than from all other sources combined, and
admitted that Mr. Rice had drawn all the provisions of the
law for that purpose.

That was the greatest crisis through which the nation has
ever passed. It was the time when all these powers which I
have referred to, and which are enumerated by the Constitution, were exercised. There was scarcely a power vested in
Congress, or in any department of the government, that was not
exercised to the fullest extent for four years during that war.
Times come in our national history when every such power
has to be exercised, when no power can be neglected; and so
far as Minnesota's conduct was concerned, in that great struggle for our national existence, she is entitled to the highest
praise and to the congratulation of this generation.

You may think it strange I have not a word to add concerning the representatives of Minnesota subsequent to the civil
war, and now, in our national Senate and House of Representatives. You are, all of you, as familiar with what they have
accomplished as I am myself. You know that by their standing and their efforts Minnesota has acquired a name and a reputation not only throughout this country but throughout the
whole earth. It is a source of everlasting commendation and
gratitude that the people have been so intelligent as to promote men so able as they have been to these exalted positions.

Looking forward, I can only express the hope that during
the next fifty years this State may be as loyal, and may be as
ably represented in both branches of the Congress of the United
States, as it has been during the past fifty years.

THE WORK OF THE MINNESOTA HISTORICAL SOCIETY THROUGH FIFTY YEARS IN PRESERVING MINNESOTA HISTORY, AND ITS DUTY TO THE FUTURE.

BY COL. WILLIAM P. CLOUGH.

Mr. Chairman, and Ladies and Gentlemen: I am in the same position as General Sanborn. I am a substitute, called in just at the eve of battle. The Anniversary Committee desired that this last address in celebration of the completion of a half century of this Historical Society should endeavor to make the public better acquainted with what it has done for the State, and with our manifest duty that this work shall continue and widen during the future years.

The first legislature of Minnesota, which met in this town fifty years ago, in September, 1849, was only small in numbers. There were twenty-seven members, all together, nine in the Council, and eighteen in the House. But they must have been a very remarkable body of lawgivers. They sat during eight weeks and four days. They had under their jurisdiction a territory almost as large as Germany or France. At that time Minnesota extended from the St. Croix, as it does now, at its eastern boundary, to the Missouri river at its western. It was without organized government of any kind, excepting that provided by the United States in accordance with the act establishing the Territory of Minnesota. It was without provision for the transfer and holding of property and the recording of titles. And still, in the short period of less than nine weeks, that small legislature completely organized the government in the Territory. It provided for its courts, for the administration of justice, for the transfer of property, for the care of the estates

of deceased persons, for the education of the youth, for the necessary roads and means of communication, and it did that all in the small space of forty-three acts. Why, legislatures much larger and supposed to be composed of men of much greater experience and ability need that today merely for the purpose of rubbing off the corners of previous legislation. But that first body of Minnesota lawgivers did its great work, accomplished all its purposes, taking legislation as a blank and filling it up completely, in forty-three acts and in fifty-two days of session.

But that legislature passed one other act, to incorporate the Historical Society of Minnesota, which was placed last in the publication of the laws passed during the session. This society was a somewhat feeble institution in its infancy. Everything was on a comparatively small scale in those days. But still the legislative act provided for a complete society for the purposes that were named by it in a somewhat general way. As was told you this afternoon, the society organized upon that basis and proceeded with its work.

It received a new impulse in the year 1856, when two further acts were passed regarding this society, and defining the work which it was to perform. Before, in the act of 1849, in a brief and general way the work and purposes and scope of the society were mentioned. In the first act passed in 1856, those purposes were expressed at somewhat greater length; but the second act in that year contained the following provision, which has been really the breath of life of the society. I will trouble you with the reading of it. It is very short and it tells the story in itself.

"Section 1. There shall be annually appropriated to the Minnesota Historical Society the sum of five hundred dollars, to be expended by said society in collecting, embodying, arranging and preserving in authentic form a library of books, pamphlets, maps, charts, manuscripts, papers, paintings, statuary, and other materials illustrative of the history of Minnesota; to rescue from oblivion the memory of its early pioneers, to obtain and preserve narratives of their exploits, perils, and hardy adventures; to secure facts and statements relative to the history, genius, progress or decay of our Indian tribes; to exhibit

faithfully the antiquities and the past and present resources of Minnesota; also to aid in the publication of such of the collections of the society as the society shall, from time to time, deem of value and interest; to aid in binding its books, pamphlets, manuscripts and papers, and in paying the necessary incidental expenses of the society."

This act is important, not merely for the small pittance which was all that it was thought could be afforded at that time from the slender revenues of the Territory for this work, but also for its recognition of a great fact, that among the educational institutions of the Territory and afterwards of the State, the Historical Society holds a prominent place.

The appropriation, you will observe, was perpetual. It has since been continued, I think, without any interruption, and of late years it has been increased, although not nearly to the amount, as we think, which should be expended upon such work. Besides the great tasks of administration of the constantly growing library, museum, and collection of portraits, another principal duty of the society, to which it has given continual attention, is the collecting and writing of history, especially the history of the State of Minnesota.

The study of history is not merely a thing of pleasure and a pastime. It is a study that is indispensable for success in the life of the individual and of the state. It is a thing which no civilized people can leave out from education and from daily use.

Everything that we see in physical nature is the result of something that preceded it. For example, the grass that grows under our feet does so because other grass grew there last year and in the years past. The beasts that walk the earth have the same forms, instincts, and habits, as their progenitors. This is a truth, so far as the physical world is concerned, which is absolute and universal. Practically, it is also universal in what we call the moral world, that is, the world of thought, of ideas, of impulses, of purposes, and consequently of men's actions. Nine hundred and ninety-nine out of a thousand of the things that every man does every day he does merely because he has previously done the same thing, or because somebody else has done the same thing before him. Is not that

true? Think of it. To say that a proposition is unusual, is to condemn it. To say that a proposition is unheard of, is to give it a knock-out blow. We are all the creatures of custom, and mankind has always been so. All of our institutions are bundles of customs. The examples of the customs are called precedents, and these control the action of men and of governments everywhere.

One of the greatest and best governments on the face of the earth has no constitution underneath it, excepting an unwritten constitution of precedents. In England, the country to which I refer, they have a kingdom and a parliament today because they have had them in antiquity. These things have gone on continuously, and the institutions which exist in England or in any other country today exist because other institutions of similar character existed in times past.

Custom, habit, and precedent, control us in every action. They control us as men and as citizens, in our daily avocations, at the ballot-box, and even on the field of battle. Can anybody doubt that the brave men who marched up San Juan hill, on the first day of July last year, were moved to greater daring because of the knowledge and recollection of what their predecessors in similar positions at Chattanooga and Atlanta and Gettysburg and in the Wilderness, had done? We must make a study of these precedents. It is as necessary to study the precedents of men's actions and of social institutions as it is to study arithmetic or grammar or mineralogy.

In these days there is a tendency in every direction to a systematic division of labor. In the workshop, in transportation, in every trade, in every profession, in every industry, this has proved very advantageous, and it is so particularly in education. It is not very long ago since the common schools were content with three studies. Men were taught those things, and they went out and battled with the world, many of them successfully. More studies were taught in the higher schools and colleges, but for a long time each institution spread itself over the entire domain of knowledge. Now the college or university divides itself into numerous branches. Now we have the classical and literary school, the scientific school, the agricultural school, the law school, the medical school, the dental

school, etc. A similar division of the work to be done is true also of those other great sources of instruction and knowledge, public libraries. Formerly a public library contained books of all classes. Literature, science, art, history, were all represented. Now a division of these subjects is being made. Some of the great new libraries, with large endowments, are confined entirely to science. In a short time others will be confined to literature, collecting poetry, fiction, plays, and essays. In a short time again others will be confined to art. The most important of all, because it affects the moral conduct of men, is the library of precedents, the library which informs us what man did under similar circumstances and under like conditions at periods in the past. That is the library of history. So many books have been written upon the subject of historical precedent that to include other subjects in the same public library makes it unwieldy and deprives each department of a large part of the good it might otherwise accomplish.

The fathers of the Territory of Minnesota and of the State appreciated this fact. They evidently foresaw and then provided for a great educational center in the State of Minnesota. In the first place, they foresaw, though imperfectly, the grand development of this Commonwealth, the beginning of which, for its first fifty years, we have reviewed today. Think of the possibilities of population for the future in our State. It is a fact worth mentioning, for purposes of comparison and to see where we may be in the future, that the area of the island of Great Britian, 88,226 square miles, only slightly exceeds that of the State of Minnesota, which is 84,287 square miles. Great Britain today is supporting, in comfort and luxury that have never been equalled in the world before, thirty-three millions of people. It would be no exaggeration to hope and to expect that Minnesota will have ten millions. And these ten millions must be educated, they must be trained, they must have all kinds of training that are necessary to fit them to be good citizens, useful men and women, qualified to do their duty under all circumstances and conditions to which they may be called.

The schools and the universities do their work. We have a great provision for them. This is a great educational center,

headed by the State University, one of the first schools of its
class in the country, and destined to become more useful and
influential, relatively, than it is today.   We have in our neighborhood also Hamline University, Macalester College, Carleton
College a short distance away, a Catholic college and a Catholic
seminary, and two Scandinavian seminaries, besides numerous
academies and the public high schools.   What could be more
fitting than to provide specially a historical library, free to all
our people, and conveniently accessible to the teachers and
students of all these institutions of learning?   That is what
the founders of the Territory and State of Minnesota provided.

It was designed that particularly the collection and preservation of the history of Minnesota should be the work of this
society, and surely there never has been any greater or more
honorable history than that of this community.   Look at it in
any aspect, in its commercial aspect, in its civil aspect, in war
and in peace.   Where is there a finer record than in Minnesota?
It is fitting that this record should be written, and that it
should be well written, thoroughly, accurately, impartially;
and there is no better arrangement for collecting the materials
of history, and for writing them fully and correctly, than a historical society like ours.   Some states have an official historian; but no individual, however successful in research and
authorship, can equal in efficiency a historical society.   Such
a society as this is made up of men of different religions, of
different politics, and of all shades of thought.   Impartiality, accuracy, the most careful investigation of all details of our
state history, can be expected from a body of that kind.   So it
has been fitting for the State of Minnesota to entrust the record of its honorable achievements, its settlement and progress,
and the illustrious careers of its public men, to a body of
this character.

This society has attempted to do the work which has been
committed to it, this great work, thoroughly well and impartially.   It has published eight volumes of its Historical Collections, comprising addresses, papers, and memoirs, on Minnesota history; and it has made a great collection of books of
history, one of the most valuable historical libraries in the
United States.

As was said this afternoon in an able paper, our society is collecting together the materials of our state history, and the best materials for use by the future historian. It is getting not merely the books of history which have been written, but it is gathering together and preserving the newspapers, which are the great source, and have been for the last century, of the materials of history. Upon this subject of the society's collection of Minnesota newspapers, I do not think too great stress can be laid. Besides, many files of newspapers from other states and countries, and some that are even far older than this society, have been acquired and are among the choicest treasures of its library; for it is recognized that the history of former times, and of other countries, is indispensable for frequent consultation by readers and students here.

If anybody will take the trouble of looking over the newspaper files of this Historical Society, I am sure that he will find much to gratify and interest him. He will learn that the newspaper is not an invention of this day or of this year or even of this century. He will find that good newspapers were published more than two hundred years ago. As an example I hold in my hand now the first volume of the "London Gazette," beginning, under the name "Oxford Gazette," November 16, 1665, and that was a fine newspaper then. This society has the complete series of it, issued semi-weekly, for nearly forty-eight years, extending to July 25, 1713. Next we have the "London Chronicle," published three times a week, for the years 1757 to 1762, inclusive. Our oldest file of an American newspaper is the "Connecticut Gazette," weekly, from June 9, 1780, to August 10, 1803, covering thus the last three years of the Revolution and the following twenty years. Of the "Columbian Centinel" (at first called the "Massachusetts Centinel"), published twice a week in Boston, we have an incomplete series extending through more than forty years, from September, 1786, to the end of the year 1827. Overlapping a part of that period, and continuing into the period that has been covered by our Minnesota newspapers, is the society's file of the "New Hampshire Patriot," from 1809 to the end of 1855. Thus for two hundred and thirty-four years, beginning in 1665, this society's library possesses, in these successive series of newspapers, an almost continuous contemporary record of the chief events of history.

I want to say to any gentleman who has not been in the habit of reading history in the newspapers but has confined himself to published books, that he loses much aid for obtaining a thorough insight and understanding of any particular event. The best account of any event, the best picture and detailed description of it, you will find, according to my experience, in the newspapers of the period.

A good illustration of the historical value of newspapers came under my observation during a visit in the State of Rhode Island last summer. There is a great historical society in Rhode Island, one of the largest institutions there; and one of the great historical events in that state was the seizure and burning of the British vessel "Gaspee" in the year 1772. That was the first overt act of the American patriots in the Revolutionary War. It preceded the Declaration of Independence by four years, and naturally it is a great event in the history of Rhode Island, and it is constantly commemorated there in many ways and on many occasions. In the reading room of their fine Historical Society building, which is situated near the buildings of Brown University, is a large painting depicting that event. On one of the walls near by is the portrait of the man who was said to be the leader of the band of patriots who assaulted and captured the ship, and it stated the date of the event to be a particular time. It seemed to me that the date was one which I had not read of before, and I asked the attendant whether it was correct. He looked at the card on the portrait, and then went off and presently brought a silver cup that had been presented to the Historical Society on the occasion of the commemoration of the same event a few years ago, and on the silver cup was another date, entirely different from that on the portrait. I thought it very strange that right at headquarters we should find two inconsistent dates of such an event, and it had a somewhat disturbing effect upon the official of the library. He proceeded to look the question up, and said, "The secretary of this society has just prepared an important paper on this subject, and it will give us the date." So that paper was resorted to, but it stated no date at all. I then said to him, "What was the name of the newspaper published in the State of Rhode Island in the year 1772?" He replied,

"The Providence Gazette was published at that ti , and we have the files." I said, "Very well, get that newspaper, and I warrant that you will find all about it and find it correctly stated." Accordingly he got down the files of the newspaper, and there we found an excellent report, just as you would find in the Pioneer Press tomorrow for any event occurring today in St. Paul within the observation of a reporter. It was short, but it was a much clearer and more specific account of the event than any I had ever seen. And in addition there was the proclamation of the British governor of Rhode Island, describing the same event and offering a reward for the capture of the offenders. The newspaper report and the proclamation gave a different date from either of those given on the portrait and on the cup; and the newspaper, having been published immediately after the event, was certainly authentic.

Now I venture to say that we make a mistake, all of us who have access to the files of newspapers, if we do not go to them for the best account of any of the events in our history. Therefore I think that one of the most valuable and useful departments of the Library of the Minnesota Historical Society is its great collection of newspapers. This is one of its best lines of work for the preservation of the history of Minnesota, well performed to the present time, and needful to be continued for future generations.

In addition to the benefit of the newspapers as mere history, and as furnishing the materials of better history in the future and of the events that are occurring today, better than we can get elsewhere, this collection is of vast business value to the State. It has been well remarked, that every piece of property, in every State, at least once in a generation, upon the average, passes through the hands of the law, under an administrator or sheriff or trustees or some legal proceedings, by which the title to the property is derived. Those proceedings are all advertised and referred to in the newspapers. Thus we have here, and the Minnesota Historical Society is perpetuating, the history of the title of every man's property in the State of Minnesota.

Ladies and gentlemen, I have detained you too long. I only intended to touch upon some features of the society's

work that had not been mentioned before, but I wanted you all to know, and we want the public to know, that this society has done good work for the people of Minnesota. This work must be continued, and it deserves the good will of the public and of the State.

Previous to the address by Colonel Clough, a song, composed by Von Suppe, entitled "My Native Land," was sung by Mr. J. Warren Turner, of Minneapolis, with piano accompaniment by Mr. Charles G. Titcomb.

After that address the audience rose and sang

AMERICA.

My country, 'tis of thee,
Sweet land of liberty,
   Of thee I sing;
Land where my fathers died,
Land of the pilgrims' pride,
From every mountain-side
   Let freedom ring.

My native country, thee,
Land of the noble, free,
   Thy name I love;
I love thy rocks and rills,
Thy woods and templed hills;
My heart with rapture thrills,
   Like that above.

Our fathers' God, to Thee,
Author of liberty,
   To Thee I sing;
Long may our land be bright
With freedom's holy light,
Protect us by Thy might.
   Great God, our King.

The Anniversary Celebration was then concluded with a benediction by Bishop Whipple.

E. F. Drake

OBITUARIES.

ELIAS FRANKLIN DRAKE.

Elias Franklin Drake was born in the village of Urbana, Champaign county, Ohio, on December 21st, 1813, and died in the seventy-ninth year of his life, on February 14th, 1892, at Hotel Del Coronado, San Diego, California. His death was the close of a long life of unusual activity and success.

About the close of the last century, Ithamar Drake, the grandfather of the subject of this sketch, removed from Pennsylvania to Warren county, Ohio, with his wife and four children, Henry, Abraham, Isaac and Mary. This was during the pioneer period of Ohio, and Ithamar Drake, like the great number of pioneers, engaged in farming, having purchased a tract of land which was heavily timbered. He was successful and became a prosperous and contented farmer. His children were reared on the farm. The family were members of the regular Baptist church, and in intelligence, morals, and religious life, were much in advance of the general average of pioneers in southern Ohio at that day. Subsequently and at the early settlement of Indiana, Ithamar Drake, with his son Isaac and his daughter Mary, who married Harvey Pope, removed to Shelby county, Indiana.

The son, Dr. Henry Drake, remained in Ohio, married Hannah Spining, and was the father of Elias F. Drake. Henry Drake had a thirst for knowledge, and although educational opportunities were limited, he acquired a good English education and studied Latin, Greek, and music. His father having furnished him with the necessary money, he studied medicine and was just beginning to practice his profession, when he died; leaving his widow with four young children and with little means of support.

Hannah Spining, the mother of Mr. Drake, was the daughter of Mathias Spining, who was a native of New Jersey and

was an active and ardent patriot in the Revolution. He fought
in the American ranks, suffered from the outrages committed
by the British troops in New Jersey, and became so imbued
with hostility to the English that he could never forgive
them nor forget the wrongs done. He married Hannah Haines,
a daughter of one of the leading families of New Jersey. After
the close of the Revolution, he with his wife settled in Warren
county, Ohio, upon a tract of land which was granted to him
by the government for his services in the war.* Here he
raised a large family in prosperity. He was a conscientious
Christian, originally a Presbyterian, but subsequently a member of the Christian Church.

The four children of Dr. Henry Drake were Ithamar, born
in 1811, Elias, born in 1813, Maria, born in 1815, and Henry,
born in 1818. Upon the death of the father, about 1820, his
widow and children were given a home upon Mathias Spining's
farm in a small house built by Elias Spining, a brother of Mrs.
Drake, and for whom the subject of this sketch was named.
Hannah Drake was a woman of strong character, who bravely
undertook the task of educating her children and giving them
such advantages as were within her power. There were in
those days no free schools, and none of any sort except in winter. Mrs. Drake boarded the schoolmaster to pay for the tuition of her children.

At the early age of seven began the life work of Elias F.
Drake. During the spring and summer he worked on the
farm, and attended school in the winter. There was little or
no leisure time during winter or summer. Farm products
were raised and sold for sustenance, and the mother spun wool
and flax for clothing. While a boy, for some months Mr. Drake
was employed in a printing office at Lebanon, the county seat
of Warren county. After a few months' trial, the printing
business not agreeing with his health, he returned to the farm.
Shortly after, in 1828, at the age of fifteen years, he became a

---

*An obituary notice, written by Judge Francis Dunlevy and published
in 1830 in the Lebanon Star, gives a full account of the Revolutionary services of Mathias Spining. Upon examination of the land records it appears
that on December 7th, 1779, John C. Symmes conveyed to Mathias Spining
200 acres near Lebanon, the deed reciting that the consideration was "$200
in certificates of debts of the United States." This land is the tract referred to above as being granted by the government. It would seem probable that these certificates were received for services in the Revolution. Mr.
Drake in his lifetime stated that his grandfather Spining had received his
land through the government for services in the Revolution.

clerk in the general store of Henderson & Hardy in Lebanon, where he remained for three years, acquiring some knowledge of business and employing his spare time in reading and studying.

In the winter of 1831-32 he formed a partnership under the name of Jameson, Eddy, Drake & Co., and went into business in Lebanon, conducting a general store. In February, 1832, Mr. Drake and his senior partner, Mr. Jameson, started for New York and Philadelphia to purchase a stock of goods. In those early days such a trip was not an ordinary occurrence and occupied much time, the travel being by stage and boat to Baltimore. On this trip Mr. Drake, for the first time and at the age of eighteen, visited the cities of Cincinnati, Wheeling, Baltimore, Philadelphia, and New York. He retained vivid recollections of his experiences on this trip and of places which he visited. He passed at Bordentown the residence of Joseph Bonaparte, who, in company with Prince Murat, was on the same boat with Mr. Drake, and their features were distinctly remembered by him.

After a short time it was found that the business of Jameson, Eddy, Drake & Co. was not sufficiently large for so many partners, and Mr. Drake sold out. With a friend he then made a journey through Indiana to Indianapolis and other places. On his return to Lebanon, he found the place in excitement owing to cholera, which had that year (1832) made its appearance. He took part in the care of the sick, a companion afflicted with the disease dying in his arms. For the following three years Mr. Drake was employed in the store of Samuel Hixon. This ended his life in Lebanon. He had now attained his majority. Without the advantages of a complete education, which is now placed within the reach of all, he had made the most of his opportunities. He had improved his brief school days, and his leisure time had been employed in reading and studying the books within his reach. He acquired habits of study which never left him in after life. In the main a self-educated man, his knowledge and information were accurate and extensive. Trained in early years in the school of adversity, he had already acquired when he became a man those habits of industry and frugality which characterized his life,

and which were the foundation of the fortune that he accumulated. At the age of twenty-one years he had already visited
the chief cities of his country, and had gained an insight into
their resources and future possibilities not possessed by many
men of his time.

In 1835 Mr. Drake went to Columbus, Ohio, and became
chief clerk of the state treasurer, Joseph Whitehill, who had
lived near Lebanon. In this capacity he had much responsi-
bility thrown upon his shoulders. Although a Whig in politics, he was selected by the Democratic Governor Lucas in the
fall of 1836 to visit Washington on business for the State of
Ohio with the President of the United States, Andrew Jackson,
with whom he had a personal interview. He returned to Columbus in time to cast his first presidential vote for General
Harrison in 1836. It may be mentioned in passing that Mr.
Drake, like his ancestors and most of his relatives, was a Whig,
and he remained one till the organization of the Republican
party, which he joined, and of which he continued to be a member during the remainder of his life. While in the Ohio Treasury, Mr. Drake began the study of law, the late Noah H.
Swayne, associate justice of the United States Supreme Court,
being his preceptor. By rising at five in the morning and
studying at night he was able to keep up his studies, and
was admitted to the bar at Delaware, Ohio.

In 1837 Mr. Drake accepted the position of cashier of the
Bank of Xenia, which subsequently became a branch of the
State Bank of Ohio. This position he filled for over eleven
years. Xenia was a bright and thriving country town in
Greene county, about twenty-four miles from Lebanon. Mr.
Drake identified himself with the place, and was soon one of
its most influential citizens. He was a member of the town
council, served in various military offices, organized and was
captain of a fire company, was chief officer in two turnpike
roads, was trustee of the Presbyterian church, became president of the Dayton and Xenia Railroad Company and of the
Dayton and Western Railroad Company, and was largely instrumental in the construction of the Little Miami and Columbus and Xenia railroads. In 1841 he served as a member of
the Whig Central Committee of Greene county, and was secretary of a public meeting called to observe May 14th as a day

of fasting and prayer on the occasion of the death of President Harrison. During the same year he was president of the Greene County Agricultural Society. In 1843 he was active in organizing a so-called "Home League" for the township. These leagues were very common, their object being the "encouragement of American enterprise and the protection of American industry and capital against foreign competition." The members were pledged to buy no goods but those of American manufacture. Mr. Drake was appointed a delegate to the state convention. To his dying day he remained a strong supporter of the principle of protection.

In 1841, Mr. Drake married Frances Mary, the youngest daughter of Major James Galloway of Xenia. The death of his wife in the spring of 1844 left him a widower with one child, Sarah Frances, who subsequently became the wife of Mr. Charles S. Rogers.

During his residence in Xenia, Mr. Drake served for three terms in the legislature of Ohio, and he was prominent in legislative and political work. More particular reference to his public services will be made in the latter part of this sketch.

In 1848 Mr. Drake was offered and induced to accept the position of president of the Columbus Insurance Company, then a popular institution owned and controlled by some of the leading men of Ohio. He soon found that the company was in a hopelessly embarrassed condition, and it shortly afterward failed and went out of business. After a two years' residence in Columbus, he returned to Xenia and formed a company to improve, for a summer watering place, springs near Xenia, called Tawawa or Xenia Springs, and built a hotel and many cottages. The enterprise proved unsuccessful, and the hotel was subsequently converted into "Wilberforce College."

About this time Mr. Drake formed a business engagement with Andrew De Graff in the construction of railroads. From this time, till shortly before his death, he was almost exclusively and continuously engaged in building and operating railroads. He practically saw the beginning of railroads in this country, and was one of the most active and successful of railroad men in undertaking and successfully carrying through railroad enterprises. In company with Mr. De Graff,

41

he built the Pennsylvania and Indianapolis railroad and the Greenville and Miami railroad. He organized and became president of the Dayton, Xenia and Belpre Railroad Company, constructing the road from Xenia to Dayton. The roads of the Dayton and Western Railroad Company, the Cincinnati, Lebanon and Springfield Turnpike Company, the Xenia and Columbus Turnpike Company, and the Xenia and Jamestown Company, were all constructed under his administration. His business required much traveling, and he became thoroughly acquainted with many of the prominent men of the country and with the large cities of the eastern states. In the year 1860, while in New York on business with Valentine Winters of Dayton, he met Andrew De Graff, who, in company with Edmund Rice and William Crooks of St. Paul, was seeking for some one to build the railroad from St. Paul to Minneapolis which is now a portion of the Great Northern railway. Mr. Drake and Mr. Winters determined to visit St. Paul and did so in July, 1860, and then made an agreement to build the railroad. In September they returned with supplies and materials and began the construction of the road, which they completed on July 2nd, 1862, being the first ten miles of railroad constructed in the State of Minnesota. Mr. Drake returned to Xenia, where his family had remained, and, after closing up his business matters in Ohio, removed in 1864 to St. Paul, where he continued to reside till his death.

While residing in Xenia, on August 21st, 1856, Mr. Drake married Caroline McClurg, the daughter of Alexander McClurg of Pittsburg, Pa. He purchased and fitted up a large, comfortable home at Xenia, where four children by his second wife were born, and where with his family he lived seven happy years before his removal to St. Paul.

Shortly after his removal to St. Paul, Mr. Drake became associated with Horace Thompson, James E. Thompson, John L. Merriam, and others, in the building of the St. Paul & Sioux City railroad and the Sioux City & St Paul railroad and their tributary roads. For more than sixteen years he was president of the companies owning these roads and their branches. Under the most discouraging circumstances, and during the financial panic of 1871 and the grasshopper plague

in southern Minnesota, these gentlemen carried through their enterprise, which has resulted in adding materially to the prosperity and influence of the city of St. Paul. These railroad companies are the only ones then existing in Minnesota which did not become insolvent and pass into the hands of receivers. To a great degree the credit for the successful prosecution of these enterprises is due to Mr. Drake. The roads were finally completed, and in 1880 were united with the system now known as the Chicago, St. Paul, Minneapolis & Omaha railway. Upon the occasion of Mr. Drake's retirement from the presidency of the St. Paul & Sioux City Railroad Company, on March 3d, 1880, the directors in appreciation of his services adopted and spread upon their records the following resolutions:

Resolved, That the retirement of the Hon. E. F. Drake from the presidency of this company, after a continuous service of more than sixteen years, is an event that demands a. formal expression of our high appreciation of his most efficient services as such president, and as the leading stockholder, director, and promoter of the enterprise that has so long associated him with us.

During the long years of financial embarrassment and distress which has compelled the bankruptcy and reorganization of so many well founded and ably conducted railroad companies, the financial affairs of the St. Paul & Sioux City Railroad have been so administered as to protect and preserve all the interests and investment of the stockholders, and to continue and improve its accommodations to the people, and generally to meet fully its obligations to the state, and to effect the purposes of its organization and construction.

Resolved, That in the recent negotiations with other powerful and friendly railroad interests to be this day consummated, Mr. Drake has crowned his long and eminently successful administration by an achievement of which he and we may all be proud, and for which he is entitled to the gratitude of every stockholder in the road, and of every citizen of St. Paul or of Minnesota.

From this time Mr. Drake took little active part in the management of railroads, but devoted himself to the care of his various properties. In 1882 he took a needed rest and with his family spent a year abroad.

During his nearly thirty years of residence in St. Paul, Mr. Drake was at all times active in promoting the interests of the city and was prominently identified with all public matters. He served many years as director of the Merchants' National Bank, the St. Paul Trust Company, the St. Paul Fire & Marine Insurance Company, and other financial institutions. From its organization he was one of the most active and efficient mem-bers of the St. Paul Chamber of Commerce. He took deep in-

terest in the Minnesota Historical Society, of which he was a councilor from 1868 until his death, and president for the year 1873.

During his entire life he took part in political affairs, and was frequently chosen to fill political positions of importance. He was a member of the Republican convention at Baltimore which nominated Mr. Lincoln for his second term, and was also a member of the Republican convention at Chicago which nominated President Garfield. In this latter convention he is credited with being the author of the resolution which broke the "unit rule" and made the nomination of Garfield possible. In 1873 he was elected to the Senate of Minnesota and served two years.

His record as a legislator deserves more than a passing notice. In Ohio he was three times chosen a member of the lower house of the legislature from Xenia, in 1844, 1845 and 1848. In his second term he was speaker of the House, being then the youngest speaker who had ever served in Ohio. The journals of the Ohio legislature bear ample testimony to his sound judgment and ability.

In the state elections in 1844 the Whigs were successful, their candidate for governor, Mordecai Bartley, defeating the Democratic candidate, David Tod, who during the campaign had earned the nickname of "Pot-metal Tod" by stating in a speech that "anything which bore the government stamp as money would answer all purposes of a currency, even if it were pot-metal." In the House the Whigs had a good working majority. Mr. Drake soon showed himself to be an active, intelligent, and influential member. As chairman of the Committee on Incorporations, most of the important legislation passed through his hands. The bill creating the State Bank of Ohio, of which he was largely the author, received his active support, and was the means of placing the finances of the state on a sound basis. He was the author of the general railroad law which is substantially in force in Ohio today. Many questions of national importance were considered in this session of the legislature, and Mr. Drake's speeches and votes, generally in entire accord with his party, demonstrate in a remarkable manner his keen foresight and sound political views. The an-

nexation of Texas, then under consideration in Congress, was a burning question. The Whigs opposed and the Democrats favored annexation. A committee of the House introduced a resolution protesting against annexation upon the following grounds: "1· Because such proceedings would be unconstitutional and void; 2. Because it would involve our country in a war with Mexico without just cause; 3. Because it would make our country liable for the debt of Texas without any sufficient indemnity; 4. Because it would involve us in the guilt, and subject our country to the reproach, of cherishing and perpetuating the results of slavery." This protest received Mr. Drake's hearty support except as to the first ground. He was undetermined whether a treaty of annexation would be void or not. On his motion the words "and void" were stricken out, and the protest was then adopted by 38 to 31, a strict party vote.

The Democratic majority at a preceding session of the legislature had adopted resolutions censuring John Quincy Adams for presenting a petition asking for a dissolution of the Union. A resolution was adopted on December 20th, 1844, rescinding this resolution, by a vote of 40 to 22, two Democrats voting aye. In support of the resolution Mr. Drake showed the absurdity of the former resolution by reading from the proceedings of Congress, which showed that Mr. Adams, in presenting the petition, repeatedly expressed his hostility to its object, and declared his wish to have it referred to a select committee in order that a suitable report might be drawn up adverse to the prayer of the petition. In answer to a remark by a Democratic member that he would be willing to censure those of his own party under similar circumstances, Mr. Drake inquired of the member whether "he had forgotten the conduct of his nullifying friends of the South, in openly threatening a dissolution of the Union and expressing their determination to have Texas, either with or without the Union."

On December 31st, 1844, he opposed an amendment to resolutions relating to the Oregon difficulty with Great Britain, which protested against the surrender by compromise or otherwise of any territory south of latitude 54° 40'. To have adopted and enforced the amendment would have precipitated a war with Great Britain. On January 2nd, 1845, Mr. Drake

voted with the minority against a resolution to print certain public reports in the German language. The opposition claimed that the resolution was tainted with demagogism. He voted against a resolution declaring a right to "alter, amend, or repeal" existing charters of incorporation, upon the ground that such action would be void under the United States Constitution, and the courts shortly after expressly so held. A bill to license and regulate taverns caused much dicussion and was vigorously opposed by the liquor interests. Mr. Drake spoke and voted in favor of rigid restrictions of the liquor traffic. During this session Tom Corwin was elected United States Senator, receiving Mr. Drake's active support.

For the session of 1845-46 Mr. Drake was chosen speaker of the House, the Whigs again having a majority in that body. The Xenia Bank, of which Mr. Drake was cashier, had in the meantime become a branch of the State Bank under the law passed at the preceding session. This bank law was vigorously opposed by the Democrats, and under a provision of the State constitution which provided that "no judge of any court of law or equity, secretary of state, adjutant general, * * * or person holding any office under the authority of this state * * * shall be eligible as a candidate for or have a seat in the General Assembly," they vigorously but unsuccessfully contested Mr. Drake's right to a seat and his election as speaker. In those days party politics greatly delayed and hampered legislation. The minority, by dilatory proceedings, were enabled to confuse and obstruct legislation. Mr. Drake possessed a thorough knowledge of parliamentary law, and by his prompt and accurate rulings aided in the expedition of public business. He naturally incurred the active hostility of the Democratic members, but at the end of the session without a negative vote a resolution was adopted tendering the thanks of the House to Mr. Drake "for the able and impartial manner in whish he has presided over the deliberations during the present session."

It is interesting, in view of the prominence recently given to the ruling of Speaker Reed in Congress in counting members present who refuse to vote as part of a quorum, to note that Mr. Drake while speaker made the same ruling. During the

session a bill was passed, less than a quorum voting. A Democratic paper having reported that the speaker and the House,
without having a quorum, undertook to pass a bill, Mr. Drake
in the House, referring to this newspaper report, said: "Now
I appeal to every candid man who hears me to say whether this
report, though true as far as it goes, does not in fact convey
to the reader a falsehood. It leads its readers to the conclusion that the House and its speaker have violated the constitution and their oaths in passing a bill without a quorum
present. What would have been a true record? By adding
the following report: Before the vote was declared, Messrs
Higgins and Vallandigham appeared within the bar, and the
clerk, by order of the speaker, called their names, but they did
not vote; whereupon the speaker said, 'There is no quorum
voting, but there is a quorum present, and, a majority of all
present having voted in the affirmative, the bill is passed.'"

In January, 1846, a resolution was offered to the effect that
all territory held by the national government purchased or
conquered is subject to national control and to be governed by
such institutions as the national will may dictate. The resolution was obviously aimed against the extension of slavery.
Mr. Drake offered an amendment, "that the State of Ohio, by
the foregoing declaration, distinctly declares that she seeks
not in any manner to interfere with the domestic institutions
of her sister states," which amendment was adopted, and the
resolution as amended was adopted, receiving Mr. Drake's
support. Mr. Drake procured the passage of a resolution for
the formation of a sinking fund for payment of the state debt.

On January 24th, 1846, he with sixteen other members
signed and presented a protest against an act which had been
passed to divorce one Dunbar from his wife. The protest says,
"No cause for the divorce exists, except that the wife is insane,
not hopelessly insane, but so insane that her confinement in
the Lunatic Asylum is necessary, and she is unable to provide
or care for herself. Against this mockery of everything sacred
in the dearest relations of life we protest, because, 1. The bill
violates a private contract by which the wife was entitled to
the aid and comfort of her husband; to his protection and
support until death should separate them; and to a share of his

estate and earnings; and the bill, being in violation of this obligatory contract, is unconstitutional, null, and void. 2. The passage of the act is a usurpation of judicial power and is therefore unconstitutional, null, and void. 3. It impairs confidence in the relation of husband and wife by adopting as a principle that insanity, disease or misfortune, and not fault, shall be sufficient cause to justify the desertion and abandonment of the party thus overcome by misfortune. The bill is unjust in principle, immoral in its tendency, and destructive of the best interests of society. 4. It is unwise, unpolitic, and inexpedient, to grant special acts of divorce by the Legislature."

On a bill to prevent gambling, Mr. Drake did not hesitate to object to those provisions which prohibited the sale of all but a certain description of playing cards, and which rewarded informers. On February 9th, 1846, he voted in favor of the repeal of the state fugitive slave law; but he was in the minority on this question. In the same month he proposed an amendment to the tax law, which was adopted and is still in force, to the effect that merchants should be taxed on the average amount in value of their stocks of merchandise for the whole year, instead of the amount at any one time.

Mr. Drake served for the third and last time in the legislature of Ohio in the year 1847-48. He was not then a candidate for the office of speaker. As during the earlier sessions, he took an active part in legislation. On a bill to amend the registry law he took strong ground in favor of a complete registration concluded before election day. Upon constitutional objection being made to such registration, Mr. Drake said: "The gentleman from Hamilton has read from the constitution in support of his position, but what are the provisions of the constitution? Not that the elector shall vote when he pleases and where he pleases without inquiry or restriction. No such thing. It only guarantees to the citizen the rights of an elector. What are the rights of an elector? Nothing more nor less than the right to deposit his vote under the same rules and regulations as are provided for every other citizen. If a more strict construction could properly be made, why do we not hear indignant thunders from the gentleman on the other

side at the law passed by his own friends to provide for the purity of elections? That act declares that the citizen 'shall not vote in any county where his family does not reside.' It matters not how much he is.identified with the place of his own residence. Where does the legislature get this authority? Your law declares that the voting in another state shall disqualify the voter and debar him from exercising the right in Ohio. Where is such power derived? From the same constitution under which the friend of a registry law finds power to declare that the voter shall take certain steps to prove his right to vote. No argument can be fairly urged against this law that does not exist with equal force against all laws in anywise restricting the right of the voter. This is no party question. It is one in which all should unite with honest purpose to keep pure the sacred privilege of the ballot box."

Senator Corwin, in the United States Senate, opposed the war with Mexico, and was credited with having said, "If I were a Mexican I would tell you: Have you not room in your own country to bury your dead men? If you come into mine, we will greet you with bloody hands and welcome you to hospitable graves." Some foolish member of the House presented a petition asking for the resignation of Senator Corwin and his confinement in a lunatic asylum. Other members hostile to Corwin foolishly supported the petition, and a long debate ensued. At the close, Mr. Drake cleverly demonstrated the absurdity of the proceeding, and, compelling his opponents to admit that if they were Mexicans they would surely oppose the enemies of their country, caused it to be entered on the record that they admitted that if they were native Mexicans they would fight against the Americans, thus taking the same position which Mr. Corwin had taken in the Senate. Mr. Drake at this session again brought forward a measure to provide for a sinking fund for payment of the public debt, and succeeded in having a bill passed for that purpose.

On a question of submitting to the voters of a county a loan to a railroad company, with the proposed limitation to voters who owned a certain amount of property, Mr. Drake said his democracy did not lead him to make property a qualification for exercising the right of voting upon any subject in

which the whole public was interested, and he therefore opposed the proposed qualification.

To the general tax law Mr. Drake offered an amendment providing that every "city or town corporation shall specify upon its records the amount required for such purpose, and it shall not be lawful to use such specific fund for any other purpose than the one for which the same was specifically levied." Although Mr. Drake's amendment was not then adopted, subsequent legislatures recognized its wisdom, and it has now long been a part of the law in Ohio.

Much important legislation was proposed and discussed while Mr. Drake was a member of the Ohio legislature, and no member took a more active part in framing the laws; and the history of the past fifty years has demonstrated that he was uniformly in favor of those laws which have since been most beneficial to the people. He voted with a minority to allow colored persons to testify in cases in which a white person was involved. In 1848 he introduced and strongly advocated resolutions denouncing the Mexican war as unnecessary and unjust, deploring a war which had for its sole object the acquisition of territory by conquest, and protesting against the extension of slavery. He favored laws increasing educational privileges and providing for libraries in all school districts, providing for roads and turnpikes, regulating judgments and executions, settling estates of deceased persons, and relating to many other kindred matters.

In 1873 he was elected a state senator in the Minnesota legislature and served two years. The legislature was largely Republican, and elected a United States senator. Mr. Drake favored Senator Ramsey, who was chosen by the Republican caucus, but was defeated by the friends of Governor Davis, the election resulting in the selection of Judge McMillan. At this time the granger element was in full control, and immediately engaged in legislation hostile to railroads. A law regulating railroad charges (Laws, 1874, Chapter 26), radical in its character, was passed by an almost unanimous vote of the Senate. The only negative votes were cast by Mr. Drake and Mr. Ignatius Donnelly, the former voting against the law because in his judgment it was too radical, and the latter because the law was not radical enough to suit him. Mr. Drake both voted

and spoke against the law, predicting that if it passed it would prove unwise and unsound and be speedily repealed. His prediction was realized, as at the next session of the legislature the law was repealed (Laws, 1875, Chapter 103), by almost as unanimous a vote as passed it.

Because of his position as a railroad man and his open opposition to the views of the majority upon railroad questions, Mr. Drake appears to have been deprived of all influence in the Senate, at the commencement of his term. His legislative experience, his fairness and integrity, his keen foresight and ability, however, commanded respect and support, and when he finished his term no man in the Senate was more influential. As in Ohio, so in Minnesota, he took an active part in all legislation, and at all times cast his vote and used his influence for the passage of those laws which provide for wise and honest government,

Mr. Drake was instrumental in securing to the State of Minnesota five hundred thousand acres of land. Governor Marshall in his annual message to the legislature, January 10th, 1867, thus refers to the matter: "Hon. E. F. Drake, early last year, called my attention to the fact that under a half forgotten law of Congress (the act of September 4th, 1841), public lands to the amount of five hundred thousand acres were granted to certain States for internal improvements; the act provided further, that new States thereafter admitted should receive a like quantity of lands, deducting any lands granted to such states for internal improvements during its territorial period. I gave Mr. Drake a letter to the Secretary of the Interior, requesting facilities for investigating the matter, which resulted in the Secretary conceding the right of the State to the lands, and giving a letter of instructions for their selection. I commend this valuable service to the State, of Mr. Drake, to your attention for such acknowledgment or compensation as shall seem to you appropriate."

These lands were duly selected, and the fund arising from the sale became the basis of settlement in 1881 of the suspended debt of the State under the Five Million loan of 1858 to railroads. It is probably true that no private citizen has ever rendered to the State so valuable a material service as Mr. Drake rendered in securing these lands.

The late Cyrus Aldrich, member of Congress from Minnesota in 1861-62, had an informal talk with the Secretary of the Interior in regard to the right of the State to these lands, but the view then taken was that the grants of several miilion acres to the Territory of Minnesota in 1857, to aid in the construction of railroads, cancelled, under the terms of the act of September 4th, 1841, any right to these five hundred thousand acres. The matter was not further investigated until Mr. Drake successfully dealt with it.

In 1875 a discussion arose in the Minnesota Senate concerning the disposition of these lands, which led to an extended debate upon the repudiation of the Railroad Aid bonds of 1858. Mr. Drake took strong ground in favor of the prompt payment of the bonds, and delivered an able speech upon the question. At that time, however, the legislature would not take steps to remove the stain upon the name of the State; and it was not till the extra session of 1881 that the matter wes settled and adjusted.

Amidst his other occupations Mr. Drake found time to devote to the militia service. While residing at Lebanon, Ohio, he served as adjutant of a regiment, and became chief of the colonel's staff. Subsequently, at Xenia, he was colonel of a regiment, and served on the general's staff.

Mr. Drake left surviving him his widow and five children, all of whom reside in St. Paul. The eldest, Sarah Frances, the only child by his first wife, as already stated, married Mr. Charles S. Rogers. The elder son, Henry Trevor Drake, married in 1882 Miss Emma Bigelow, daughter of Mr. Charles H. Bigelow, and is engaged in business in St. Paul. Alexander McClurg Drake, the younger son, is also engaged in business in St. Paul. He was for many years connected with his father's affairs. The two remaining children are daughters. Mary, the elder, married Mr. Thomas S. Tompkins in 1886; and Carrie, the youngest of the family, married Mr. William H. Lightner in 1885.

From this summary and review of the important events in Mr. Drake's life the reader can form a fair estimate of his character. He was a man of unusual executive ability. He not only originated large enterprises, but he had the ability and

industry to carry them to a successful completion. He was not disheartened by unforeseen obstacles and discouragements, but, with a never failing confidence in the future, he tenaciously adhered to his course and ultimately won success. His mind was remarkably clear and logical, and his judgment sound. No man was more often applied to for advice by his friends and neighbors; and many citizens of St. Paul will bear testimony to the fact that his advice, freely given, was judicious and beneficial to those seeking it. Trained under stern religious influences, tinctured with the Puritan doctrines, he had however a broad and liberal mind, which neither favored nor supported fanaticism or bigotry. Though himself not a church member, he actively and liberally supported the Baptist Church, of which his second wife and their children were members. Like all positive men, he had strong prejudices founded upon his honest and sincere convictions. Yet he never allowed his prejudices to influence his reason, and no man was more open to conviction when in error. He was pre-eminently a man of affairs, and during his long life there were found no periods of idleness. Of a most sociable character, he was entirely free from personal vices, and was temperate in all his habits.

Mr. Drake was a very domestic man. He found his greatest happiness in his family circle, where perfect harmony prevailed, and where a devoted wife and loving children joined in giving to him what he most prized, a happy home.

For a year and a half prior to his death he was in failing health; and in November, 1891, with his wife and her sister, Miss McClurg (who had long been a devoted member of his family), he went to California in the hope that the change of climate might prove beneficial. In February he rapidly lost strength, and died peacefully on the 14th, his wife and her sister being at his bedside. The remains were brought to St. Paul and buried in the family lot in Oakland cemetery. The extent of the loss to the city, and the shock and grief in the community caused by his death, may be gathered from the extended notices in the press.

WILLIAM H. LIGHTNER.

HENRY MOWER RICE.

Death has taken from our membership since the last meeting* an honored associate, one of the most illustrious men in the history of Minnesota. Henry Mower Rice died at San Antonio, Texas, where he was sojourning for his health, January 15th, 1894, in the seventy-seventh year of his age.

Mr. Rice was named in the act of October 20th, 1849, incorporating the Minnesota Historical Society, and he was its president three terms, for the years 1864 to 1866. He has been very helpful in upbuilding the Society during all its history.

For more than half a century Mr. Rice had been identified in active business enterprises, and in the most important public functions, in the Northwest and the Territory and State of Minnesota. He was the delegate of the Territory in Congress four years, 1853 to 1857, and the United States senator from the admission of the state in 1858 for five years. He was prominently connected with the most important treaties with the Indians by which their rights to the lands of Minnesota were extinguished. In Congress he secured the liberal land grants in aid of our magnificent system of railroads, by which they were secured almost in advance of settlements. No man in our history did more to lay broad the foundations of the state. His name will be cherished in all time as that of a benefactor of the millions who are to possess and enjoy this fair land as their heritage.

A man of remarkable forecast of mind, of great refinement and courtliness of manners, of fine bodily presence, he was a natural leader of men; yet he was modest and retiring. He sought little for himself. His ambition was in connection with the advancement of public interests and the prosperity and welfare of his fellow men. During the great struggle for na-

---

*This obituary sketch was read at the monthly meeting of the Executive Council, February 12, 1894.

Yours Respectfully,
Henry M. Rice.

tional life his loyalty to the Union, and his labors as a member
of the military and other important committees of the United
States government, were most honorable and most useful.

The Minnesota Commandery of the Military Order of the
Loyal Legion, soon after its organization, November 4th, 1885,
honored itself and sought to honor him by electing him one of
the first of the limited number who, by the constitution of the
Order, may be members from civil life. In the language of the
constitution of the Order, he was chosen from those who "in
civil life during the Rebellion were especially distinguished for
conspicuous and consistent loyalty to the national government,
and who were active and eminent in maintaining the supremacy of the same." No language could more fittingly characterize Mr. Rice.

Henry Mower Rice was born in Waitsfield, Vermont, November 29th, 1817. He was of honorable ancestry, descended
from Edmund Rice, who came from Bankhamstead, Hertford-
shire, England, and settled in Sudbury, Mass., in 1638 or 1639.
Through a maternal ancestor he was descended from the family
which produced Warren Hastings. His father died when he
was but twelve years of age, the oldest of ten children.

At the age of eighteen he came west to Detroit, Mich., with
the family of General Justus Burdick, a friend of his father,
with whom young Rice had made his home after his father's
death. In 1836, in his nineteenth year, he was engaged in the
surveys for the government canal at Sault Ste. Marie, to make
navigable the entrance to lake Superior. The following year
he went with General Burdick's family to Kalamazoo, Mich.,
where he was engaged in trade in that new settlement for two
years. In 1839 his adventurous spirit led him to go farther
west. Two hundred miles of the journey through the wilderness he made on foot, suffering much hardship. In his travels
he reached St. Louis, where Kenneth McKenzie, connected
with Indian trade and the sutler's store at Fort Snelling, engaged him to take care of McKenzie's business there. Mr.
Rice wrote to his boyhood friend, Roswell P. Russell, then at
Kalamazoo, to join him. After a journey of much hardship,
having their Mackinaw boat frozen in at La Crosse, they
reached Fort Snelling November 5th, 1839.

Mr. Rice left Fort Snelling in May, 1840, with the United States troops ordered to the new Winnebago Reservation in northern Iowa to establish Fort Atkinson. He was appointed sutler of the post. This position he relinquished in 1842 to engage in the Indian trade. In this trade he was connected with Colonel Hercules L. Dousman of Prairie du Chien. Later he was a partner of B. W. Brisbois in a trader's outfitting store at Prairie du Chien, and in 1847 he was made a partner of P. Chouteau, Jr., & Co., the great fur traders.

The white settlements of Iowa in 1846 began to demand the removal of the Winnebago Indians. Mr. Rice, with a delegation of chiefs, went to Washington and concluded a treaty for the sale of the reservation, he signing the treaty in place of a chief, a distinguished mark of the confidence of the Indians.

In 1847, as United States commissioner, he negotiated treaties with the Chippewas of the upper Mississippi and of lake Superior for cessions of their lands. He took up his residence at Mendota in 1847. In 1848 he was engaged in removing the Winnebago Indians from Iowa to their new reservation above Sauk Rapids on the Mississippi and Long Prairie rivers.

March 29th, 1849, he married Matilda Whitall of Richmond, Va., after which he made his home at St. Paul, Minn. He engaged extensively in trade with the Ojibway and Winnebago Indians from 1847 to 1852.

In 1852, when the confirmation of the treaties of 1851 with the Sioux for their vast possessions in Minnesota was in danger of failing, his assistance was sought in securing the consent of the Indians to modifications of the treaties required by the Senate of the United States; and, although he had never been connected with these Indians in trade or otherwise, and was not a beneficiary under the treaty as were others to the extent of hundreds of thousands of dollars, his great tact and ability speedily secured the consent of the Sioux to the Senate amendments. Thus, in the fall of 1852, all of Minnesota west of the Mississippi river and south of the Ojibway country was opened to white settlement.

In 1853 Mr. Rice was chosen delegate in Congress, and he was re-elected in 1855. With great efficiency he secured land grants in aid of our great system of railroads, and got land

offices established conveniently for settlers in greater numbers than had ever before been allowed in new and sparsely settled countries. He got the pre-emption laws extended to unsurveyed lands. He procured the enabling act of 1857, under which the Territory became a State, in which was confirmed to the State two sections of land in every township, and also two townships of land for a State University. He took his seat in the United States Senate on admission of the State in 1858, for a term ending March 3rd, 1863.

At the breaking out of the Civil War he severed his relations, which had been intimate, with Breckenridge, Clay, Toombs, and others of the South, and loyally and ably sustained the national cause.

As a member of the military, finance, and other important committees of the Senate, his business experience and ability were of the highest value to the Union cause. Henry Wilson, chairman of the military committee, said that to Mr. Rice more than any other member was due the credit of those practical measures for providing clothing, subsistence, and camp equipage, and for mobilizing our great armies.

After his retirement from the Senate, by published letters in 1863-64 of marked ability and the most fervid patriotism, he upheld the national cause until its triumphant success.

In 1865 he was the candidate of his party for governor, but the large ascendancy of the opposite party precluded success. He avowed at the time that he accepted the nomination as a representative of the unhesitating Union sentiments of his party, and to prevent the ascendancy of the reactionary element.

It is worthy of note that, although his sentiments were in full accord with the great party in control of the state and nation from the clash of arms in 1861 onward and if he had openly allied himself with that party, as did Matt. Carpenter, Daniel S. Dickinson and others, he would have been honored with high places of trust and emoluments, he chose to forego all such advantages and to remain, as he had been from the beginning of his public career, associated with the Democratic party. It is a striking example of his disinterestedness and freedom from self-seeking that he preferred to remain

42

with the minority, and to exert his influence to promote in that party cordial support of those in authority in a vigorous prosecution of the war, and for a sound financial policy after the war in honorable fulfillment of national obligations.

In 1887 and 1888 he was a United States commissioner to make settlement with the Ojibway Indians in matters between them and the government, rendering most valuable service.

He was chosen treasurer of Ramsey county at a time which called for the services of a faithful, fearless officer. He discharged the duties several terms with the utmost fidelity.

He was repeatedly chosen president of the Chamber of Commerce of St. Paul, and was in all ways devoted to the public interests of the city which was so long his home.

His last public service was within two or three months of the close of his life, when he acted in conjunction with Governor Ramsey and H. S. Fairchild in fixing values of the land taken by the State for a new capitol building.

Thus has closed, in the fullness of years and honors, the life of one who will have a foremost place in the records of our history, and in the hearts and memories of those who knew him in life, as one of the founders and benefactors of our State.

WILLIAM R. MARSHALL.

Charles E. Mayo

CHARLES EDWIN MAYO.

"Cape Cod, the bared and bended arm of Massachusetts, behind which the State stands on her guard, with her back to the Green mountains, and her feet planted on the floor of the ocean, boxing with northeast storms," has been the home for many generations of sturdy, brave, and fearless men. Inured to hardships, coming to these shores for conscience' sake, the New Englander has stood for what is best in our newer civilization.

It has been said of Brewster township, on Cape Cod, that the tide ebbs out a greater distance than at any other place in the world, and that it has been the home of more sea captains than any other town, considering the number of its population.

The subject of this sketch, Charles Edwin Mayo, was born at Brewster, Massachusetts, October 26th, 1827, the son of Jeremiah Mayo and Mary Paddock Clark Mayo. His was an ancestry of which to be proud, and from which he inherited many strong traits. He was lineally descended from nine of the passengers of the Mayflower. These were Elder William Brewster, for whom his native town was named, with his wife Mary; Alice and William Mullens, with their daughter Priscilla; John Alden, Thomas Rogers, and Stephen and Giles Hopkins.

His colonial ancestry contained thirty-eight names, including men who played a prominent part in the affairs of state, members of the General Court, governor and governor's assistants, captains of companies in King Philip's war and the Pequot war, and of Miles Standish's company.

One of these worthies, Governor Thomas Prence, was governor of the colony for twenty years. Bishop Samuel Seabury, the first bishop of the English church in this country, was one of his ancestors, who had a great and moulding influence on church and state.

Mr. Mayo's father, Jeremiah Mayo, was a sea captain, sailing from Boston to foreign ports. He visited the battlefield of Corunna a few days after the battle beween the French and English, and saw the prisoners that were taken in the fight, a miserable, wretched looking lot. He was familiar with the details of the battle, and would grow eloquent as he spoke of the heroism of Sir John Moore. Among his son's autographs, that of Sir John Moore was greatly prized, probably because of his early admiration for this hero.

In 1815 Captain Jeremiah Mayo visited Havre just after the battle of Waterloo, and, on being approached by the emissaries of Napoleon in regard to bringing him to this country, he agreed to do so, knowing that, if caught, his vessel and cargo would be confiscated. He heard before sailing, however, that Napoleon had surrendered himself to the English. Many voyages were made to Russian and European ports.

In the home at Brewster there were hung on the walls a map of the United States and a facsimile of the Declaration of Independence, as means of furnishing food for thought for the young children of the family.

Many nights when a boy, Charles would copy the signatures on the Declaration of Independence, and after a few trials became quite expert in the imitation of any of them.

In 1835 the Brewster Academy was opened, and Charles Edwin Mayo began his school training. Among the text books then in use was Goodrich's History of the United States, with Emerson's Questions. The class in grammar used Pope's Essay on Man. Other studies were natural philosophy, chemistry, rhetoric, botany, algebra, and logic. Much attention was paid to composition and declamation. In the fall of 1837 Mr. Benjamin Drew, of Plymouth, superseded Mr. Washburn, the previous teacher. On opening his school Mr. Drew wrote upon the blackboard, "Order is Heaven's first Law," and to this motto he strictly adhered, as did also his pupil, the subject of this sketch, through life. During the many expeditions made with his teacher, Mr. Drew, his taste was formed for the best in literature, which he always retained. It was this habit, then formed, which was more fully gratified when he removed

to Boston, where he was able to obtain books and information which could not be obtained in his native town.

In 1842 he was sent to school at Sandwich, Mass., and there his teacher, Mr. Crowell, wrote to his father: "I wish to write a word regarding your son. . . . . . I love your son, and I wish him to be educated. My great reason is, because it seems to me he should be; he has the mind, the habits, the qualities, that ought to be cultivated. . . . . I must say I can almost envy his talents in view of his age." His should have been a professional life. Charles was a member of the First Parish church of Brewster, then Congregational, and his father was an active man in its affairs.

In 1844 Charles left for Boston, to enter the hardware store of Montgomery Newell. During this first year in Boston he joined the Mercantile Library, and attended regularly the Lyceum lectures; his evenings were spent in reading and study. It was always his desire to see and hear the best, and he never lost an opportunity of hearing men of note, who were so numerous at that time. During his stay in Boston he heard such men as Sumner, Choate, Webster, Phillips, Holmes, Garrison, Pierpont, Parker, Burlingame, Frederick Douglass, and also Jennie Lind, and all the noted actors and actresses of the day. Here he also heard Louis Kossuth, whom Whittier styled

> . . . . "the noblest guest
> The Old World's wrong has given the New World of the West."

In no other city of our country is so much interest felt in the preservation of historical memories, and so much effort expended to snatch from oblivion the buildings and sites of earlier days. Mr. Mayo, surrounded in these formative days with the love of the past, early showed his attachment for the places and persons that had helped to found the strong, stable national government of which we are all justly proud. It was during his stay of seven years in Boston that he became associated with his cousin, Charles Mayo, in accumulating historical and genealogical notes of the Mayo family; and in that work his natural love of old documents and newspapers was fostered, so that his friends, knowing this, made him the

recipient of many papers of value, all of which were his most loved and prized possessions.

Deciding that a drier climate might be more beneficial to his health, he moved to Cincinnati in September, 1852, where he remained during the winter; and in the spring of 1853 he made a visit, by boat, to New Orleans, spending a month on the trip. Upon his return he stopped for a few days in Cincinnati, and then embarked for St. Paul, Minnesota, on the steamboat "Nominee," of which Russell Blakeley was captain, arriving here May 27th, 1853. Here he lived to see the change from a frontier western town to the present city. Soon after coming to St. Paul Mr. Mayo engaged in the hardware business, entering the store of Francis S. Newell, but spending a portion of the first summer here in assisting Mr. Halsted in surveying Warren and Winslow's addition. His tall stature, six feet four inches, served him well as a surveyor, Mr. Halsted saying that he was the best chainman he had ever employed. In the fall he entered business for himself with Mr. Elkanah Bangs and Mr. F. S. Newell, under the firm name of Charles E. Mayo & Company.

The following anecdote will illustrate his kindly nature. In the summer of 1854 he was called to a frame house in the rear of his store, by the wife of a sick man, who wanted his help. He went and found the man sick with cholera, without proper bed, furniture, medicine, or care, which he at once proceeded to give, carrying over to the house furniture and a mattress from his own room, calling a doctor, and remaining with them until the man's recovery was assured.

His mother, writing him soon after this act of charity, said: "A charitable deed done to a fellow creature, a stranger, sick with cholera, though nothing more than was your duty to do, gave me more heartfelt satisfaction than mines of gold would have done."

His sister, having come west to make a visit, wrote: "Charles and I started from St. Paul January 22nd, 1856, for Boston. We rode in a covered sleigh four days, and one night in a stage coach, before we reached Dubuque." What a difference between the time it then took to travel and that of today!

Almost immediately after coming to St. Paul he became associated with those whose interests, intellectually, were identical with his own, and in November, 1855, he became a member of the Minnesota Historical Society, of which society he remained an active member until his death. He was elected a member of the Executive Council of this society in February, 1864, and continued in the Council through his life. He was secretary of the society from February 19th, 1864, to January 21st, 1867, being succeeded by J. Fletcher Williams; was president for the year 1872; and from 1891 to his death was second vice president.

His research in history and genealogy was very deep, and his broad mind and retentive memory enabled him to master any subject to which he turned his attention. He was applied to for genealogical information by people from all parts of the country.

The Mayflower Society, the Cape Cod Historical 'Society, to which he was elected in 1882, the Pilgrim Society of Plymouth, which, as their certificate of membership states, was organized December 21st, 1820, "in grateful remembrance of the first settlers of New England, who came here December 21st, 1620," all claimed him as a member. It was under the auspices of the last named society that the Faith Monument at Plymouth was erected, to commemorate the landing of the Pilgrims.

Mr. Mayo became a member of, and Genealogist for, the Society of Colonial Wars in Minnesota. During one of his many visits to his native town, in 1895, he copied, with the help of others the inscriptions on the tombstones in the old burial ground, which were rapidly becoming obliterated. These he published three years afterward, with copious notes, in a pamphlet of 83 pages, entitled "Mortuary Record from the Gravestones in the Old Burial Ground in Brewster, Mass."

For some years Mr. Mayo was a member of the St. Paul Library Board, and served one year as its president. It was while on this board that he became interested in securing a course of entertainments for the benefit of the Library. Noted speakers and authors were induced to come to St. Paul and

regale their audiences with the pleasure their readings gave for an evening. Mary Scott Siddons, John B. Gough, Henry Ward Beecher, Horace Greeley, Camilla Urso, and many others, were among the number.

Mr. Mayo was married in St. Paul, May 7th, 1861, to Caroline E. Fitch, who survived him but eight months. Two daughters and one son are left to mourn their loss.

Just after his marriage and during the Civil War, he and his wife were deeply interested in the work of the Sanitary Commission, and in providing for the soldiers' families that were left at home without means of subsistence. After his marriage he was a regular attendant at Christ Episcopal Church.

He was associated in business, at different times, with Mr. J. P. Pond, Mr. H. M. Smyth, and Mr. Charles H. Clark.

In July, 1889, he was appointed United States Appraiser for this district, under the Collector of Internal Revenue, Colonel Charles G. Edwards, and served in that capacity until his death ten years later. His judgment in matters pertaining to his duties was seldom questioned, and in such cases as were appealed his decisions were almost always sustained.

His cheerful disposition was a constant source of happiness to his friends and family. His rugged frame and mind accepted the heritage of his sturdy ancestors, and his whole life was given to living up to the high standard set by them. How well he succeeded the members of the Historical Society know. That he was ever willing to assist in any way the young men with whom he came in contact, many now living can attest.

In his death, April 23rd, 1899, his family lost a kind husband and indulgent father; the city, an upright, moral and broad-minded citizen; and the Historical Society a genial, capable, and valued friend.

EDWARD C. DOUGAN.

RUSSELL BLAKELEY.

The last pages of this volume, excepting its index, were in type, when death removed another in the series of presidents of this society, one of its early and most valued members. Captain Blakeley had been well known, trusted, honored, and beloved by the people of Minnesota during more than half a century. Before Minnesota acquired its name and organization as a territory, he began his important service in the steamboat navigation of the Upper Mississippi; and during the fifteen years of his connection with the Galena and Minnesota Packet Company he brought here many thousands of the pioneers and founders of our commonwealth. In addition to large business activity, he had always a lively interest in promoting the intellectual and moral welfare of his city and state.

Within the latest five years of his life, when the care of business had been chiefly laid aside, Captain Blakeley wrote, in accordance with earnest solicitations by his associates in this society, two extended articles for its eighth volume of Historical Collections, giving his reminiscences of the old days of steamboat travel and freighting on the Mississippi and the Red river of the North. His portrait is presented in that volume as the frontispiece of his paper, "History of the Discovery of the Mississippi River and the Advent of Commerce in Minnesota"; and the same article includes photogravures of eleven steamboats which plied on the Upper Mississippi, bringing immigrants to this state, before the close of the civil war. After that time, immigration came mostly by railways and wagon roads.

Russell Blakeley was born in North Adams, Mass., April 19th, 1815, being the son of Dennis Blakeley and Sarah Samson Blakeley. On the paternal side he was a descendant from

Samuel Blachley, who was a pioneer of Guilford, Conn., in 1650, removing thence about the year 1653 to New Haven. Another writer has directed attention to qualities which he received by inheritance, being "on both sides of Puritan ancestry and descended from two of the oldest families of Plymouth, Mass., and New Haven, Conn. His remote ancestors were somewhat prominent in the early affairs of the New England colonies. Later some of them took part in the French and Indian War, and when the War of the Revolution came it would seem that nearly all of the able-bodied male members of both the Blakeley and the Samson families fought for liberty and independence."

In 1817 Dennis Blakeley removed with his family to Leroy, Genesee county, N. Y., where Russell received a common school education and grew to manhood. For three or four years, from 1832 to 1835, he was employed as a merchant's clerk in Batavia and in Buffalo, N. Y.

At the age of twenty-one years, in the autumn of 1836, he removed with his father to Peoria, Illinois, and remained there nearly three years. In the summer of 1839 he removed to Galena, Illinois, and engaged in mining and smelting lead, in the employ of Capt. H. H. Gear, during the next five years. He then went to Austinville, Wythe county, Virginia, and was there engaged in lead smelting until the early summer of 1847, when he returned to Galena.

June 8th, 1847, Russell Blakeley began his experience in steamboating as clerk of the steamer Argo, under Capt. M. W. Lodwick, making regular trips from Galena to St. Paul and Fort Snelling. After the loss of his steamer the next autumn, a partnership was formed in the following winter, including Messrs. Campbell, Smith, and Henry Corwith, of Galena; Col. H. L. Dousman, Brisbois, and Rice, of Prairie du Chien; H. H. Sibley, of Mendota; Capt. M. W. Lodwick, and Mr. Blakeley. They bought the steamer Dr. Franklin, and began in the spring of 1848 the regular carrying trade of the Galena and Minnesota Packet Company, under M. W. Lodwick as captain and Russell Blakeley as clerk. In 1851 the latter succeeded Captain Lodwick as master of the Dr. Franklin. In 1853 Captain Blakeley was transferred to the command of the Nominee, and in 1854 to the Galena. When the

Illinois Central railroad was completed to the Mississippi river
at Dunleith (now East Dubuque), Ill., in 1855, he was appointed agent and traffic manager at Dunleith for the packet
company. His connection with this company continued until
1862, when its business was sold out.

December 9th, 1851, Captain Blakeley was married to Ellen
L. Sheldon, daughter of Major John Pitts Sheldon of Willow
Springs, Lafayette county, Wisconsin. She was born in Detroit, Michigan, October 26th, 1831, and died at Thomasville,
Georgia, March 28th, 1892. During the first ten years after
marriage, their home was in Galena, excepting the summer
of 1856, when it was in St. Paul. They removed to this city
in 1862, and two years later Captain Blakeley built the fine
stone residence at the corner of Jackson and Tenth streets,
which was ever afterward his home.

During the winter of 1855-6, he became a partner with
J. C. Burbank of St. Paul in express and commission business. In 1858 this firm, J. C. Burbank and Co., contracted
with the United States government to carry the winter mail
between Prairie du Chien and St. Paul; and in the spring
of 1859 they succeeded to all the mail service of Allen and
Chase, having adopted a corporate name as the Minnesota
Stage and Northwestern Express Company. In 1862 they
admitted John L. Merriam as a third partner. Five years
afterward, when the building of railroads had considerably diminished their business, Messrs. Burbank and Merriam withdrew from the staging and expressing, which then came under
the management of Captain Blakeley and C. W. Carpenter, the
latter having previously been the confidential clerk of the
company. By them a stage line was extended to Fort Garry,
Manitoba, in 1870. They continued in business in Minnesota
until 1878, when the railroads had virtually superseded all the
former main stage routes in this state.

In 1877 this company was reorganized under the corporate
title of the Northwestern Express, Stage and Transportation
Company, in which N. P. Clark and Peter Sims became interested, with Captain Blakeley as president and C. W. Carpenter as secretary and treasurer. They entered into contract with the Northern Pacific railroad company to run a
stage line and transport freight from Bismarck, Dakota, on

that railroad, to Deadwood in the mining district of the Black
Hills, a distance of 250 miles through the Sioux Reservation.
By this route they carried the mails, express, passengers, and
freight brought by this railroad for the Black Hills, until 1881,
when the Chicago and Northwestern railway company completed its line to Pierre on the Missouri river.

For the next four years this company, under the direction
of Captain Blakeley and Mr. Carpenter, who had purchased
the interests of the other stockholders, carried mail, passengers, freight, etc., between Pierre and the Black Hills, owning for this purpose 300 horses, 500 mules, and 1,000 work
oxen, besides also hiring for the freighting business at times
nearly as many more.

Another transfer of location of this business was made in
1886 to the terminus of the Fremont, Elkhorn and Missouri
Valley railroad, a part of the Chicago and Northwestern system, on its extensions to western Nebraska and northerly by
a branch to the Black Hills. With the completion of this
branch railroad, in 1891, the last opportunity for employment
of such methods of transportation of this magnitude closed.
The stock and vehicles that had been used were therefore
gradually disposed of and the business terminated, the oxen
being grazed for a year on the ranges west of Pierre and sold
as beef on the Chicago market. At this time of retirement
from active business, Captain Blakeley had attained the age
of seventy-six years.

During the last ten years of this transportation company's
operations, they carried as express matter, under strong guard
of messengers, practically all of the gold and silver product
of the Black Hills district, the values at times reaching $300,-
000 for a single trip.

Other financial enterprises in which Captain Blakeley had
interests included the First National Bank of St. Paul, being
one of its original stockholders; the St. Paul and Sioux City
railroad, of which he was also an original stockholder, and
was a director from 1866 to 1880; the St. Paul, Stillwater and
Taylor's Falls railroad, being a charter member and the first
president of the company organized for its construction; the
St. Paul Fire and Marine Insurance Company, in which he was

a director during more than thirty years; and the Rock County Farming Company, in which he was a large stockholder and president, joining with Mr. Horace Thompson in the purchase of 22,000 acres of land. This last venture entailed considerable loss, following the death of Mr. Thompson, its business manager.

Captain Blakeley aided in organizing the St. Paul Library Association, and was its first president. He was active in founding the St. Paul Chamber of Commerce, and was a member of its board of directors during twenty-one years, being its president for the last two years, and being recognized at the time of his retirement as the father of that organization. He was president of the St. Paul Bethel Association, of the Oakland Cemetery Association, and of the Old Settlers' Association of Minnesota.

He became a member of the Minnesota Historical Society in 1864, and was a member of its council continuously from that date until his death. He was president of this society in 1871, and was a vice president continuously since 1876. No other member was more devoted to its interests, and during his last years he greatly enjoyed reading in its Library and there meeting old friends whom he had brought as pioneers in the early years of Minnesota.

Fletcher Williams, in his History of St. Paul, published in 1876, remarked: "If Captain Blakeley would write a faithful account of steamboating in those days, with his personal reminiscences of men and events, it would make an interesting chapter of our pioneer history." This was done, as already mentioned, in the years 1896 to 1898, when two valuable historical papers were prepared by Captain Blakeley for this society. In his studies for the second paper, relating to the Upper Mississippi, he carefully reviewed the records of the earliest explorations of this region, beginning with Groseilliers and Radisson in the years 1654 to 1660.

Politically, Captain Blakeley enthusiastically supported the principles of the Whig party until 1856, then becoming a Republican. He voted in the presidential campaign of that year for Fremont, and four years later for Lincoln. He was repeatedly chairman of the State Central Committee, and of the Ramsey County Committee for the Republican party.

Religiously, he firmly believed in universal salvation. He aided to organize the Universalist State Convention in 1866, and ever afterward was a member of its executive board of trustees, being for many years the president of its meetings. He was the president of the First Universalist Society of St. Paul since 1866.

Tracing his lineage from the first Pilgrims of Plymouth, Mass., he became a member of the Society of Mayflower Descendants of New York.

Four children were born to Captain and Mrs. Blakeley in Galena, Illinois, and six in St. Paul. Eight of these survived their father, namely, Henry, born November 27th, 1854; William, born December 17th, 1857; Sheldon, born July 1st, 1860; George Samson, born October 11th, 1862; John Marvin, born June 14th, 1864; Ellen, born November 27th, 1865, married to Thomas L. Wann, April 26th, 1887; Frank Drummond, born December 18th, 1867; and Marguerite Elizabeth, born October 6th, 1872, married to Harold P. Bend, October 28th, 1897.

The latest work of Captain Blakeley was a compilation, chiefly from the Library of the Historical Society, supplemented by much correspondence, showing the ancestry of himself and his children. This work, which is left in manuscript, he intended to publish after its revision by others of his kindred.

During the last few months, most of his bodily powers gradually failed with the weakness common to old age; but his hearing, sight, and mental powers, remained nearly in their ordinary vigor till a few days before his death, which occurred at his home in St. Paul, February 4th, 1901. He went cheerfully from this mortal life, with clear Christian faith in a better and immortal future life.

WARREN UPHAM.

OTHER DECEASED MEMBERS OF THIS SOCIETY,

1898-1901.

FRANKLIN G. ADAMS was born in Rodman, Jefferson county, N. Y., May 13th, 1824, and died at his home in Topeka, Kansas, December 2d, 1899. He was elected a corresponding member of this society February 8th, 1897. He was brought up on a farm, and had only a common school education; but after removing to Cincinnati, in 1843, he spent the next several years as a school teacher, and as a law student, graduating from the law department of the Cincinnati College in 1852. He came to Kansas in 1855; was register of the United States Land Office in Topeka; was probate judge of Atchison county; and from 1876 until his death was the very efficient secretary of the Kansas State Historical Society.

LEVI ATWOOD was born in Chatham, Mass., in 1824, and died at his home in that town September 3d, 1898. During many years he was an editor of the Chatham Monitor; and he was town clerk and treasurer twenty-six years. April 10th, 1876, he was elected a corresponding member of this society.

WILLIAM M. BUSHNELL, elected to life membership in this society April 14th, 1890, was born in Lafayette, Stark county, Illinois, January 23d, 1853, and came to Minnesota, settling in St. Paul, in 1874. He was engaged here in the sale of agricultural implements and machinery during eleven years, and afterward in real estate business. In 1889 he was president of the State Agricultural Society. He died January 1st, 1901, in Monterey, Mexico.

ALEXANDER H. CATHCART was born in Toronto, Canada, July 24th, 1820; and died at his home in St. Paul, October 3d, 1899. At the age of eleven years he began as an apprentice

in the retail dry goods business, which he followed about fifty years. In 1841 he removed to Montreal, and later to New York City, whence he came to St. Paul in 1850, being one of the earliest merchants here. He was a charter member of the St. Paul Chamber of Commerce. January 15th, 1856, he was elected a life member of this society. In 1864 he was elected to its Executive Council, and served six years. Later, he was again a councilor from 1882 to 1885, and from 1888 to 1897.

ROBERT CLARKE, publisher, bibliographer, historian, and archæologist, died at his home in Cincinnati, Ohio, August 26th, 1899. He was elected a corresponding member of this society November 9th, 1868. He was born in Annan, Scotland, May 1st, 1829; came, with his parents, to Cincinnati in 1840; was educated at Woodward College; was author and editor of numerous books of Ohio history; and was publisher of many important historical works.

ELLIOTT COUES, who was elected an honorary member of this society May 14th, 1894, was born in Portsmouth, N. H., September 9th, 1842, and died in Baltimore, Md., December 25th, 1899. He graduated at Columbian University, Washington, D. C., in 1861; entered the United States Army as a medical cadet in 1862, and two years later became an assistant surgeon. From 1876 to 1880 he was secretary and naturalist of the U. S. Geological and Geographical Survey of the Territories, under direction of Dr. F. V. Hayden. During thirty years Dr. Coues was active as an author and editor of works of ornithology and other branches of zoology; and in recent years he was editor of new editions of the reports of Lewis and Clark and of Pike, and the journal of Alexander Henry, works of great importance for the early history of the Northwest.

CHARLES P. DALY, jurist, was born in New York City, October 31st, 1816; and died at Sag Harbor, N. Y., September 19th, 1899. He had only a scanty school education, and early went to sea before the mast, thus serving as a sailor three

years. Later he became a mechanic's apprentice, and afterward studied law, being admitted to the bar in his native city in 1839. He became justice of the court of common pleas in 1844, and first judge in 1857; and was chief justice of New York from 1871 to 1886, his term expiring by limitation of age, when he returned to the practice of his profession. Justice Daly had been during many years president of the American Geographical Society, up to the time of his death; and was the author of numerous pamphlets and books. He was elected an honorary member of this society in 1856.

WILLIAM DAWSON was born in County Cavan, Ireland, October 1st, 1825. After completion of his education, he came to America at the age of twenty-one years, and settled as a civil engineer near Peterborough, Ontario. Three years later he removed to the United States, and was engaged as a school teacher and as a country merchant in the South, latest at Laurel Hill, Louisiana, until the beginning of the Civil War in 1861. Coming then to the North and locating in the city of St. Paul, he was actively engaged here as a banker during thirty-five years. He served several terms in the city council, and during three years, 1878 to 1881, was mayor of this city. He died here suddenly, from apoplexy, on the morning of February 19th, 1901. Mr. Dawson was elected a life member of this society December 8th, 1879.

SAMUEL S. EATON was born in Barton, Vermont, June 27th, 1825, and spent much of his early life in Canada, where his father was engaged in lumbering. He went to California in 1849, remained there two years, and then returned to the East and was in the insurance business during about three years in Buffalo, N. Y. In 1885 he came to Minnesota, settling in St. Paul, and through the remainder of his life was prominent in the insurance business here, becoming the first secretary of the St. Paul Fire and Marine Insurance Company. He was elected a life member of this society April 14th, 1879. He died at his home in St. Paul, December 5th, 1899.

WILLIAM H. EGLE, the eminent historian of Pennsylvania, was born in Harrisburg, Pa., September 17th, 1830; and died

43

at his home in that city, February 19th, 1901. He was elected to honorary membership in this society November 12th, 1894. After receiving a public school education he was in succession a compositor, state printer, editor and physician, graduating from the medical department of the University of Pennsylvania in 1859. He served during the Civil War as a surgeon of Pennsylvania volunteers. Since 1871 he became largely engaged in historical researches, and from 1887 to 1900 was the state librarian of Pennsylvania. During his administration, the library was removed from the capitol to a separate new building. He was editor of the Colonial and State Archives, second and third series; and was author and compiler of many important works of history, biography and genealogy.

CHARLES D. ELFELT was born in Millerstown, Pa., August 29th, 1828; and died in St. Paul, April 28th, 1899. He came to Minnesota, settling at St. Paul, in 1849, and during many years was engaged in the wholesale dry goods trade, in company with his brothers, for which they erected a large building at the corner of Third and Exchange streets. Mr. Elfelt had been a member of this society and actively interested in its progress during all its history. His name appears in the earliest published list of members, in the first issue of the society's Annals, dated 1850. He became a life member January 15th, 1856, and was a member of the Executive Council since 1889.

MAHLON N. GILBERT was born in Laurens, Otsego county, N. Y., March 23d, 1848. He was a student three years in Hobart College, Geneva, N. Y.; but at the beginning of his senior year, in 1869, was obliged to relinquish his studies because of ill health. In 1875 he graduated from the Seabury Divinity School, Faribault, Minn. After six years of pastorates in Deer Lodge and Helena, Montana, he was called to Christ Church in St. Paul, and this city was ever afterward his home. In 1886 he was elected assistant bishop of Minnesota. He became an annual member of this society in 1883, and a life member January 9th, 1888. He died at his home

after a short illness of pneumonia, March 2d, 1900. His earnest and noble life had deeply endeared him to all who knew him. An address which he delivered to this society had been printed before his death in the early part of this volume (pages 181-196).

WILLIAM WIRT HENRY, a grandson of Patrick Henry, was born at Red Hill, Charlotte county, Va., February 14th, 1831; and died in Richmond, Va., December 5th, 1900. He was elected a corresponding member of this society February 8th, 1897. He graduated from the University of Virginia; was admitted to the bar in 1853, and practiced law during many years; was president of the Virginia Historical Society, and of the American Historical Association; and was author and editor of the "Life, Correspondence, and Speeches of Patrick Henry."

CHARLES J. HOADLY, during forty-five years state librarian of Connecticut, and since 1895 president of the Connecticut Historical Society, was born in Hartford, Conn., August 1st, 1828, and died at his home in that city October 19th, 1900. He graduated from Trinity College in 1851; and was appointed librarian of that college in 1854. The next year he was appointed state librarian, succeeding Dr. J. Hammond Trumbull. He copied and edited, with valuable annotations, sixteen volumes of the Colonial and State Records of Connecticut. He was elected an honorary member of this society November 8th, 1897.

JOHN R. JONES was born in Champaign county, Ohio, May 18th, 1828; and died at his home in Chatfield Minn., June 26th, 1900. He was one of the pioneers of Fillmore county, locating at Chatfield in 1854, as a young lawyer, and soon became the official county attorney. This position he resigned in 1857, having been elected to the State Senate. In the Sioux war of the years 1862 to 1865 he enlisted as a private, was mustered in as the captain of Company A in the Second Minnesota Cavalry, participated in several battles with the Indians, and was promoted to the rank of major. In the

ensuing years he built up a very extensive law practice. He became an annual member of this society in 1879, and was elected to life membership December 8th, 1884.

WILLIAM H. KELLEY was born in Boston, Mass., May 9th, 1819; and died at his home in St. Paul, April 3d, 1900. He came to Minnesota in 1855, and to this city in 1856, which was thenceforward his home, excepting an interval of five years' residence in the South. During many years he was the chief bookkeeper of the First National Bank of St. Paul; and he was connected with this bank, before and after his absence in the South, for more than thirty years. Mr. Kelley was much interested in the work of this society, and was its actuary, in care of the library and museum, in 1858 and 1859. December 26th, 1863, he was elected its secretary for the remaining month of the term left vacant by the resignation of Dr. Neill; and from 1864 to 1874 he was a member of the Executive Council. At the organization of the St. Paul Library Association, in 1863, Mr. Kelley became its secretary; and in 1882 he was elected secretary of the board of directors of the City Public Library, and continued in that position until about a year before his death. One of his recreations was the study of botany and the collection of a herbarium, which, after his death, was conditionally donated by Mrs. Kelley to this society's museum. It includes about 2,000 specimens, mostly collected in St. Paul and its vicinity.

PATRICK H. KELLY was born February 2d, 1831, in County Mayo, Ireland, and died at his home in St. Paul, October 23d, 1900. He emigrated to Montreal, Canada, at the age of sixteen years, and remained there about one year. Next he was a clerk and merchant nine years in the village of Mooers, N. Y. In 1857 Mr. Kelly, with his brother Anthony, came to Minnesota. The two brothers were in the grocery business at St. Anthony during the next six years. In 1863 Mr. Patrick Kelly removed to St. Paul, and was here engaged as a wholesale grocer during the ensuing thirty-seven years, until his death. He was a most public-spirited citizen, and in many ways contributed greatly to the advancement of the commercial, edu-

cational, and political interests of St. Paul and of Minnesota. He was elected a life member of this society March 12th, 1877.

JOHN JAY LANE, of Austin, Texas, who was elected a corresponding member of this society February 8th, 1897, died in that city July 17th, 1899. He was a resident of New Orleans before the Civil war. During the last twenty years of his life he resided in Austin, being engaged in journalism as correspondent of several newspapers. He was secretary of the board of regents of the University of Texas during many years, and in 1891 published a history of that university (322 pages).

EDWARD GAY MASON was born in Bridgeport, Conn., August 23d, 1839; and died at his home in Chicago, December 18th, 1898. He graduated at Yale college in 1860, studied law in Chicago, and became prominent in the practice of law in that city. He was elected a corresponding member of this society May 14th, 1883. He became a member of the Chicago Historical Society in 1880, and was its president during the last eleven years of his life, being elected to that office in November, 1887.

FRANK BLACKWELL MAYER, artist, was elected a corresponding member of this society at a very early date, probably in 1851. He was born in Baltimore, Md., December 27th, 1827; and died at his home in Annapolis, Md., July 28th, 1899. After studying with celebrated painters in Paris, he made a tour of the western frontier of the United States, and was present at the treaty made by Governor Ramsey with the Sioux Indians at Traverse des Sioux. July 23d, 1851. A picture of the scene of the treaty, which he painted for this society, is displayed in its library.

DELOS A. MONFORT was born in Hamden, N. Y., April 6th, 1835; and died in Atlantic City, N. J., Aug. 26th, 1899. He first visited Minnesota in 1854, and three years later came here to reside, settling in St. Paul, which was ever afterward his home. He was first engaged with the banking firm of Edgerton and Mackubin, and afterward was cashier of

the People's Bank.   From 1864, the date of organization
of the Second National Bank, he served during nearly thirty
years as its cashier and a part of the time as vice president.
In 1893 he succeeded the late E. S. Edgerton as president of
this bank, which position he held to the time of his death.
He was elected a life member of this society January 13th,
1890, and was a member of its Executive Council since January 19th, 1891.

AMOS PERRY, who was elected a corresponding member
of this society December 10th, 1894, was born in South Natick,
Mass., August 12th, 1812.   He graduated at Harvard College
in 1839, and afterwards taught in New London, Conn., and
Providence, R. I.   He visited Europe several times, and from
1862 to 1867 was United States consul at Tunis.   He was
secretary of the Rhode Island Historical Society since 1873,
and its librarian since 1880.   His death occurred during a
visit to New London, Conn., August 10th, 1899.

JOHN THOMAS SCHARF was born in Baltimore, Md., May
1st, 1843; and died in New York City, February 28th, 1898.
He was elected an honorary member of this society February
12th, 1877.   He enlisted in the First Maryland Artillery of
the Confederate Army, June 1st, 1861, and served two years,
being wounded in several battles; and afterward was a mid-
shipman in the Confederate Navy.   He was admitted to the
Baltimore county bar in 1873, and practiced law in Baltimore,
and since 1897 in New York City.   He was the author of many
historical works on Maryland, Delaware, the cities of Philadelphia and St. Louis, the Confederate States Navy, etc., the
earliest being "Chronicles of Baltimore," published in 1874.

ISAAC STAPLES was born in Topsham, Maine, September
25th, 1816; and died at his home in Stillwater, Minn., June
27th, 1898.   At the age of eighteen years he began work on
his own account in lumbering on the Penobscot river.   In
1853 he came to Minnesota, locating in Stillwater, and was
engaged there, and on the St. Croix river and its branches,
in extensive and prosperous lumbering, farming, and manu-

faĉturing industries. He continued in active business until
a year or two before his death. He was elected to this society,
as a life member, April 14th, 1890.

GEORGE C. STONE was born in Shrewsbury, Mass., November 11th, 1822, and died in Duluth, Minn., October 25th, 1900.
At the age of fourteen years he removed, with his father and
family, to St. Louis, Mo. After reaching manhood, he was
engaged in mercantile business, and as a banker, in Bloom-
ington (now Muscatine), Iowa, in Chicago, and in New York
and Philadelphia. In the year 1869 he came to Duluth, and
thenceforward was actively interested in the upbuilding of
that city, and in the development of the natural resources of
northeastern Minnesota. To Mr. Stone, perhaps more than
to any other one man, was due the railroad building and mining which have placed Minnesota in the front rank of the
states of the Union in respect to the production of iron ore.
He was elected a life member of this society June 11th, 1883.

WILLIAM S. STRYKER, who was elected to corresponding
membership in this society February 8th, 1897, was born in
Trenton, N. J., June 6th, 1838; and died October 29th, 1900.
He graduated at Princeton in 1858; served in the Civil War;
was admitted to the bar in 1866; and was adjutant general
of New Jersey during more than thirty years, from 1867. He
was president of the Society of Cincinnati in the State of New
Jersey, and of the New Jersey Historical Society; was compiler of "Officers and Men of New Jersey in the Revolutionary
War," and of a similar but larger work, in two volumes, giving
the roster of this state in the Civil War; and was author of
numerous historical pamphlets and books, including a volume
published in 1898, entitled "The Battles of Trenton and
Princeton."

GEORGE W. SWEET was born in Hartford, Conn., September 20th, 1823; and died in Havre, Montana, March 14th, 1898.
He came to Minnesota during President Pierce's administration as register of the United States Land Office at Sauk
Rapids. He was a member of the second state legislature

in 1859-60. Later he resided in St. Paul, and was the attorney of the Northern Pacific Railroad Company during the building of its line from St. Paul to Bismarck, North Dakota. Afterward he lived in Bismarck, platted that town, and practiced law there. In 1890 he removed to Havre, and was also engaged there in the practice of law. He was elected to life membership in this society May 6th, 1858.

CHARLES L. WILLIS was born in Erie, Pa., August 18th, 1819; and died at his home in St. Paul, June 29th, 1898. He graduated at the Harvard Law School in 1847, and came to Minnesota in 1850, settling in St. Paul, where he ever afterward resided. During many years he was engaged in the practice of law, and also had considerable interests in real estate here, and in Superior and Ashland, Wisconsin. He was elected a life member of this society January 15th, 1856.

JOHN C. WISE was born in Hagerstown, Md., September 4th, 1834; came to Minnesota in 1859, settling at Mankato, where through the remainder of his life he was an enterprising and influential editor; and died at his home in that city November 17th, 1900. He began publication of the Mankato *Record* in 1859, and was its editor nine years. In 1869 he founded the Mankato *Review*, which he edited thirty-one years, until his death. He was a prominent Democrat, was a delegate to the presidential nominating conventions in 1872 and 1884, and was the postmaster of Mankato during a part of each of the administrations of President Cleveland. He was elected to life membership in this society January 10th, 1898.

INDEX.

Lightning Source UK Ltd.
Milton Keynes UK
UKHW021402051118
331796UK00014B/893/P